INSIDERS' GUIDE®

OFF THE BEATEN PATH® SERIES

Off the Beaten Path®

EIGHTH EDITION

new jersey

A GUIDE TO UNIQUE PLACES

WILLIAM G. AND KAY SCHELLER

INSIDERS' GUIDE®

GUILFORD, CONNECTICUT
AN IMPRINT OF THE GLOBE PEQUOT PRESS

Although thorough efforts have been made to verify hours of operation and admission charges and rates, these items often change at the whim of proprietors or as a result of governmental budgets. Therefore, call ahead for current information before traveling.

Maps provided are for reference only and should be used in conjunction with a road map. Distances suggested are approximate.

To buy books in quantity for corporate use or incentives, call **(800) 962–0973, ext. 4551,** or e-mail **premiums@GlobePequot.com.**

INSIDERS' GUIDE®

Text design by Linda Loiewski
Maps created by Equator Graphics © Morris Book Publishing, LLC
Text illustrations by Carole Drong
Spot photography throughout © Tom Till/Alamy

ISSN: 1538-1188
ISBN-13: 978-0-7627-4055-0
ISBN-10: 0-7627-4055-8

Manufactured in the United States of America
Eighth Edition/First Printing

Help Us Keep This Guide Up to Date

Every effort has been made by the authors and editors to make this guide as accurate and useful as possible. However, many changes can occur after a guide is published—establishments close, phone numbers change, hiking trails are rerouted, facilities come under new management, etc.

We would love to hear from you concerning your experiences with this guide and how you feel it could be improved and be kept up to date. While we may not be able to respond to all comments and suggestions, we'll take them to heart, and we'll make certain to share them with the authors. Please send your comments and suggestions to the following address:

The Globe Pequot Press
Reader Response/Editorial Department
P.O. Box 480
Guilford, CT 06437

Or you may e-mail us at: editorial@GlobePequot.com

Thanks for your input, and happy travels!

To Alice and William G. Scheller,
two New Jerseyans who helped immensely
in researching and revising this book

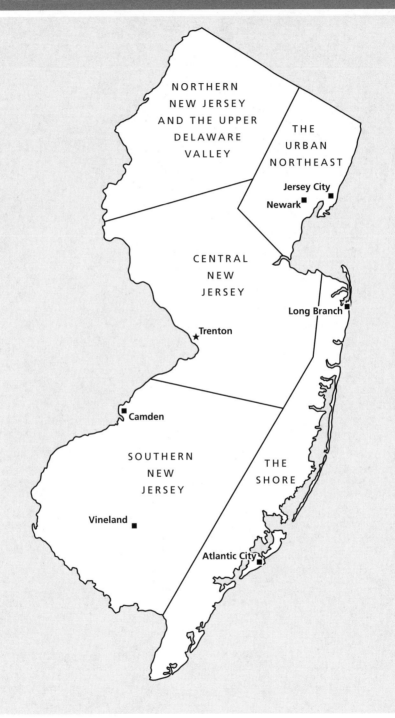

NORTHERN
NEW JERSEY
AND THE UPPER
DELAWARE
VALLEY

THE
URBAN
NORTHEAST

■ Jersey City
Newark ■

CENTRAL
NEW
JERSEY

Long Branch ■

★ Trenton

Camden ■

SOUTHERN
NEW
JERSEY

THE
SHORE

Vineland ■

Atlantic City ■

Contents

Introduction

This eighth edition marks seventeen years of *New Jersey Off the Beaten Path*. What's new for 2006? We've discovered museums filled with antique bicycles and snowmobiles, a gallery of African art, excursions in antique railroad cars and hot-air balloons, a rock-and-roll tour of the Jersey shore, and an ice-cream parlor with a singing waitstaff. And what's to eat? How about Malaysian food in Edison, Ethiopian in New Brunswick, and Japanese in Dennisville? As in our seven previous outings, we've found that the Garden State is full of surprises while remaining true to its past, and that it can still revel in its stereotypes while standing the conventional wisdom on its head. That old Jersey joke might ask, "What exit?"—but that ramp off the turnpike or the parkway is just as likely to lead to a colonial village or a wildlife preserve as to an all-night diner or a factory outlet.

With a population of some eight and a half million, a healthy economy based on both service and manufacturing industries, and a steady influx of immigrants from all parts of the world, the Garden State often seems to be a place where change is the only constant. But much of New Jersey defies rapid transformation. People throughout the Middle Atlantic states can still enjoy what remains one of the most beautiful beaches in the world, the 120-mile stretch of white sand that extends from Sandy Hook to Cape May, where the ocean is bracing but (at least by July) never forbiddingly frigid, where good Italian restaurants are as thick as they are in Naples, and where you can turn your back on the machines that ate your quarters in Atlantic City and enjoy gorgeous expanses of federally protected salt marsh. The Pine Barrens, the heart of which has also been protected from development, are still splendidly desolate almost to the point of eeriness, and the exurban lanes of southwest Jersey, around Greenwich, are in much the same league as the byways of up-country New England, even if the terrain is a bit flatter. If you want more rugged country, there are always the Kittatinny Mountains that stand sentinel above the Delaware Water Gap, away up north near the New York and Pennsylvania borders.

For such a small state, New Jersey has a tremendously varied topography. The black basalt cliffs called the Palisades tower formidably above the Hudson River at the state's northeastern gateway and slope westward toward the great marshy basin of the Hackensack Meadows. More than 270 species of birds have been observed in the Meadows, hundreds of acres of which have been preserved despite the encroachment of condos, office parks, and a football stadium. The Great Swamp, near Chatham and Summit in the north-central part of the state, is the site of an even more impressive preservation effort. Here more than 6,000 acres of primeval freshwater wetlands were set aside under federal protection after citizens rallied, more than thirty years ago, to keep out a projected jetport.

Nor has New Jersey any apologies to make when it comes to historical associations. This was an old and well-settled place by the time of the American Revolution; during the century and a half that went before, Dutch and English settlers in the north and Swedes in the south had been hewing farms and homes out of the land of the Lenni-Lenape Indians. Men smelted iron in the Pine Barrens and the Ramapo Mountains in the middle of the eighteenth century, and the Revolution was barely over when Alexander Hamilton stood at the Great Falls of the Passaic and decided that here would be built America's first planned industrial city.

All too often we tend to limit our geographical notions of the War for Independence to the early battlefields of Massachusetts and the political arenas of Philadelphia, but more of that eight-year struggle took place in New Jersey

You Know You're from New Jersey If:

- You don't think of citrus when people mention "The Oranges." *
- A good, quick breakfast is a hard roll with butter.
- You remember that the "Two Guys" were from Harrison. **
- You know what a "jug handle" is. ***
- You don't go "to the shore," you go "down the Shore." And when you're there, you're not "at the shore"—you're "down the Shore."
- Even your school cafeteria made good Italian subs.
- You've gotten on the wrong highway trying to get out of the mall.
- You've had a Boardwalk cheese steak and vinegar fries.
- You've never pumped your own gas. ****

For You Non–New Jerseyans:

* Orange, East Orange, South Orange, West Orange—all are towns near Newark. There is no North Orange.

** Two Guys from Harrison, a now-defunct discount store chain—"Two Guys" for short.

*** An exit ramp shaped like one.

**** Self-service pumps are illegal in New Jersey.

than anywhere else, and the state well earned its title "Cockpit of the Revolution." Here the Continental army waited out winters as devastating to morale as the one at Valley Forge; here George Washington accomplished what has been called the greatest strategic retreat in military history; and here, at Christmastime in 1776, the American commander-in-chief won the Battle of Trenton after his legendary crossing of the Delaware.

New Jersey's role in the Industrial Revolution was no less impressive. Basic resource-extraction enterprises, such as the mines at Ringwood and Batsto, soon began to be eclipsed by manufacturing, with Paterson rising to become the nation's preeminent weaver of silk and its second most important builder of locomotives (after Philadelphia). Railroads have figured prominently in New Jersey ever since John Stevens demonstrated America's first working steam locomotive on his Hoboken estate in 1824. The state became vital to rail enterprises such as the Pennsylvania and Erie Railroads and the Delaware, Lackawanna, and Western, which operated electric passenger trains perfected by the Wizard of Menlo Park (New Jersey), Thomas Edison. Today the petroleum, petrochemical, and pharmaceutical industries are among the state's largest employers.

The purpose of this book is to distill New Jersey's wonderful diversity—geographic, ethnic, historical, and industrial—into the description of selected sites in the five major areas of the state. These places haven't been chosen because they're the major New Jersey attractions; the premise of the Off the Beaten Path® series is the discovery of places many guidebooks overlook. You'll find some familiar spots, but our hope is that most of the territory covered in these pages will be as new as the perceptions it may inspire. If, while following this guide, you drive along the turnpike, eat in a diner on Route 9, and pop a Bruce Springsteen CD into the CD player, that's all right. Just remember, there's a lot more to New Jersey than those stereotypical experiences suggest.

The Poetry of New Jersey Names

When it comes to being celebrated in song, New Jersey has been shortchanged. There's no Jersey equivalent of "Moonlight in Vermont," and New Jerseyans have to be envious when they hear Gladys Knight sing "Midnight Train to Georgia" or the Bee Gees harmonize on "Massachusetts." There is, of course, John Pizzarelli Jr.'s whimsical "I Like Jersey Best"—but our favorite, if little-known, paean to New Jersey is the late folk legend Dave van Ronk's "The Garden State Stomp." "Stomp" consists of nothing but a litany of New Jersey town names—Allamuchy, Piscataway, Parsippany, Egg Harbor—a long, mellifluous celebration of Indian, Anglo, and Dutch nomenclature that only a map of Jersey could have inspired.

Please be sure to call ahead when making travel arrangements, as prices, and hours and dates of operation change. To help with planning, we have used a scale for the prices of restaurants and accommodations. Entrees (without beverage) are classified as inexpensive, less than $10; moderate, $11–$20; and expensive, more than $21. For motels, bed-and-breakfasts, and hotels, prices are per night: inexpensive, less than $40; moderate, $41–$80; and expensive, more than $81.

We hope you enjoy exploring New Jersey as much as we have—and that the next eight editions of *New Jersey Off the Beaten Path* find the Pine Barrens just as desolate, the surf at Ship Bottom every bit as invigorating, and the state's restaurants offering cuisines we haven't even heard of yet, much less sampled. For us, *that* would define progress.

New Jersey Information

Travel Information

New Jersey Division of Travel and Tourism
20 West State Street, Trenton 08625
(800) VISITNJ or (609) 777–0885
www.visitnj.org

Preferred Inns of New Jersey
P.O. Box 108, Spring Lake 07762
(732) 449–3535
www.njinns.com
(a free directory is available)

New Jersey Campground Association
29 Cooks Beach Road, Cape May Court House 08210
(800) 2–CAMP–NJ for free guide
www.njcampgrounds.com

Area Codes

All local calls made in the 973, 732, 862, 848, 551, and 201 area codes require callers to dial the area code plus the seven-digit number for calls within these area codes.

Average Temperatures

32.1 degrees Fahrenheit December–February
51.6 degrees Fahrenheit March–May
74.4 degrees Fahrenheit June–August
57.1 degrees Fahrenheit September–November

Transportation

Major Airports

Atlantic City International Airport, (609) 645–7895; www.acairport.com

Newark Liberty International Airport, (973) 961–6000; www.panynj.com

Trains:

Amtrak, (800) USA–RAIL; www.amtrak.com

New Jersey Transit Passenger Rail System:

northern New Jersey, (973) 772–2222

southern New Jersey, (800) 582–5946

out-of-state, (973) 762–5100

www.njtransit.com

Major Newspapers

Jersey Journal (Jersey City)

Star-Ledger (Newark)

Herald News (Passaic County)

Bergen Record (Hackensack)

Philadelphia Inquirer (Philadelphia, Pennsylvania—read widely in southern New Jersey)

Population

8,698,879 (2004 estimate)

Tourism Information

New Jersey Commerce & Economic Growth Commission

Office of Travel & Tourism

20 West State Street

P.O. Box 820

Trenton 08625

(609) 777–0885

www.visitnj.org

Some Selected World Wide Web Addresses in New Jersey

General information:

www.state.nj.us

Free travel publications:

www.visitnj.org

Statewide events and New Jersey Transit information:

www.state.nj.us/travel

Preferred Inns of New Jersey:

www.njinns.com

New Jersey Audubon Society:
www.njaudubon.com

New Jersey Campground Owners Association:
www.njcampgrounds.com

New Jersey Road Map:
www.online96.com/towns/lbi/njmap.html

The Urban Northeast

New Jersey's heavily urbanized northeastern corner often serves the popular imagination as a metaphor for the entire state. It might just as well represent all the United States—not because the entire country is as densely populated as New Jersey, but because, at its best, it is as richly textured and heterogeneous as New Jersey's contribution to the New York metropolitan area. One of the most striking aspects of this compact region is its racial and ethnic diversity; remember that Ellis Island is only a few hundred yards from Jersey City. People come here, people stay, people pass through on their way to somewhere else. (Union City, once a Swiss preserve, is now largely a Cuban community.) Within this chapter we'll visit the home of an Italian labor organizer, farmhouses that belonged to the earliest Dutch settlers, and a rich display of African art and artifacts.

Dense population, with the complicated patchwork of cities, suburbs, and industrial districts that it engenders, seldom gets good press, and there's no denying that it has spawned its share of problems. But an often-overlooked virtue of the Jersey metropolis is its variety, the quickness with which one environment gives way to another. When so many towns and cities are this close together, even locals usually have to admit that there is plenty they haven't seen (or maybe even heard of)

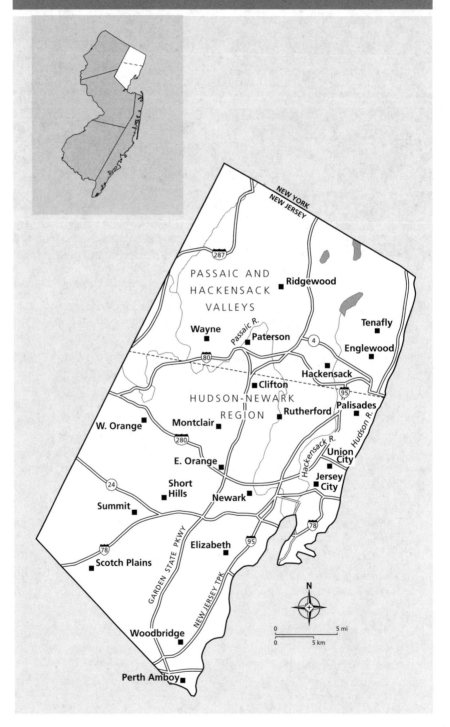

right within their county limits. Distances don't shrink under these circumstances; they expand: People in eastern Wyoming probably know more about
western Wyoming than the folks in Hoboken know about Hackensack.
   Note: The orientation in this chapter is roughly north to south.

Passaic and Hackensack Valleys

The **Palisades** are the dark, beetling cliffs that begin near the border of
Hudson and Bergen Counties and continue northward into New York State.
The Palisades are more than just the foreground for the Jersey sunsets that sell
terraced Manhattan apartments; they are a window into deep geological time
and the focus of one of the region's earliest and most successful preservation
movements. They're also a great place to take a hike.

   By the mid-nineteenth century extensive quarrying operations were set
up, and before long the southerly reaches of the cliffs were all but obliterated.
Fortunately, early preservation activists persuaded the states of New York and
New Jersey to purchase the Palisades, along with the land at their base and
summit. Quarrying stopped in 1900, and by 1909 **Palisades Interstate Park**
had been dedicated.

THE URBAN NORTHEAST'S TOP PICKS

Palisades	The Montclair Art Museum
Waterford Gardens	Presby Memorial Iris Gardens
Hiram Blauvelt Art Museum	Aviation Hall of Fame and Museum of New Jersey
Steuben House	
USS *Ling*	Park Performing Arts Center
The African Art Museum of the S.A.M. Fathers	Afro-American Historical Society Museum
Great Falls/S.U.M. National Historic Landmark District	South Mountain Reservation
Lambert Castle	Turtle Back Zoo
American Labor Museum	Watchung Reservation
Van Riper–Hopper Museum	First Presbyterian Church
Dey Mansion	Bible Gardens of Israel

The best way to enjoy the Palisades today is to hike along either the Long Path, which runs along the crest of the cliffs and offers lovely views of the Hudson and the New York shore, or the Shore Path, which follows the riverbank at the base of the towering rocks. To begin the latter route, which is marked with white blazes and extends 10 miles northward into New York State, park at the Englewood Boat Basin, just north of the New Jersey approach to the George Washington Bridge. A good access point for the Long Path is 5 miles north (via Route 9W) at the turnoff for the Alpine Boat Basin. At Alpine, both trails are connected by a steep switchback path. Whatever you do, stick to marked paths such as this one when ascending or descending in the Palisades. Much of the rock is loose and makes for extremely dangerous climbing.

Waterford Gardens in Saddle River is likely to be different from any garden center you've ever seen. Its exclusive focus is water plants—day- and night-blooming tropical water lilies, lotuses, floating plants, and aquatic border plants—as well as ornamental fish.

The company's displays of its living wares are beautifully arranged along the banks of the Saddle River, in an array of ponds and pools that are more suggestive of a pristine bayou than the vicinity of exit 163 on the Garden State Parkway. Best of all, you don't have to be shopping for water lilies to visit the gardens. They're open to casual visitors—although we suspect that many of those visitors won't be so casual once they start thinking about the possibilities of water gardening, and that lily ponds will start appearing in more and more suburban backyards.

Waterford Gardens, 74 East Allendale Road, (201) 327–0721, is open Monday through Saturday 9:00 A.M.–5:00 P.M. and Sunday 9:00 A.M.–4:00 P.M., after Easter through July 31; the rest of the year, Monday through Saturday 9:00 A.M.–5:00 P.M. Admission is free.

The Making of the Palisades

The grand, dark cliffs called the Palisades, which dominate the New Jersey side of the Hudson River from the George Washington Bridge to the New York State border and beyond, had their origin 190 million years ago, when molten rock forced its way upward into fissures in layers of sandstone and shale. The molten material cooled beneath the surface, hardening into a rock called *diabase*, before being exposed by erosion. The columnar, prismlike structure of the cliffs is a result of the contraction and vertical splintering that took place as the rock solidified. That structure also gave the formation its name: To early settlers, the cliffs resembled a palisade, a military enclosure made of sharpened stakes driven into the ground.

The **Saddle River Inn,** housed in a rustic yet elegant 150-year-old barn, is consistently voted one of the state's best restaurants. It seats just seventy diners and offers artfully prepared cuisine and excellent service. French/continental specialties might include an appetizer of seared foie gras and an entree of chateaubriand for two with sautéed mushrooms and roesti potatoes. Guests are invited to bring their own wine, and jackets are required.

The Saddle River Inn, 2 Barnstable Court, (201) 825–4016, is open for lunch Wednesday through Friday, and dinner Tuesday through Saturday. Reservations are highly recommended.

Our friend, ardent gardener and writer Betsy Hays, told us about the **Celery Farm Natural Area** in Allendale. Technically not a garden, and no longer a working celery farm, this 107-acre wildlife sanctuary is ablaze with wildflowers and home to a multitude of critters, including warblers, mink, and bullfrogs. Owned by the Borough of Allendale, it's located on the Franklin Turnpike (Route 507), just north of the intersection with East Allendale Avenue. Open dawn to dusk. Free.

Bergen County's only eighteenth/nineteenth-century house, the **Hermitage,** is a National Historic Landmark. The original structure, built circa 1740 as a two-story brownstone, was owned by British officer James Marcus Prevost and his wife. Their visitors included George Washington and Aaron Burr, who married Mrs. Prevost here after the British officer died.

The Hermitage

In 1807 the Hermitage was purchased by Dr. Elijah Rosencrantz for his bride, Cornelia Suffern. The family of the doctor—who became one of the area's leading industrialists—occupied the home for the next 160 years. In 1847 one of his sons, Elijah Jr., hired architect William Ranlett to renovate the Hermitage. Ranlett "razed most of the existing structure, added a wing, and remodeled the home into the romantic Gothic Revival mansion" that stands here today.

The home's last owner, Mary Elizabeth Rosencrantz, died in poverty in 1970, refusing to sell the Hermitage to developers because she believed her home should be a legacy to the public: She bequeathed it to the State of New Jersey upon her death. Today the landmark, due to the hard work of the Friends of the Hermitage, is a fine interpretive museum of America's late Victorian era.

The Hermitage, 335 North Franklin Turnpike, Ho-Ho-Kus, (201) 445–8311, www.thehermitage.org, is open for tours Wednesday through Sunday 1:00–4:00 P.M.; last tour at 3:15. Admission is $5.00 for adults and $3.00 for children ages six through twelve. Call for information on special events such as Revolutionary War reenactments and Civil War encampments held there throughout the year.

The ***James C. Rose Landscape Research and Study Center*** in Ridgewood was designed and built in the early 1950s by James Rose (1913–1991), the premier figure in American landscape architecture for more than half a century. Tossed out of Harvard for creating "modern" designs, Rose went on to design hundreds of exquisite gardens, write several books, and receive accolades from his clients and peers as well as from the Japanese, who related to his spare, integrated living space and garden designs.

Rose's approach successfully integrated the outdoor and indoor environments and didn't require large pieces of acreage to do so. The Ridgewood home and garden is actually a "tiny village" of three buildings built on an area half the size of a tennis court. Rose's experimental landscape seamlessly fuses the outdoors and indoors and was intended to constantly evolve. Over the nearly forty years that Rose, his mother, and sister lived on the property, the design changed dramatically. After visiting Japan to participate in the World Design Conference, for instance, Rose was inspired by Buddhism and Eastern design to add a roof garden and *zendo,* a hall for the practice of and training in zen.

During the last decade of Rose's life, the property fell into disrepair and was almost ruined by fire and flood. Since 1993, under the leadership of Dean Cardasis (James Rose scholar, landscape architect, and associate professor at University of Massachusetts, Amherst) and a dedicated group of volunteers, the site is being rehabilitated. The center serves students, scholars, and the general public as a catalyst for examining elemental questions about the nature of design.

The Rose Center, 506 East Ridgewood Avenue, (201) 446–6017, is open to the public for self-guided tours on the first and third Saturday and Sunday, May through October, 10:00 A.M.–4:00 P.M. Admission is $8.00 per person.

One hundred and twelve kinds of pancakes? You can count them, but we'd recommend not wasting your time when you could be eating them at ***Country Pancake House & Restaurant***, 140 East Ridgewood Avenue, Ridgewood, (201) 444–8395. Not to be missed (or avoided at all costs, depending on your inclination): Heavenly Celestial Body Pancakes, with almonds, white chocolate chunks, and whipped cream. They're open daily 6:30 A.M. through dinner.

A water treatment plant may not be your idea of the perfect setting for a garden, but unusual settings beget unusual gardens, and the half-acre xeriscape garden here fits the bill. *Xeriscape* is from the Greek word *xero,* which means "dry," and all the plantings at the ***United Water Xeriscape Garden*** at Haworth Water Treatment Plant thrive on little water.

A joint project of DeRosa Landscaping of Montvale and the Rutgers Cooperative Extension Service, the low-maintenance landscape has a short walking path that winds past shrubs, rock gardens, and perennial grasses; under a canopy of trees; and along a riot of colorful flowers including lavender, bleeding hearts, and black-eyed Susans, to a duck pond.

United Water Xeriscape Garden, 200 Lakeshore Drive, Haworth, (201) 767–9300, is open daily from dawn to dusk. Admission is free.

Step into a world where elephants roam the African veldt, Canada geese glide tranquilly across fog-shrouded ponds, and a snow leopard looks down from his lofty perch high in the Himalayas. In 1957 conservationist Hiram Blauvelt donated his private wildlife art and big-game collection to focus awareness on issues facing the natural world and to showcase the artists who are inspired by it. Today the ***Hiram Blauvelt Art Museum,*** in Mr. Blauvelt's 1893 turreted, shingle-style carriage house, exhibits a large collection of Audubon folios, works by artists such as Carl Rungius and Charles Livingston

AUTHORS' FAVORITE ATTRACTIONS IN THE URBAN NORTHEAST

The African Art Museum of the S.A.M. Fathers	Hiram Blauvelt Art Museum
American Labor Museum	Steuben House
The Hermitage	William Paterson University

Bull, and magnificent dioramas. The big-game collection includes a large display of North American mammals.

The Hiram Blauvelt Art Museum, 705 Kinderkamack Road, Oradell, (201) 261–0012, is open Wednesday through Friday 10:00 A.M.–4:00 P.M., and Saturday and Sunday 2:00–5:00 P.M. Closed holidays. Admission is by donation.

Although the **Steuben House** was named for the Prussian-born hero of the American Revolution, Maj. Gen. Baron Friedrich von Steuben, the house dates to 1713, well before the general's birth. The oldest part of the house was built by Johannes Ackerman of Hackensack. In 1752 a new owner, Jan Zabriskie, expanded the building to its present size and gave it its graceful gambrel roof. In 1939 the structure was restored and opened as a museum.

The Steuben House is an appropriate showplace for the collections of the Bergen County Historical Society, which include eighteenth-century furnishings and a trove of antique toys distinguished by what is said to be the oldest doll in the United States—"Betsy Coxe"—made of wax about the year 1700.

Directly in front of the Steuben House is an 1888 iron bridge (closed to traffic) occupying the site of the original "New Bridge" of 1774 that figured so prominently in the retreat of American troops late in 1776.

The Steuben House, 1209 Main Street, River Edge, (201) 487–1739, is open Wednesday through Saturday 10:00 A.M.–noon and 1:00–5:00 P.M.; Sunday 2:00–5:00 P.M. Admission is free.

Just a few miles downriver from Steuben House is a relic of another war—the submarine **USS Ling,** riding peacefully at anchor in the Hackensack River. The *Ling* was brought here for restoration in 1973 by the Submarine Memorial Association after being decommissioned by the U.S. Navy in 1971.

The 312-foot *Ling* was commissioned in June 1945, during the closing days of World War II. She made one Atlantic patrol before the war's end and was kept in reserve until her recommissioning in 1960 as a naval training vessel. Her home port during this era was the Brooklyn Navy Yard, from which she made her last voyage, through New York Harbor and Newark Bay into the tidal mouth of the Hackensack, after the Navy agreed to donate the vessel to the Memorial Association rather than consign her to scrap.

The *Ling* stands as a monument to the diesel era of American submarine operations and to the men who served as submariners. She has 2,040 tons displacement, 6,400 horsepower, and accommodations for twenty-four torpedoes and a crew of ninety-five officers and men. Visitors can board the *Ling* and see the engine and control rooms, the torpedo rooms, and the close quarters of the crew.

The USS *Ling* and adjacent New Jersey Naval Museum, Borg Park, 78 River Street, Hackensack, (201) 342–3268, is open 10:00 A.M.–4:00 P.M. Saturday and Sunday (tours begin at fifteen minutes after the hour; last tour at 3:30 P.M.).

USS *Ling*

Admission to the submarine is $7.00 for adults, $3.00 for children under twelve. Admission to the museum and grounds is free.

Traditionally, many Christian missionaries to Africa regarded the peoples and cultures among whom they worked as inferior to those of the West. Their artifacts were often judged ugly, and objects having any connection with so-called pagan religious practices were frequently collected and burned.

At ***The African Art Museum of the S.A.M. Fathers,*** the Society of African Missions in the United States instead offers a display of art and artifacts that emphasizes the beauty and richness of African cultural expression.

Wandering about the museum, we learn that masks of the Wee people in Liberia, which may at first glimpse seem strange or grotesque, were in fact used as a social control. Each mask represented a specific spirit who wanted to be involved in human affairs. The masks were teachers of the values of tradition and law and the need to preserve those values. Helmet masks of the Baule in the Ivory Coast, which represent horned animals, are used in dances to protect the village, to discipline women, and at funeral ceremonies.

The African Art Museum of the Society of African Missions (S.A.M.), 23 Bliss Avenue, Tenafly, (201) 894–8611, is open daily 9:00 A.M.–5:00 P.M. Donations are welcome.

Even New Jersey trivia lovers might be hard-pressed to name the state's tallest growing tree. It's the moisture-loving tulip tree, which grows up to 200 feet and each May and June sprouts elegant, six-petaled flowers. There are

Note: Schedules may vary; call ahead.

Cherry Blossom Festival, Newark;
April; (973) 263–3500

St. Ann's Italian Festival, Hoboken;
July; (201) 659–1114

**New Jersey West Indian
Caribbean Carnival,** Jersey City;
August; (201) 547–5003

Hambletonian Day, Meadowlands
Racetrack, East Rutherford; August;
(201) 935–8500; www.meadowlands.com

Sunset Jazz Series, Camden;
August; (856) 757–9400

Newark Black Film Festival,
Newark Museum; August;
(973) 596–6493

many fine specimens at ***Lost Brook Preserve,*** a 380-acre sanctuary of ponds, plants, woods, wildflowers, and unique rock formations in the middle of urban Tenafly.

The preserve's diverse habitat is a haven for wildlife, including white-tailed deer, Eastern cottontail rabbits, and water snakes. It's a popular spot for bird-watchers, particularly during fall and spring migrations when it provides a welcome rest stop for a wide variety of bird species. The preserve's newest attraction is the enclosed butterfly habitat in front of the visitor center.

Lost Brook Preserve, Tenafly Nature Center, 313 Hudson Avenue, Tenafly, (201) 568–6093, is open daily dawn to dusk. The parking lot closes at 5:00 P.M. The visitor center is open Monday 1:00–5:00 P.M., Tuesday through Saturday

If the Carp Are Jumping, It's Springtime on the Passaic

All too often, North Jersey's Passaic River is portrayed as an example of an urban waterway lost to pollution and streamside blight. But the Passaic does have its pristine stretches. It rises near the Great Swamp and passes through part of that wilderness preserve. Farther downstream the Passaic meanders through an area on the borders of Essex and Passaic Counties called Great Piece Meadow—not a meadow so much as an impenetrable swamp, all the more remarkable for being within a few miles of Route 46 and the giant Willowbrook Mall.

About the only way to get into the heart of Great Piece is by canoe. We've done it in early April and seen one of the true primeval spectacles of northern New Jersey: carp, usually thought of as sedate bottom feeders, jumping like trout during their spring spawning season.

9:00 A.M.–5:00 P.M., and Sunday 10:00 A.M.–5:00 P.M. (if volunteers are available). Closed holidays. Admission is free.

Flat Rock Brook Nature Center, a 150-acre nature preserve with volcanic bedrock formations, cliffs, ponds, and meadows, is an oasis in the urban north that's home to diverse plant and animal life. The Backyard Habitat for Wildlife exhibits native plants selected to provide food for wildlife *and* be ornamental. There are 3.2 miles of hiking trails (maps are available), and small kids will love the 800-foot Quarry Boardwalk in front of the center at 443 Van Nostrand Avenue, Englewood, (201) 567–1265. Picnic area and trails are open from sunrise to sunset. The visitor center and greenhouses are open Monday through Friday 9:00 A.M.–5:00 P.M., Saturday and Sunday 1:00–5:00 P.M. Admission is free.

The Passaic Falls, located in the heart of the city that they created—Paterson—are the focus of the *Great Falls/S.U.M. National Historic Landmark District.* ("S.U.M." stands for Society for the Establishment of Useful Manufactures, the industrial development organization founded along with Paterson in 1791.)

Here the waters of the Passaic River, which has its source nearly 50 miles upstream in the Great Swamp, crash over a 280-foot-wide chasm to continue toward tidewater at Newark Bay. During the Revolution on July 10, 1778, George Washington and Alexander Hamilton came to stand on the rock ledge opposite the falls and marvel at their fury. To Hamilton, however, the falls were more than a scenic wonder. Once independence was won, he was quick to propose that the waters of the Passaic should be harnessed as a source of power for the nation's first planned industrial city. In 1791 the settlement above and below the cataract was incorporated and named for William Paterson, New Jersey governor and signer of the Declaration of Independence.

Paterson's founders selected French engineer Pierre L'Enfant to design Paterson's industrial infrastructure. L'Enfant came up with an ingenious system of raceways, but the plan was never completed to his specifications due to its

A Real Beat Town

Paterson's claim to literary celebrity is nearly always linked with William Carlos Williams's epic poem of the same name. But the Silk City also figures in the defining work of the Beat Generation, Jack Kerouac's *On the Road.* Early in the novel Kerouac's autobiographical hero, Sal Paradise, refers to "Paterson, New Jersey, where I was living with my aunt." Soon afterward, Sal makes Paterson his point of departure for his first trip to the West Coast. Kerouac knew the city through his friend, Paterson native Allen Ginsberg. The poet appears in *On the Road* as "Carlo Marx."

You Know It's Easter in Paterson When . . .

Throughout the cities and suburbs of northern New Jersey, the days right before Easter bring the delicious aroma of Easter Pie. Perhaps not as well known as baskets and dyed eggs but beloved by the descendants of the Italian immigrants who populated this part of the Garden State, Easter Pie ("pizza piena," or "full pie" in the language of the old country) is an over-the-top celebration of the end of Lent. It keeps in the fridge for at least a week, and serves equally well, hot or cold, as breakfast, lunch, and dinner. Here's our family recipe, courtesy of Bill's mom. It makes six pies, so you can give them to friends and family as Easter presents.

Crust:
   2 teaspoons salt
   black pepper (optional)
   7 cups flour
   1½ cups butter, chilled and cut in pieces
   ¾ cup lard
   8 egg yolks plus enough ice water to equal 2 cups

Filling:
   1 pound sopressata (coarse, cured Italian salami-like sausage), skin removed, diced
   1 pound prosciutto, diced
   1½ pounds mozzarella, sliced or diced
   1½ pounds fresh ricotta (sold in Italian markets as "basket cheese"), sliced
   6 hard-boiled eggs, sliced
   1 dozen eggs
   ½ gallon milk
   freshly ground black pepper
   1 egg yolk mixed with 2 tablespoons water, for brushing

To make the crust, sift salt and pepper (if using) into the flour, and work in the butter and lard with your fingers. Add the egg-water mixture, stirring until it forms a ball. The dough should be soft, but not sticky. A little more flour may be added if necessary. Refrigerate for several hours or overnight.

Roll out half of the dough and line six 9-inch pie or cake pans (they should be 2 to 3 inches deep), leaving a little overhang. Set oven at 350 degrees.

Fill pastry-lined pans half full with sopressata, prosciutto, mozzarella, ricotta, and sliced eggs. Beat eggs with milk, adding black pepper to taste. Pour this mixture over ingredients in pans, filling to within ½ inch of top. Roll out remaining dough and cover each pan, sealing edges tightly. Make several slashes in top for steam to escape. (If you have dough left over, you can use it to decorate the tops. Mom puts crosses on for Easter, with a Star-of-David variation for her Jewish daughter-in-law and grandson.) Brush with egg-water wash and bake for 40 minutes or until crust is lightly browned. Allow to cool slightly before cutting, so the filling can set. If you use a deeper pan, increase baking time to 1 hour.

considerable expense. Eventually Connecticut industrialist Peter Colt finished the job. It was well into the 1820s before Paterson's first significant industry—cotton—gained a foothold, but before long the millraces were supplying water-power to a host of burgeoning enterprises. The locomotive industry would prosper here throughout the remainder of the nineteenth century, and the silk industry even longer. By 1900 the "Silk City" would be the fifteenth largest in the United States.

The Great Falls Historic District is primarily concerned with the legacy of Paterson's industrial heyday. Sites within the district include the falls themselves and several of the more important mills that once dominated the area: the **Rogers Locomotive Erecting Shop** (now housing the Paterson Museum, described below); the wheelhouse of the **Ivanhoe Paper Mill;** the home of John Ryle, who first introduced silk manufacturing to Paterson; the **Benjamin Thompsen House** (circa 1835); the **Phoenix Mill Complex;** the two remaining stories of the 1836 mill in which Samuel Colt built his first regular production revolvers; and the impressive Beaux Arts **City Hall.**

Guided group tours start at the **Great Falls Cultural and Historic Center,** 65 McBride Avenue; (973) 279–9587. The center is open year-round Monday through Friday 9:00 A.M.–4:00 P.M.

The **Paterson Museum**'s collections of photographs and artifacts document the textile and locomotive-building industries, as well as Paterson's short-lived involvement in Samuel Colt's firearms enterprise. Perhaps the most famous of the museum's holdings, however, are the two earliest experimental submarines, built in 1878 and 1881 by John P. Holland, father of the modern submarine. The museum's interests also range to the natural and social history of the North Jersey area, and one of the state's finest mineral exhibits includes a fluorescent display in a simulated mine.

Finally, two most fitting exhibits stand in the courtyard outside the Paterson Museum building—Alco-Cooke locomotives, built just across Market Street from the Rogers plant. Number 299 was built in 1906 to help in the construction of the Panama Canal.

The Paterson Museum, 2 Market Street, (973) 321–1250, is open Tuesday through Friday 10:00 A.M.–4:00 P.M., Saturday and Sunday 12:30–4:30 P.M. There is a suggested donation of $2.00 for adults.

The Texas weiner was reportedly "invented" in Paterson, and **Libby's,** near the Passaic Falls, carries on the Silk City's culinary tradition, serving up delicious dogs heaped with their special sauce (beef, onions, peppers, and spices). Tuck into a couple with the works, but save room for the homemade rice pudding. The restaurant, at 98 McBride Avenue, is open Monday through Saturday 10:00 A.M.–1:00 A.M. and Sunday 11:00 A.M.–1:00 A.M.

In its industrial glory days at the turn of the twentieth century, Paterson supported a comfortable capitalist class. None of the silk barons lived so lavishly as Catholina Lambert, a man whose home, appropriately enough, has come to be called *Lambert Castle.* Today the home of the Passaic County Historical Society, this great sandstone pile still stands in lordly isolation on the brow of Garret Mountain, looking down over the mills and the city that made its builder rich.

Lambert built his Garret Mountain castle, which he called Belle Vista, in 1892; four years later he built the 70-foot tower (closed to visitors now) that still stands behind the house. Belle Vista became more than a home for Lambert and his family; it was also a magnificent art museum. Lambert died at the castle in 1923, at nearly ninety years of age. His house and grounds were acquired by the Passaic County Park Commission in 1928, and the building was opened as a museum six years later.

In 1997 the castle and grounds underwent a $5.5 million restoration. The first floor of the castle is now interpreted as a historic house, with period rooms and an exhibit on Catholina Lambert. The art gallery on the second floor traces the development of Passaic County. There's also a recently restored three-story atrium/art court. A research library in the basement is open by appointment. The castle serves as an excellent starting point for an exploration of the 575-acre *Garret Mountain Reservation,* jewel of the county's park system, and there's a spectacular view of New York from here.

The Lambert Castle Museum is on Valley Road, Paterson; (973) 247–0085. It's open Wednesday through Sunday 1:00–4:00 P.M. Admission is $5.00 for adults, $4.00 for seniors, and $3.00 for ages twelve to eighteen. The grounds are open daily dawn to dusk.

When Beer Flowed through Fire Hoses

Mention Prohibition beer barons and most people think of Chicago. But Paterson, a city that supported five major breweries back before the Volstead Act became law, had its own underworld brewmaster. He was Waxey Gordon, a one-time pickpocket and mob enforcer who set up shop in the city's old Sprattler & Mennel Brewery on Marshall Street. In order to avoid the suspicion that would have been aroused by a constant stream of trucks loading at the brewery, Waxey and his boys ran high-pressure fire hoses through the city sewers to distribution points around town.

The operation was even dramatized in an episode of TV's *The Untouchables.* But it was an income tax evasion rap, and not a raid on his brewery, that finally brought Waxey down. He was released from prison in 1940, and died at Alcatraz in 1952 while awaiting trial for heroin distribution.

Lambert Castle

More than seventy nationalities live within Paterson's $8\frac{3}{10}$ square miles, and adventurous diners can sample foods of the world without leaving city limits. In a few blocks, you can sample *acili ezme* (hot and spicy chopped vegetables) at **Alaturka Turkish Cuisine** on Main Street, (973) 523–6060, (and enjoy live music on weekends); *alcappura* (fried pastries of green bananas, pork, and seasonings) at Pepé Mercado's Puerto Rican restaurant, **Rincon Criollo,** on East Eighteenth Street; hop over to **Lin's Place** on Park Avenue for West Indian fare; and finish up with some down-home Southern fare at **E & A Restaurant** on Straight Street. Along the way there are Lebanese bakeries, falafel stands, sub shops, and even homemade ice cream at **Guernsey Crest** on Nineteenth Avenue. You might leave Paterson broke, but you won't leave hungry.

The other side of Paterson's industrial past is told in a far less imposing structure than Lambert Castle, located in the nearby town of Haledon. This is the 1908 Victorian home of Italian immigrants and mill workers Pietro and Mario Botto. Designated a national landmark, the Botto house is home to the **American Labor Museum.**

The Bottos were silk workers carrying on a trade learned in the "old country," Italy. It was a tough life. Workers suffered with low wages, long hours, poor lighting, and harsh production demands. In 1913, when one of Paterson's companies tried to introduce the four-loom weaving system, workers realized that at least half of them would be put out of work. Spontaneously, they walked off their jobs and onto picket lines. One by one the mills were closed by the strikes and 25,000 people were out of work.

During the 1913 Paterson silk strike, Pietro Botto opened his doors to leaders of the Industrial Workers of the World (the IWW or "Wobblies"), such as William "Big Bill" Haywood and Elizabeth Gurley Flynn. For as long as the strike lasted, thousands of Paterson mill workers would stand outside the house while Haywood and the others stirred them with oratory from its balcony.

The American Labor Museum's collections of photographs, union memorabilia, tools, and household artifacts document not only the silk strike itself, but the way of life of a generation of working-class immigrants.

The American Labor Museum/Botto House National Landmark, 83 Norwood Street, Haledon, (973) 595–7953, is open Wednesday through Saturday 1:00–4:00 P.M. or by appointment. Admission is $3.00. Come at least forty-five minutes before closing time.

The ***Van Riper–Hopper Museum*** in Wayne is a fine example of New Jersey Dutch colonial architecture. The one-and-one-half-story building, built in 1786 by Uriah Van Riper, has five lower rooms and four upstairs bedrooms in the main section of the house. The three rooms in the frame section are the former slave quarters. Typical of the New Jersey Dutch style, the house faces south, and the majority of windows are in the front to receive full benefit of sunlight. As was the custom with Dutch houses of the time, all additions were made to the side of the house rather than the rear.

There are six fireplaces throughout the house. During the year the fire in the huge basement fireplace, which contains a Dutch oven, was never allowed

Home-Fries Memories

Growing up in Paterson in the 1950s, I lived just a few blocks from a factory that turned out one of New Jersey's most famous products—diners. Standing on East Twenty-seventh Street and watching a gleaming, freshly minted stainless-steel eatery roll out of the Silk City Diner Company's plant was every bit as exciting as watching a new battleship slide down the ways. After all, I had a proprietary interest in Silk City diners: My grandfather, John Marchitti, owned one. For two decades his Hiway Diner, on Route 4 in nearby Fairlawn, was a beacon to truckers, salesmen, families, and travelers of all sorts. I learned how to make home fries at the Hiway and how to craft the perfect Taylor ham and egg sandwich. A world that could use more of John Marchitti's counterside jokes hasn't heard them for more than thirty years now, and I'm told that the Hiway Diner is someplace out in Pennsylvania. If any readers know just where, let me know and I'll be off quicker than it takes to fire up a griddle.

—Bill Scheller

A Bad Year for Paterson

On February 8, 1902, fire broke out in the streetcar barns near Paterson's Market Street. By the time the blaze was extinguished, the Silk City had lost nearly five hundred buildings, including the heart of the business district. The city's Beaux Arts City Hall, then only eight years old, was heavily damaged—it survives today, but with extensive postfire renovation.

Patersonians were barely beginning to tally the damages when, on March 2, the Passaic River roiled over its banks and carried away many of the mills, homes, and bridges that had not been lost in the fire.

to die out for fear it would bring bad luck. Only on New Year's Day was the fireplace cleaned out, and then a new fire was promptly built.

The walls in the Van Riper–Hopper House are 20 inches thick and made of local fieldstone. The floors are wide pine planks. Open ceilings are supported by heavy hand-hewn beams. A mortar of clay, straw, and hair holds the stone walls in place, and the plaster of the inside walls is an inch thick.

The homestead was saved from destruction in 1964 after the Passaic Valley Water Commission planned the *Pointview Reservoir,* which now provides a waterfowl sanctuary and attracts devoted bird-watchers (who still reminisce about the rare sighting of a Hudsonian godwit). Flower and herb gardens are maintained by Wayne garden clubs.

Colonial hearth-cooking demonstrations are held periodically at the circa 1740 *Mead–Van Duyne Museum,* a colonial stone house, which was moved 7 miles to the grounds of the Van Riper–Hopper House in 1974 to make room for highway expansion.

The Van Riper–Hopper Museum is at 533 Berdan Avenue, Wayne, (973) 694–7192. It is open by appointment and most Tuesdays and Thursdays from 9:00 A.M. to 4:00 P.M. There is a suggested donation of $5.00 for adults and $2.00 for children.

You may love some of the fourteen sculptures on the campus of *William Paterson University*. . . . You may love them all. . . . Or you may hate them all. But as long as you have some feeling about them, they've served their purpose. They've all been chosen as part of the school's Sculpture on Campus program, initiated to create an environment in which sculpture—whose development has generally been perceived as provocative and controversial—can be discovered, discussed, and, if necessary, challenged. Among them: Albert E. Henselmann's *Untitled,* Lyman Kipp's *Yoakum Jack,* Michel Gerard's *Mary Ellen Kramer Memorial Sculpture,* and Tova Beck-Friedman's *Magna Dea.*

whoneedsniagara?

Paterson's Great Falls of the Passaic River is one of the largest waterfalls east of the Mississippi.

The university's Ben Shahn Center for the Visual Arts houses several galleries for exhibits in a wide variety of media, and it also houses the college's African and Oceanic art collections. The center hosts an Art at Lunch slide lecture series seven Thursdays each semester. Call the center at (973) 720–2654 for a schedule. The center is open September to the end of May, Monday through Friday 10:00 A.M.–5:00 P.M.

The William Paterson University of New Jersey is on Pompton Road in Wayne; (877) 978–3923.

There is a house in Wayne where George Washington not only slept but spent part of 1780 planning strategy as the Revolution drew toward its decisive final year. This is the **Dey Mansion,** a graceful brick Georgian home, built about 1740 for Bergen County militia commander Col. Theunis Dey. A visit here is as instructive of how a comfortable country family lived in America in the latter half of the eighteenth century as it is of the circumstances in which the commander-in-chief conducted his councils of war and lived out his days far from his own Virginia home. Period furnishings, weapons, prints, and documents all help to tell the tale.

The Dey (pronounced "die") Mansion, 199 Totowa Road, (973) 696–1776, is open Wednesday through Friday 1:00–4:00 P.M. and Saturday and Sunday 10:00 A.M.–noon and 1:00–4:00 P.M. The last tour begins at 3:30 P.M. Admission is $1.00; children under ten are free.

Albert Payson Terhune's estate, Sunnybank, is gone now; it was torn down in 1969. But **Terhune Sunnybank Memorial Park** in Pompton Lakes—on the lake's western shore—serves as a memorial for the man who immortalized his collie, Lad, in such books as *Lad, A Dog* and *Lad of Sunnybrook.* And Lad himself is remembered, buried beneath a small marble marker that reads LAD, THOROUGHBRED IN BODY AND SOUL, 1902–1918.

A visit to the **Yogi Berra Museum & Learning Center** "ain't over till it's over." You'll learn not only about the record-setting career of Yogi Berra, catcher for the Yankees during their glory years in the 1950s and later manager of both the Yankees and the Mets, but also about New Jersey's many connections to America's national pastime.

The Yogi Berra Museum & Learning Center, on the campus of Montclair State University, 8 Quarry Road, Little Falls, (973) 655–2377, is open Wednesday through Sunday noon–5:00 P.M.; closed major holidays. Admission is $6.00 for adults, $4.00 for children and students.

The area's ethnic diversity is also evident at ***Corrado's Family Affa***. at 1578 Main Avenue in Clifton; (973) 340–0628. This huge, warehouse-style grocery store is jam-packed with foods from every nation: prosciuttos and mozzarellas, chayotes and tomatillos, kosher knishes, Afghani flatbread—and on, and on, and on.

Diners can take the sting out of the prix-fixe tab of $65 for a three-course dinner at ***Café Matisse*** by bringing along their own bottle of wine; bottles at the wine boutique, Vin de Matisse, start at just $10. The BYOB establishment is serving up some of the area's most creative contemporary American and European fare: appetizers such as smoked duck carpaccio with pan-roasted foie gras or grilled, smoked salmon on salted currant rye bread. Entrees include honey-roasted Chilean sea bass and pan-charred veal fillet in a Pinot Noir demi-glace; succulent desserts include goat-cheese cake with hazelnut sabayon, and spicy macadamia nut bread pudding with coconut-rum sauce. An a la carte menu is also available every night except Saturday.

Café Matisse, 167 Park Avenue, Rutherford, (201) 935–2995, is open for dinner Tuesday through Sunday.

Hudson/Newark Region

When American art began to claim serious critical attention in the early 1900s, a farsighted New Jersey collector and the remarkable institution he inspired were in the forefront of efforts to make works by American painters accessible to the public. The collector was William T. Evans, who in 1909 offered the town of Montclair twenty-six paintings on the condition that a museum be built to house them. The building request was met, and today the Evans collection forms the nucleus of ***The Montclair Art Museum.*** Opened in 1914, this was the first art museum in New Jersey to be open to the public, and it remains one of the few institutions of its kind to limit its concentration entirely to American art—including an excellent collection of Native American art and artifacts.

Montclair was the home of the great landscape painter George Inness, and many of his most familiar works depict the Montclair environs. Most appropriately there are twelve Inness canvases in the museum's collection of more than a thousand paintings, watercolors, and other works. Also represented are such American luminaries as John Singleton Copley, Winslow Homer, Reginald Marsh, John Singer Sargent, Childe Hassam, Robert Henri, William Morris Hunt, and James McNeill Whistler. In addition the museum houses a 14,000-volume research library.

The Montclair Art Museum, 3 South Mountain Avenue, (973) 746–5555, is open Tuesday through Sunday 11:00 A.M.–5:00 P.M., closed Monday and major holidays. Admission is $8.00 for adults, $6.00 for students and senior citizens,

The Montclair Art Museum

free for children under twelve. The museum is free to all every Friday 11:00 A.M.–1:00 P.M. No charge for parking.

In 1796 Israel Crane, at the age of twenty-two, constructed a turnpike that opened New Jersey's heartland to early trade; he also built a Federal-style mansion that was to become home to seven generations of his family. Today the ten-room **Israel Crane House** has been restored to look as it did between 1796 and 1840, and uniformed docents are on hand to provide a glimpse into life during that period.

On the premises are herb and pleasure gardens, an 1818 house converted into a country store, and a crafts building.

The Israel Crane House, 108 Orange Road, Montclair, (973) 744–1796, is open Thursday through Saturday 1:00–4:00 P.M., and Sunday 2:00–5:00 P.M. Admission is $5.00 for adults, $2.00 for children ten and under. Group tours are available by reservation. Thanksgiving, Christmas, the Fourth of July, and the changing seasons are celebrated with traditional foods, music, and decorations. Call for details.

Less than a mile from the Crane House, at 30 North Mountain Avenue, **Evergreens: The Schultz House Museum** was designed by Michael Le Brun, architect of the Metropolitan Life Insurance Tower in New York City. The unusual residence, built in 1896, is a blending of several architectural styles; it includes Tudor and colonial revival details. There is a shingle style carriage house in the rear. Tours of Evergreens are given at 3:00 P.M. on the first and third Sunday of the month between April and October. Advance registration is required, and tickets are $8.00 for adults and $4.00 for children ten and under. For information, call the Israel Crane House at (973) 744–1796.

Eagle Rock County Reservation, just a half mile from the Crane House, provides a magnificent view of the Manhattan skyline.

If you happen to be in or around Montclair between the middle of May and early June, don't leave without visiting the National Historic Trust Site *Presby Memorial Iris Gardens* in Mountainside Park. These gardens are the legacy of Montclair citizen Frank H. Presby, a breeder of irises and a founder of the American Iris Society.

Having begun with a modest planting that included several of Presby's own iris hybrids, the gardens have grown to include six species with more than 4,000 varieties of irises, including some that date from the 1500s. If you wish to refresh your memory of spring's iris pageant, return to Presby Gardens in September and October, when the remontant (reblooming) irises come into bloom.

Admission to the Presby Memorial Iris Gardens, 474 Upper Mountain Avenue, Upper Montclair, (973) 783–5974, and Mountainside Park, is free. The grounds are open in season 10:00 A.M.–8:00 P.M. Call for information on times to see the iris displays. Donations are welcome.

If you need a little spice in your life, head over to *Spice it Up!,* 229 Glenridge Avenue, (973) 744–3344. More than 250 spices from around the world—from the mundane to the exotic—are sold in bulk, beginning at a half-ounce. Most range in price from $2.00 to $4.00 an ounce. The shop's knowledgeable owners will be glad to give you advice on what to use to perk up your bland chicken breast. Call for hours.

If you've ever thought about what it would be like to be an air traffic controller (but lack the tolerance for stress and superhuman doses of responsibility that go with it), head over to the *Aviation Hall of Fame and Museum of New Jersey* in Teterboro. Teterboro Airport, one of the nation's busiest facilities that serves private and commuter aircraft, needed a new control tower a while back. Instead of tearing down the old one, though, authorities incorporated it into the Aviation Hall of Fame. Now, after looking over the Arthur Godfrey collection of aviation artifacts and watching films of historic events in New Jersey aviation history, visitors can head upstairs and witness takeoffs and landings from the same perch controllers used for years. There's even an audio hookup, broadcasting the directions that controllers in the new tower are giving to incoming pilots.

(The Arthur Godfrey connection with Teterboro, by the way, is both famous and infamous. One day the radio and television personality buzzed the tower in a fit of temper, and later he recalled the event in a song called "Teterboro Tower.")

ιe Education Center adjacent to the control tower has a facsimile control
r; aircraft, helicopter, and rocket exhibits; and hands-on airplanes to "fly."
ιν. / Jersey–built piston, jet, and rocket engines and a military aviation display
dominate the Great Hall. There's a Hall of Fame, where exhibits present avia-
trixes such as Amelia Earhart and Kathryn Sullivan (the first woman to walk in
space), and astronaut Buzz Aldrin, a native New Jerseyan.

The Aviation Hall of Fame and Museum of New Jersey, Route 46, (201) 288–
6344, is open Tuesday through Sunday 10:00 A.M.–4:00 P.M. Admission is $6.00
for adults, $4.00 for senior citizens and children over two.

Teterboro sits on the fringes of a vast tract of land that was for centuries an
uninhabited and virtually uninhabitable wilderness, even after populous cities
and suburbs sprang up all around it. Variously called the Hackensack Meadows,
the Secaucus Meadows, or simply the Meadowlands or Meadows, the marshy
basin that surrounds the estuarial reaches of the Hackensack and Passaic Rivers
constitutes a remarkable ecosystem that is, unfortunately, famous chiefly for the
ways in which it has been abused over the past hundred years.

Construction of any magnitude was stymied because the Meadows' foundation consists of up to 200 feet of unconsolidated muck. Within recent memory railroads and their attendant structures were the only substantial fabricated
works in the Hackensack Meadows.

In spite of this construction problem, people did find some uses for the
Meadows, and the uses they found were responsible for the dubious reputation
the area once carried. Fifty years ago, when you were driving on the turnpike
through the Meadows on a hot summer day, you would roll up your windows
(this was before auto air-conditioning) when you got near Secaucus because
of the stench of the pig farms that occupied the edges of the Meadows. And if it
wasn't the pigs, it was the garbage—communities in North Jersey long ago took
to using the Meadows as a giant solid-waste landfill. Finally, as if pigs and
garbage weren't enough, there were all the jokes about missing mobsters who
were spending eternity beneath the marsh grasses.

In the early 1970s everything started to change. Construction engineers figured out how to build on the Meadows' soil, and the Hackensack Meadows
Development Commission (HMDC) was formed. The Meadowlands were
zoned, divided, and conquered.

didyouknow . . . ?

It is believed that Snake Hill in the
Hackensack Meadows is the eroded
stump of an ancient volcano.

Fortunately the planners who
undertook the development of
the Meadows found room for the
preservation of one of the more
undisturbed tracts as the multi-
ple-use *Richard DeKorte State*

Park. It includes hiking and
nature-observation trails as well
as a miniwilderness wildlife-management area. For all the depre-
dations of the past, the Meadows
are still a fine place for birding.
You can even borrow a pair of

Connie Francis, Frankie Valli, Paul Simon,
Whitney Houston, and Philip Roth all hail
from Newark.

binoculars at the **HMDC Environmental Center,** where there are informa-
tive exhibits and a large, glassed-in wing that overlooks the wildlife-management areas.

The HMDC Environmental Center is located at the end of Valley Brook
Avenue in Lyndhurst; take the Polito Avenue exit off Route 17 South. The center
is open Monday through Friday 9:00 A.M.–5:00 P.M. and Saturday and Sunday 10:00
A.M.–3:00 P.M. The boardwalk and trails are open daily, May through September,
8:30 A.M.–7:00 P.M.; October through March, 8:30 A.M.–4:00 P.M.; and April, 8:30
A.M.–6:00 P.M. For more information call the center at (201) 460–8300.

For a historical perspective on the Meadowlands and environs, visit the
Meadowlands Museum in Rutherford. This small institution, which is housed
in a Dutch colonial farmhouse, maintains files of historical photographs and documents that are available to researchers if not currently on display. In addition
to the first-floor exhibits, which change three or four times a year, the museum
also features reconstructions of colonial and turn-of-the-twentieth-century
kitchens on its lower level as well as exhibits of antique toys and dolls and New
Jersey minerals on the second floor.

The Meadowlands Museum, 91 Crane Avenue, Rutherford, (201) 935–1175,
is open January through June and September through December, Monday,
Wednesday, and Saturday 1:00–4:00 P.M. and Sunday 2:00–4:00 P.M.; in July and
August hours are Monday through Thursday 1:00–4:00 P.M. and Sunday
2:00–4:00 P.M. Closed major holidays. A donation of $2.00 per adult and $1.00
per child is requested.

Head east now to the bluffs above the Hudson River at Weehawken.
Known to motorists as the town on the New Jersey side of the Lincoln Tunnel
and to aficionados of Edward Hopper's paintings as the setting for his *East
Wind over Weehawken,* this is where the career of Alexander Hamilton, the bril-
liant American statesman, Federalist Papers writer, and first U.S. secretary of the
treasury, was cut short in a duel with Vice President Aaron Burr. Burr, who felt
that his recent candidacy for the governorship of New York had failed largely
because of the vociferous criticism of his old enemy Hamilton, made the formal
demand for satisfaction; the two men met at what was then a secluded spot on
the Jersey side of the Hudson on the morning of July 11, 1804. Pistols were the

weapon of choice. Hamilton's shot missed; Burr's did not. The author of the Federalist Papers died a day later, while Burr, his political career finished, left the area and began his descent into the shadows of American history.

The actual **Hamilton-Burr Duel Site,** which is marked today by a small park and a modest tablet, is on John F. Kennedy Boulevard East (also called by its old name, Hudson Boulevard East). Nearby is **Veterans' Memorial Park,** where there is a more impressive monument and bronze bust of Hamilton. Historical considerations aside, this is a particularly scenic spot at dusk on a late fall or winter afternoon, when lights twinkle on across the river in Manhattan.

If you've always wanted to visit the Ginza but haven't had a chance, plan a stop at **Mitsuwa Marketplace** (formerly Yaohan Plaza), a mall whose vendors specialize in Japanese (and other) goods. The centerpiece here is a giant market filled with exotic produce, fresh fish and noodles, and imported packaged goods. Go there hungry; the food concessions are a bit more eclectic than the shops, offering everything from sushi to kung pao chicken to Korean hot pot. The mall, at 595 River Road in Edgewater, (201) 941–9113, is open Sunday through Friday 9:30 A.M.–8:00 P.M. and Saturday 9:30 A.M.–9:00 P.M.

If you're more in the mood for black bean soup, *ropa vieja* (stewed, shredded flank steak), or *bistec de Palomilla* (pan-seared marinated sirloin steak), you're in luck. **Azucar** serves up fine traditional Cuban fare in an upbeat and lively spot. The restaurant, at 10 Dempsey Avenue, Edgewater, (201) 886–0747, is open for lunch Wednesday through Friday and dinner Tuesday through Sunday. BYOB. Reservations accepted for parties of three or more.

In 1915 Pope Benedict XV issued a plea for world peace, and the Reverend Joseph N. Grieff, pastor of Holy Family Church in Union Hill (now Union City), responded. He envisioned a production of an "Americanized" Passion play, modeled on the one presented every ten years since 1680 in Oberammergau, Bavaria. Thus began Union City's annual—and the country's oldest—Passion play. In 1931 the **Park Performing Arts Center** was built specifically for the Passion play, which is now performed here each Easter season. The 1,400-seat Moorish-style opera house also hosts other cultural events throughout the year.

The Passion play tells the story of the last days of Jesus as he preached, journeyed to Jerusalem, presided at the Last Supper, and was crucified. The play received an overhaul in 1985, when Father Kevin Ashe rewrote the script to alter the anti-Semitic reputation Passion plays had earned over the years. "The Park Theater's Passion play is an art form that teaches a lesson to Christians," Father Ashe states. "In times of social unrest, the play teaches us that we all come from the same roots. Christ himself was Jewish."

The center is at 560 Thirty-second Street, Union City; call (201) 865–6980, or go to www.parkpac.org, for a schedule of events.

Union City has a large Hispanic population, so it's no surprise that some of New Jersey's best Latin restaurants and grocery stores are here. Mexican tortillas, Chilean empanadas (crusty turnovers), Colombian *batidos* (a drink of whipped milk, fruit, and sugar)—the 3½-mile route along Bergenline Avenue running toward West New York is a Latin fresser's dream come true.

The 20,000-square-foot grocery store **Mi Bandera** (518 Thirty-second Street off Bergenline Avenue) is a great place to stock up on provisions such as molé (a Mexican sauce made of chocolate and spices) and tomatillos. If you prefer to have the cooking done for you, the restaurant upstairs serves fabulous *chicharrones* (fried pork cracklings), *sancocho* (Cuban meat, yucca, and corn stew), and other Latin specialties. If you're in town on Saturday, stop at **Celso's Cafe** (4900 Bergenline Avenue) for some delicious empanadas (beef, onion, and egg turnovers). Or stop in at **La Isla Cigars** (505 Forty-second Street off Bergenline Avenue), buy a hand-rolled cigar from Berto Ale, who learned his trade in Cuba, and meander up Bergenline smoking and grazing.

The Hoboken piers immortalized in Elia Kazan's 1954 movie *On the Waterfront* were once among the busiest on the East Coast. From the mid-nineteenth century until the beginning of World War I, two ocean liner companies, Hamburg-American and North Germany Lloyd, owned docks here and landed so many German immigrants that the city earned the nickname "Little Bremen." (By the mid-1850s, almost one-quarter of the city's population of 7,000 was German.) World War I's American Expeditionary Forces sailed from Hoboken to Europe. During the war, almost 3,500 workers were employed here, working on the new steel ships that required more skilled labor.

Since World War I, the piers have been home to several companies, including Bethlehem Steel (1938–1980), but by the 1970s the rising popularity of containerization and the lack of space on the Hoboken docks were the death knell for the steel company and its employees. The company sold the shipyard to the Braswell Corporation in 1982, but after a few years it also closed its doors. A lingerie manufacturer purchased the site with plans to convert it to luxury housing, and a wrecking crew had actually demolished a corner of the 1890 Machine Shop—the oldest building on the waterfront—before it was stopped by members of the community.

Today the Machine Shop is home to the ***Hoboken Historical Museum,*** 1301 Hudson Street, (201) 656–2240, which hosts exhibits, lectures, and walking tours of piers left largely intact. Call for admission fees and a schedule of tours. The museum is open Tuesday, Wednesday, and Thursday 2:00–9:00 P.M., Friday 1:00–5:00 P.M., and Saturday and Sunday noon to 5:00 PM. Admission is $2.00. Museum guests receive two hours of free parking at the Fourteenth Street lot. Take a ticket from the machine and request a token at the museum.

Frank Sinatra is immortalized on a "hall of fame" of photographs at ***Leo's Grandevous Restaurant,*** just a few blocks from the one-time home of the "Chairman of the Board" (his birthplace, at 415 Monroe Street, has been torn down; his boyhood home at 841 Garden Street is still standing). While you're there, you can chow down on some fine, moderately priced Italian dishes, including stuffed calamari and spinach ravioli, or have a drink at the bar, where someone is bound to spin a tale about their days with Frank. The restaurant, at 200 Grand Avenue and Second, (201) 659–9467, is open for lunch weekdays and dinner nightly.

We don't know if Mr. Sinatra ever ate at ***Schnackenberg's Luncheonette,*** but we can well imagine him stopping by for a cup of coffee back in the 1930s when Henry and Dora first opened their luncheonette. Today, it's operated by their daughter, Betty, who has done very little redecorating, and judging by the prices—$1.20 for a peanut butter and jelly sandwich and fifty cents for coffee—has not changed the menu or prices much, either. It's at 1110 Washington

Hoboken Terminal

Thousands of workers take commuter trains in and out of Hoboken every day, but how many stop to take a look at the station? Built in 1907 for the Delaware, Lackawanna, and Western Railroad, Hoboken Terminal was one of the great transportation temples of the age. Much of the exterior—especially on the Hudson River facade where the DL&W ferries used to dock—is copper, its surface aged to a mellow green. Inside, the 90-by-100-foot main waiting room is lavishly decorated in limestone and bronze. The ferry concourse, now being restored, once contained a restaurant with river-facing balcony, a sumptuous barbershop, and even an emergency hospital.

Out beneath the 607-foot train sheds, prosaic New Jersey Transit commuter cars now depart on short suburban runs—a far cry from the glory days, when crack overnight trains like the *Phoebe Snow* sallied out of Hoboken on their way to the cities of the Midwest.

Street, Hoboken, (201) 659–9836, and open Monday through S
A.M.–5:00 P.M.

Many folks believe that tiny, informal, and brightly lit *La Isla* i
Hoboken (104 Washington Street, 201–659–8197) offers the best C...... .a.. .... m
the state. Among the favorite dishes: ground beef or chicken empanadas, garlic
shrimp, and roast suckling pig with sweet potatoes (generally served only at
Saturday dinner). Sunday brunch, served 11:00 A.M.–4:00 P.M. September through
June, is a standout. The restaurant is open Monday through Saturday 7:00
A.M.–10:00 P.M. BYOB.

City Bistro, one of the many upscale restaurants attracted to Hoboken in
recent years, serves up fine food and a spectacular view of Manhattan. There
are three floors here, but, weather permitting, opt for the roof deck, sit back,
and enjoy. The food is contemporary American with French and Italian
touches, including appetizers such as fried calamari with aioli sauce. Seared
diver scallops and grilled sirloin steak are just a few of the well-prepared
entrees. The restaurant, at 56-58 Fourteenth Street, (201) 963–8200, is open for
lunch Monday through Friday, Saturday and Sunday brunch, and dinner
nightly. Free three-hour parking.

As we go to press, the HBO series *The Sopranos* is heading into its last
season. Here's a ride that fans of Tony and the gang won't want to miss: bus
tours that take in the show's hot spots, including Big Pussy's Auto Body
Shop, Satriale's Pork Store in Kearny, and the Club Bada Bing in Lodi (which
is actually called the Satin Dolls and doesn't have nude dancers, but it does
sell T-shirts). Many of the locations are created for filming, although one of
the tours stops for refreshments at Sorrento's bakery in Lodi, where Tony
and the boys buy their *sfogliatelles* (cheese-filled pastries).

On Location Tours (www.screentours.com) offers a four-hour tour that
leaves Saturday and Sunday at 2:00 P.M. from Manhattan's Times Square. The
cost is $42, and advance reservations (highly recommended) can be made by
calling (212) 209–3370.

Jersey City's *Afro-American Historical Society Museum* focuses on
New Jersey's African-American people, places, and events, with changing as
well as permanent exhibits. Among the latter: a 1930 kitchen reflecting the
heart of an urban black home for that time and period; black dolls from the
African Diaspora (some dating back more than 125 years); sculptures and
paintings; and civil rights artifacts and collections of the 1950s and 1960s.

In addition to exhibits, the museum hosts lectures and programs relating
to the black experience, and sponsors a Kwanzaa program each December.
The New Jersey Afro-American Historical and Genealogical Society, Inc., meets
at the museum on the second Saturday of each month at noon.

katynmemorial

At Exchange Place, the busy centerpiece of Jersey City's revived business district along the Hudson River waterfront, stands one of the most stark and unsettling statues to ever commemorate a historic event. It is a standing soldier, his face frozen at the moment of death, impaled on a bayonet. The statue memorializes the execution of 11,000 Polish army officers by Soviet troops in the Katyn Forest during the spring of 1940. It serves as a reminder that Jersey City's considerable Polish population refuses to forget the betrayal, devastation, and slaughter that was its fate during World War II.

The Afro-American Historical Society Museum, 1841 John F. Kennedy Boulevard, (201) 547–5262, is open Monday through Saturday 10:00 A.M.–5:00 P.M. In July and August, Monday through Friday 10:00 A.M.–5:00 P.M. Admission is free.

Whether or not you're a Jersey chauvinist who thinks the state flag should fly from Liberty's crown, it's nice to know that you can get out to Liberty Island and the **Statue of Liberty** without having to sail from the Battery. The Circle Line operates a ferry that leaves **Liberty State Park,** off exit 14B of the New Jersey Turnpike, and stops at Ellis Island State Park and the Statue of Liberty. The ferry operates frequently, but the times change with the seasons, so call ahead. (If you wish to visit both Ellis and Liberty Islands, it's recommended that you take an early boat. A time pass is required to visit the Liberty Island promenade and/or observatory. Call (866) 782–8834 for a reservation.) The ferry operates every day except Christmas. The fare is $11.50 for adults, $9.50 for senior citizens, and $4.50 for children ages four to twelve. The best time to go is in the morning, before the crowds arrive. Parking is $5.00. Call Liberty State Park at (201) 435–9499 for more information or check their Web site at www.libertystatepark.com.

The carhops are gone now, but little else at the **White Mana** has changed since 1939 (it originally opened at the World's Fair). Dedicated patrons continue to pack the tiny, classic diner for the house specialty, a grilled burger with onions on a soft bun, with pickle chips on the side (75 cents each). The key to the burger's popularity? "The grill is saturated with onions, seasoned with onions . . . the more seasoned, the better burgers," says the day cook, Larry McMillan, who has been grilling Mana

heavystuff

Jersey City boasts two of the "world's biggest" of their kind: the largest concrete monument, a 365-ton fountain erected in 1911 at the main entrance to Lincoln Park; and the 2,200-pound Colgate Clock, whose 50-foot face overlooks the Hudson River on Hudson Street.

burgers for more than twenty years. The diner, (201) 963–1441, is at Manhatta and Tonnelle Avenues in Jersey City.

Newark, New Jersey's largest city, has two major troves of regional historical materials, the Newark Museum and the lesser known **New Jersey Historical Society.** This society is the repository of what has been called "an unparalleled collection of New Jerseyana," and the sheer bulk and diversity of its holdings support the claim. Here is a library of 80,000 volumes, open to the public for reference use, and a collection of 2,000 maps, 22,000 prints, and 1 million manuscripts, including the original New Jersey charter of 1664. The society owns 300 portrait and landscape paintings and thousands of drawings, as well as furnishings, silver, glass, and porcelain of New Jersey manufacture.

The New Jersey Historical Society, 52 Park Place, (973) 596–8500, is open Tuesday through Saturday 10:00 A.M.–5:00 P.M. Admission is free.

The magnificent **Cathedral Basilica of the Sacred Heart** is a church of superlatives: It's the fifth largest in the country, has the second largest rose window in the United States (37 feet in diameter), and has the state's largest church organ. It's also considered by many to be the purest example of classical French Gothic architecture in the Western Hemisphere. Organ recitals are given throughout the year (the schedule is on their Web site: www.cathedralbasilica.org/concerts), and admission is $10. Tours of the cathedral are offered after the concerts or by appointment. The cathedral is open daily 9:00 A.M.–7:00 P.M. The National Historic Site is at 89 Ridge Street, Newark, (973) 484–4600.

It's rumored that pals Joe Pesci and Robert De Niro stop in at **Dickie-Dee Pizza** at 380 Bloomfield Avenue whenever they get a craving for one of Jersey's finest pies. We're not sure what kind they order, but we can heartily endorse the special, as well as the great antipasto and the house special—deep-fried

sailaway

Five state-owned marinas are administered by New Jersey's Park Service. They include Forked River State Marina in Forked River, (609) 693–5045; Fortescue State Marina in Fortescue, (609) 447–5115; Leonardo State Marina in Leonardo, (732) 291–1333; Liberty Landing Marina in Jersey City, (201) 985–8000; and Senator Frank S. Farley State Marina in Atlantic City, (609) 441–8482.

hot dogs. The sandwiches, on circular loaves of bread, are also great. The restaurant is open for lunch and dinner; (973) 483–9396.

In nearby Bloomfield, you can satisfy your hankering for an old-fashioned peanut butter and jelly sandwich ($2.00) and wash it down with an ice-cream soda at **Holsten's Brookdale Confectionery,** an old-fashioned ice-cream parlor

nnewark

e has plenty of open
usual for people to
Jersey with pavement.
torical as well as a visual
reason for the connection: The first application of asphalt for street paving in the United States was in Newark, in 1870.

that makes its own candy and ice cream. Those with more sophisticated palates can opt for burgers, double-decker sandwiches, and omelettes. Save room for Holsten's special: four scoops of ice cream topped with fruit salad, hot fudge, whipped cream, and a cherry ($6.50). The Confectionery, at 1063 Broad Street, (973) 338–7091, is open Monday through Saturday 11:00 A.M.–11:30 P.M. and Sunday noon– 10:00 P.M.

Before leaving town, be sure to take a stroll through the lovely *Town Green Historic District,* whose large town green is lined with more than 200 handsome homes of diverse architecture, including Federal, Italianate, and Queen Anne. Contact the Historical Society of Bloomfield, 47 Clark Avenue, Bloomfield 07003, (201) 429–8387, for a map of the walking tour.

Branch Brook Park is lovely at any time of the year, but magnificent in April when 2,700 Japanese cherry trees—the largest display in the world—come into bloom. The park, at Franklin Avenue and Mill Street, Belleville, is open year-round, dawn to dusk. Admission is free. For more information, call (973) 268–3500.

The 2,047-acre *South Mountain Reservation* is the most spectacular parkland in the greater Newark area. Covering parts of Millburn, Maplewood, and West Orange, South Mountain is maintained as a balanced mix of forest, meadows, bridle and bicycle paths, and secluded hiking trails. From Washington Rock on the Crest Drive along the reservation's eastern border, there are magnificent views of the skylines of Newark and New York; on the Lenape Trail deep in the interior, it's possible to forget that there is any urbanization or even human settlement for miles.

Near the northern end of the South Mountain Reservation, on sixteen acres of land, sits *Turtle Back Zoo.* Northern New Jersey's largest zoo houses 500 animals of 200 different species, with an emphasis on animals originally found in New Jersey. The most recent exhibits have flight cages for the golden and bald eagles, and the gray wolves and black bears are presented in a naturalistic setting. More exotic animals include penguins, llamas, mouflon sheep, addaxes, and squirrel monkeys.

Admission includes the Turtle Back Railroad train ride through the scenic reservation (the train runs from mid-April through October, weather permitting), as well as access to picnic areas. There are also pony rides and a petting zoo.

The zoo is at 560 Northfield Avenue, West Orange, (973) ¯
and May, the zoo is open Monday through Saturday 10:00
Sunday 11:00 A.M.–5:30 P.M. Admission is $7.00 for adults, $?
ages two to twelve and senior citizens (ages sixty and over).

Nearby Union County has also set aside some fine parklands. The best
place to head for a day's ramble hereabouts is the roughly 2,000-acre
Watchung Reservation, located between Summit and Scotch Plains.

Although there are cultivated rhododendron plantings within the Watchung
Reservation, most of the land within its borders has been left as much as possible in its natural state. As at South Mountain, there are extensive hiking and
bridle trails; for the hardy, a 10-mile loop called the Sierra Club Trail makes a
circuit of the reservation, just within the boundaries.

Near the New Providence Road entrance to the Watchung Reservation is
the **Trailside Nature and Science Center,** a well-run facility recommended
to anyone who visits the park with children. There are exhibits on local animals, fossils, minerals, plants, and pond ecology. The center is open daily
1:00–5:00 P.M. For information contact Trailside, Coles Avenue and New
Providence Road, Mountainside 07092, (908) 789–3670. Admission is free.

At the **Stage House Inn,** a brick structure dating to 1737, chef/proprietor
David Drake combines a variety of cooking methods and ingredients from
numerous countries to create well-balanced dishes with a French flair. Among
his specialties: an appetizer of quail stuffed with lobster on a bed of lobster
risotto garnished with sautéed chanterelles; a loin of veal entree with celery
root, caramelized apples, and smoky bacon; and glorious desserts such as
apple tart tatin. The restaurant, at
366 Park Avenue, Scotch Plains,
(908) 322–4224, is open for dinner nightly. Jackets for men are
requested. The inn's new tavern
serves lunch daily.

You don't have to visit Vermont
to show the kids where the syrup
they're putting on their waffles
comes from. Each February environmental scientists at the sixteen-
acre **Cora Hartshorn Arboretum
and Bird Sanctuary** tap the
arboretum's sugar maples and boil
up batches of delicious maple
syrup. The process requires cold

feltville

An unexpected find amid the leafy glades
of Summit's Watchung Reservation is the
cluster of old wooden buildings that consti-
tute the remains of the deserted village of
Feltville. Feltville was the creation of New
York businessman David Felt, who chose
this site for a model paper-manufacturing
and printing operation, complete with
workers' housing. The place boomed from
1845 until about 1860, and has been a
ghost town since 1880. Since then, Watchung
Reservation, a county park, has come to
enclose the old industrial site.

In This Case, *with* a Paddle

My most unusual excursion through my home state of New Jersey took place in the spring of 1985, when five friends and I traveled the entire length of the Passaic River by canoe. Starting at the river's source near the Great Swamp, we made the 75-mile trip over the course of three days. Our longest portage was around the Great Falls of the Passaic in Paterson. Our strangest overnight stay was when we pitched tents on the riverbank in downtown Summit. And the successful conclusion came at Newark, when we paddled our three canoes under the Pulaski Skyway and entered Newark Bay.

—Bill Scheller

nights and warm days, so call ahead to find out when the sap is running and make a reservation ($5.00 per family). The 16½ acres of wooded grounds at the Arboretum encompass 3 miles of trails. An exhibit of stuffed and live animals is housed in the Stone House. Dogs are not permitted. It's at 324 Forest Drive, Short Hills, (973) 376–3587, and open year-round during daylight hours.

History of an abrupt and dramatic variety was made on the steps of Springfield's Presbyterian Church by its minister, the Reverend James Caldwell, during the Revolutionary War Battle of Springfield. As the battle raged over the fields, Continental troops ran out of the wadding that was used between powder and ball in the muzzle-loading muskets of the day. Caldwell, an ardent separatist and chaplain of one of the New Jersey regiments, dashed into the church and emerged with as many copies as he could carry of the then-standard Watts hymnbook. Tossing them to the soldiers at the foot of the church steps, the minister called out, "Give 'em Watts, boys. Put Watts into them." Many a Continental musket ball was seated atop a wadded page of hymns that day. Caldwell was minister of the ***First Presbyterian Church*** of Elizabeth from 1762 to 1781, when he was shot and killed. He preached with loaded pistols in the pulpit and kept a lookout in the belfry to warn of an approach of the British, who came on forays from Staten Island. The church building of Elizabeth was burned by the British and rebuilt in 1785–1787. The church burned again in an accidental fire in 1946, but the outer walls are the original 1787 structure. The inside was restored to its colonial style and is an authentic representation of Georgian architecture. The adjacent graveyard represents an unbroken continuum of history that dates back to the late seventeenth century.

The church, 42 Broad Street, Elizabeth, (908) 353–1518, houses a museum and will be opened for visitors by appointment. The grounds and cemetery are open daily during daylight hours; Sunday services are at 11:00 A.M. (10:00 A.M.

in summer); Wednesday services are at noon. In July, services are held at the circa 1820–1893 Second Presbyterian Church, 1161 East Jersey Street, Elizabeth, (908) 352–1659. Tours are offered there by appointment.

Far different, and more ancient, associations are suggested by a visit to Beth Israel Memorial Park, a Jewish cemetery in Woodbridge. Here are the **Bible Gardens of Israel,** conceived as a means of bringing the physical environment of the Holy Land to life in the New World. The vehicle used for this ambitious enterprise was horticulture; here are hundreds of the plants mentioned in the Bible, from olive, fig, and pomegranate trees to myrtle, oleander, and bay. The trees, shrubs, and flowering plants are arranged in four main gardens: the Garden of the Promised Land, the Garden of Moses, the Garden of Jerusalem (Garden of Peace), and the Garden of the Kings. Each individual specimen is identified by its Hebrew, English, and Linnean names.

In order to bring an added note of authenticity and significance to the biblical plantings, the garden's designers have incorporated boulders from Mount Canaan, Elath, and the River Jordan; stones from Aijalon, Galilee, and Mount Zion; and numerous other physical reminders of the land where the Scriptures were written. Artworks of marble, bronze, and wrought iron are tastefully integrated into the gardens.

The gardens, on Route 1 (near the Garden State Parkway), Woodbridge, (732) 634–2100, are open daily during daylight hours. Admission is free.

He Got the Benz

The stonecutters at Rock of Ages in Barre, Vermont, are used to unusual requests: They've carved granite headstones shaped like a soccer ball, an easy chair, and even a soldier's wife appearing in a puff of cigarette smoke. But the request to carve a full-size 1982 Mercedes-Benz was definitely among the more unusual.

It's a memorial for Ray Tse Jr., a Chinese boy who died at the age of fifteen, before he could receive his license. Commissioned by his brother, the thirty-six-ton monument took three Rock of Ages workers a year and a half to complete.

Ray's Mercedes is in the Asian section (the northern end) of the **Rosedale and Rosehill Cemetery,** 335 East Linden Avenue, Linden. The cemetery is open 9:00 A.M.–6:00 P.M.

Places to Stay in the Urban Northeast

Grand Summit Hotel
570 Springfield Avenue
East, Summit;
(908) 273–3000;
fax (732) 473–4228

Palace Hotel
2600 Tonnelle Avenue,
North Bergen;
(800) 548–4206 or
(201) 866–0400;
fax (201) 866–6007

The Pillars of Plainfield
922 Central Avenue,
Plainfield;
(908) 753–0922 or
(888) PILLARS;
www.pillars2.com.
Moderate.

Robert Treat Hotel
50 Park Place, Newark;
(973) 622–1000 or
(800) 569–2300;
fax (973) 622–6410;
rthotel.com.
Moderate–expensive.

Sheraton Suites on the Hudson
500 Harbor Boulevard,
Weehawken;
(201) 617–5600;
sheraton.com/suiteshudson.
Moderate–expensive.

Woodcliff Lake Hilton
200 Tice Boulevard,
Woodcliff Lake;
(800) HILTONS or
(201) 391–3600;
fax (201) 391–4572;
hiltonwoodclifflake.com.
Moderate–expensive.

Wyndham Garden Hotel
21 Kingsbridge Road,
Piscataway;
(732) 980–0400;
fax (732) 980–0973;
wyndham.com.
Moderate–expensive.

Places to Eat in the Urban Northeast

Arthur's Landing
Pershing Circle at
Port Imperial,
Weehawken;
(201) 867–0777
The menu is contemporary
American and the view
of the Manhattan skyline
is fantastic at this waterfront spot. Thursday
evening features live
jazz, and brunch is
served Saturday and
Sunday. Dinner nightly.
Expensive.

Chakra
144 Route 4 East,
Paramus;
(201) 556–1530
New American cuisine is
prepared with a deft touch,
with dishes such as grilled
octopus with sun-dried
tomatoes and port-braised
short ribs with foie gras.
Dinner Monday through
Saturday. Expensive.

Chowpatty Vegetarian Restaurant
1349 Oak Tree Road,
Iselin;
(732) 283–9020
For a snack, a quick meal,
or dessert, the Indian

restaurant/sweet shop
offers an extensive
menu ranging from the
traditional to the unusual.
Where else can you
wash down your samosa
or ragda patties with a
mango milk shake?
Lunch and dinner.
Inexpensive.

Cucharamama
233 Clinton Street,
Union City;
(201) 420–1700
Among authentic Latin-
American specialties
are poached octopus
chunks in Peruvian black-
olive sauce. Dinner
Tuesday through Sunday.
Inexpensive–moderate.

El Artesano
4101 Bergenline Avenue,
Union City;
(201) 867–7341;
www.elartesanorestaurant
.com.
An unpretentious little spot
with a long red counter as
well as table seating, and
some of the area's finest traditional Spanish fare. Lunch
and dinner daily. Moderate.

Frankie & Johnnie's
163 14th Street,
Hoboken;
(201) 659–6202
Terrific steaks and chops, a
tranquil piano bar, and a traditional steak house atmosphere. Entertainment
Tuesday through Saturday.
Dinner nightly. Expensive.

Highlawn Pavilion
Eagle Rock Reservation,
West Orange;
(973) 731–3463
American cuisine with a
European flair is the spe-
cialty at the restaurant
housed in a 1909

Florentine-style building overlooking Manhattan. Many dishes are prepared on the French rotisserie or in the wood-burning Italian brick oven. Jackets required in dining room. Pizza and foccaccia are on the menu in the piano bar. Expensive.

The Manor
111 Prospect Street,
West Orange;
(973) 731–2360
The grounds, with its formal gardens, are exquisite, and the menu—which includes lobster buffets (Wednesday through Saturday evenings), as well as a la carte selections in the Terrace Lounge—is diverse. On Sunday there are brunch and family dinner buffets. A three-course pre-theater menu includes valet parking and round-trip ferry to New York. Lunch buffet Wednesday, regular lunch Thursday and Friday, dinner Tuesday through Sunday. expensive.

Mexicali Rose
10 Park Street, Montclair;
(973) 746–9005
Bring along your own beer to wash down Mexican and Southwestern dishes including shrimp in tequila and Tijuana chicken. Lunch and dinner daily. Inexpensive.

Miyoski
21 Mercer Street,
Hackensack;
(201) 489–0007
For more than fifteen years the sushi- and sashimi-starved have been making tracks to this traditional Japanese restaurant, which also serves fine beef teriyaki, shrimp tempura, and other

popular dishes. Dinner nightly. Inexpensive–moderate.

Raymond's
28 Church Street, Montclair;
(973) 744–9263
A classic American menu with a touch of the international includes everything from cheeseburgers to mussels marinara. Lunch Monday through Friday, dinner nightly; Saturday and Sunday brunch. Inexpensive.

Restaurant Juniper
7 Ridge Road, Lyndhurst;
(201) 939–6019
For those who opt for well-prepared dishes rather than a quiet dining experience, this is the place. Juniper's contemporary menu changes with the seasons, and might include risotto with wild mushrooms and truffle oil and/or sautéed duck breast. Moderate–expensive.

Sagres Bar and Grill
44–50 Prospect Street,
Newark;
(973) 589–4070
Traditional Portuguese fare such as shrimp in garlic sauce and *carne de porco a Alentejana* (brazed pork cubes with clams) meet up with pasta specialties including penne in vodka sauce and *linguini scampi*. Live music begins at 9:00 P.M. Monday through Thursday. Dinner nightly. Moderate.

So Moon Nan Jib
238 Broad Avenue,
Palisades Park;
(201) 944–3998
Do-it-yourself cooking is elevated to an art at this authentic Korean barbecue. Waiters deliver pans of char-

coal to the table and customers grill their selections. The tiny bowls filled with condiments range from the cooling to the excruciatingly hot. Dinner nightly. Inexpensive.

Spirato Grill
500 Harbor Boulevard,
Sheraton Building,
Weehawken;
(201) 867–0101
Classic Italian dishes include black truffle and seafood risotto, and grilled chicken Napoleon. There's a fine patio for outdoor dining, and a pre-theater menu served from 5:00–6:00 P.M. Sunday brunch ($19.50) includes a complimentary cocktail. Lunch and dinner daily. Moderate–expensive.

Stony Hill Inn
231 Polifly Road,
Hackensack;
(201) 342–4085
Contemporary continental cuisine with an Italian influence is the specialty at this 1818 Dutch homestead on the National Register of Historic Places. Among the house specialties: chateaubriand for two and rack of veal. Lunch Monday through Friday, dinner nightly. Expensive.

Other Attractions in the Urban Northeast

Boxwood Hall State Historic Site
1073 East Jersey Street,
Elizabeth; (973) 648–4540

Dr. William Robinson Plantation
593 Madison Hill Road,
Clark; (732) 381–3081

East Brunswick Museum
16 Maple Street,
East Brunswick;
(732) 257–1508

**Edison National
Historic Site**
Main Street, West Orange;
(973) 736–0550

Fort Lee Historic Park
Hudson Terrace, Fort Lee;
(201) 461–1776

**Grover Cleveland
Birthplace**
207 Bloomfield Avenue,
Caldwell; (973) 226–0001

**Historic New Bridge
Landing Park**
Main Street, River Edge;
(201) 487–1739

Liberty Science Center
Liberty State Park, 251
Philip Street, Jersey City;
(201) 200–1000

**Long Pond Ironworks
State Park**
West Milford;
(973) 962–7031

**New Jersey Children's
Museum**
599 Valley Health Plaza
East, Paramus;
(201) 262–5151

Newark Museum
49 Washington Street,
Newark;
(973) 596–6550

**Thomas A. Edison
Memorial Tower and
Museum**
Christie Street and
Route 27, Edison;
(732) 549–3299

SELECTED REGIONAL INFORMATION CENTERS, CHAMBERS OF COMMERCE, AND VISITOR CENTERS IN THE URBAN NORTHEAST

Gateway Tourism Council
P.O. Box 2011, Bayonne 07002
(201) 436–6009 or (877) 428–3930

**Hudson County Chamber of
Commerce**
660 Newark Avenue, Suite 220
Jersey City 07306
(201) 386–0699
www.hudsonchamber.org

**North Jersey Regional Chamber
of Commerce**
1033 Route 46 East, Box 110,
Clifton 07013
(973) 470–9300
www.njrcc.org

**Passaic County Cultural &
Heritage Coucil**
County Community College
1 College Boulevard, Paterson 07505
(973) 684–5444

Northern New Jersey and the Upper Delaware Valley

Not too long ago it was fair to state simply that the northwestern corner of New Jersey offered a marked contrast to the heavily urbanized communities to the east. Here were dairy farms, upland pastures, dense forests, and tucked-away lakes; between one small town and another, there was only a strip of two-lane blacktop and maybe an old-fashioned roadhouse with a pair of antlers over the bar.

Now things have gotten a little more complicated, and this part of New Jersey contrasts as sharply with itself as it does with any other portion of the state. The completion of I–80 in the 1960s opened the gates for the suburbanization of Sussex and northern Warren Counties; it's no longer unusual for someone to live out past Lake Hopatcong or up near Sparta and commute to a job in New York City. Dairy farmers have sold out by the score (the actual number of farms is up in Sussex, but acreage is down—the result of smaller specialty operations that replaced dairying), and developers have moved in, building houses and pumping out press releases about the joys of living in "ruburbia," whatever that is.

Development tends to cluster along the major highways of northwestern New Jersey, and it still isn't hard to find a back road that will take you into a landscape more typical of the

NEW YORK
NEW JERSEY

NORTHERN
HIGHLANDS

206

PENNSYLVANIA
NEW JERSEY

Sussex

94

Layton

Lafayette

Ringwood

Wanaque
Res.

Newton

206

Sparta

Wanaque

Delaware R.

94

15

Lake
Hopatcong

HOPATCONG
REGION

Pequest R.

80

Hopatcong

80

46

287

Hackettstown

46

Flanders

Parsippany

Morristown

MORRIS-WARREN
HILLS

206

Washington

31

Phillipsburg

0   10 mi
0   10 km

N

rural stretches of neighboring New York State and Pennsylvania. There are still lovely country vistas along the Delaware River, from Phillipsburg north to High Point, and the most beautiful part of the upper Delaware Valley has wisely been preserved as the Delaware Water Gap National Recreation Area—a wonderful place for hiking (the Appalachian Trail parallels the river on the Jersey side) and canoeing. So don't write off Sussex and environs just yet. The suburban booster crowd may squeal with glee every time a new set of population projections comes out, but it's a safe bet that there will still be plenty of open spaces to enjoy hereabouts for quite some time to come.

Note: This region is divided into three sections: the Northern Highlands, the Hopatcong Region, and the Morris-Warren Hills.

Northern Highlands

Hard upon the Delaware River, just north of the point where I–80 crosses into Pennsylvania, is a community devoted entirely to the perpetuation and teaching of fine craft. The **Peters Valley Craft Education Center** is a cluster of twenty-two buildings, thirteen of which are on the National Historic Register, but its importance to artisans throughout America far outweighs its size. One of only three dozen such communities in the country, Peters Valley offers intensive courses—with live-in accommodations—in blacksmithing, ceramics, fiber

NORTHERN NEW JERSEY AND THE UPPER DELAWARE VALLEY'S TOP PICKS

Peters Valley Craft Education Center	Pyramid Mountain Natural Historic Area
Paulinskill Valley Trail	Four Sisters Winery
Franklin Mineral Museum, Inc.	Pequest Trout Hatchery
Stokes State Forest	Well-Sweep Herb Farm
Space Farms Zoo and Museum	Fosterfields Living Historical Farm
Van Bunschooten House	Frelinghuysen Arboretum
Ringwood Manor	Historic Speedwell
Skylands Botanical Garden	Craftsman Farms
Village of Waterloo	

ᵒme New Jerseyans
Know That . . .

• ...ey is the only state in which every county is classified as a metropolitan area.

• New Jersey has more racehorses than Kentucky.

• New Jersey has the most densely concentrated system of highways and railroads in the United States.

• Northern New Jersey has seven major shopping malls in a 25-square-mile area, the densest concentration of malls in the world.

• Union, New Jersey, boasts the world's tallest water tower.

(basketry, paper and book arts, and surface design), fine metals, photography, weaving, and woodworking. Courses range from two to nine days, with basic to advanced instruction by nationally known artists/teachers.

You don't have to be interested in actually learning a craft to come to Peters Valley; simple appreciation will do. Every Saturday and Sunday from June 1 through August 31, the studios are open between 2:00 and 5:00 P.M. so that visitors can watch resident craftspeople work and ask them questions. Evening slide lectures/presentations are held throughout the summer by workshop faculty and are open to the public free of charge. In addition, the Peters Valley Craft Store and Gallery is well stocked with the work of more than 300 American craftspeople, including the residents, and features changing displays and exhibits. The annual Craft Fair takes place during the last weekend in September. The fair includes more than 160 juried exhibitors, live music, food, and craft demonstrations. Peters Valley Craft Education Center is on Route 615, south of Layton (mailing address: 19 Kuhn Road, Layton 07851), (973) 948–5200. The store and gallery are open Friday through Wednesday 11:00 A.M.–5:00 P.M.

"We feed the deer and people, too" is the motto of the folks at the **Walpack Inn.** They've been doing both since 1949. The deer come to within 20 feet of the restaurant to feed, and because the restaurant is a giant greenhouse (hundreds of plants are suspended from the ceiling), there are plenty of windows from which to watch the animals and enjoy views of the Kittatinny Ridge.

Friday night lobster and Saturday night prime rib are house specialties. There's a great salad bar and delicious home-baked loaves of Swedish bread. Sunday dinner, ham ($17) or roast beef ($21 for a twelve-ounce cut) includes the salad bar and homemade bread. One might well imagine that the deer would be inside than out.

The restaurant, on Route 615, Walpack Center, (973) 948–9849, is open all year, Friday and Saturday 5:00–10:00 P.M. and Sunday 3:00–8:00 P.M.

In the late 1950s one of Canadian Joseph-Armand Bombardier's children died when he couldn't be transported through the snow to a hospital for an emergency appendectomy. In 1959 Bombardier built his first Ski-Doo, and thus was born the snowmobile industry. Dan Klemm is a great fan of snowmobiles. In fact, he has the world's largest collection of snowmobiles and related memorabilia. He recently doubled the size of his **Snowmobile Barn Museum** in order to exhibit more than 300 of his antique and vintage sleds, which span more than ninety years of the industry's history. The museum is on his farm, and visitors with kids who have a short attention span will be delighted to discover that they're invited to visit the barnyard and feed some of the animals. The museum, at 928 Cedar Ridge Road in Fredon, is open by appointment. Call (973) 383–1708. Admission is $7.00 for adults and $4.00 for children.

Enjoy a leisurely stroll through **The Lafayette Mill Antiques Center,** an 1850s gristmill, which houses the wares of forty dealers. Just off Route 15 in Lafayette, (973) 383–0065, it's open daily, except Tuesday and Wednesday, 10:00 A.M.–5:00 P.M.

At **Abbey Glen Pet Memorial Park,** 187 Route 94 South, Lafayette, (800) 972–3118, Saint Francis of Assisi, patron saint of animals, watches over the "Hillside Burial" area. A special section of the fourteen-acre park is reserved for seeing-eye and therapy dogs, police canines and horses, and other animals who have dedicated their lives to public service. In the "Country Burial" area, pets' names are inscribed on a Gift of Love Plaque. The park is an inspiration to all animal lovers.

AUTHORS' FAVORITE ATTRACTIONS IN NORTHERN NEW JERSEY AND THE UPPER DELAWARE VALLEY

Craftsman Farms	Ringwood Manor
Fosterfields	Space Farms Zoo and Museum
High Point State Park	Stokes State Forest
Historic Speedwell	Well-Sweep Herb Farm

...linskill Valley Trail, paralleling the Paulinskill River, ...lds, rolling hills, woods, and swamps, it passes by nearly ...ersey's plant species and offers spectacular views of the rural ...tryside. Once the bed for the New York, Susquehanna and ...this rail-trail passes by several old railroad-era buildings and still ...sts, mileage markers, and other railway relics. At milepost 89 (you... ...es from Jersey City), there's a great view of the Hainesburg Viaduct, considered... the eighth wonder of the world when it was completed in 1911.

The trail endpoints are Brugler Road near Columbia and Sparta Junction. For information contact the Park Superintendent, Kittatinny Valley State Park, P.O. Box 621, Andover 07821, (973) 786–6445.

It seems only fitting that getting to the state's last remaining glacial lake should require some effort. But knowing your effort is not going to go unrewarded counts for a lot. Forty-one-acre, spring-fed *Sunfish Pond,* a designated National Landmark, lies in a chestnut oak forest high in the Kittatinny Mountains. It's a popular spot for hikers as well as migratory waterfowl and raptors.

Several steep and rocky paths lead to Sunfish Pond (called "Hidden Lake" by Native Americans). The trailhead for one of the most popular, the Appalachian Trail, begins at a parking lot just off I–80 (exit at the rest area/parking area for Dunnfield Creek). The 3¾-mile hike to the top passes through a hemlock forest and Dunnfield Creek Natural Area and then climbs to the pond.

For information on Sunfish Pond Natural Area, contact Worthington State Forest, Old Mine Road, Delaware Water Gap, (908) 841–9575.

New Jersey's last operating zinc mine is now a National Historic Site. *Sterling Hill Mining Museum* has more than thirty acres of exhibits, displays, and historical buildings. Those persons not suffering from claustrophobia will enjoy the underground mine tour, which winds through ⅓ mile of tunnel and passes by a spectacular mineral fluorescence display. The mine is at 30 Plant

Hiking the Trail

Seventy miles of the Appalachian Trail, which stretches from Maine to Georgia, run through New Jersey. On the north the trail enters the state at Greenwood Lake, then follows the New York–New Jersey border west along the Kittatinny Ridge and continues to the Delaware Water Gap. Three-sided shelters and campsites are located at 8- to 12-mile intervals, at High Point State Park, Stokes State Forest, and Wawayanda State Park. Backpackers will find campsites at Worthington State Forest. Camping is allowed at the Delaware Water Gap National Recreation Area. For information call (973) 948–6500.

Street, Ogdensburg; (973) 209–7212. Open daily April through November and weekends in March and December 10:00 A.M.–3:00 P.M. Tours are given daily at 1:00 P.M. Admission is $9.50 for adults, $8.50 for seniors, and $7.00 for children under the age of seventeen (not recommended for children under six). A collection area is open to visitors the last Sunday of each month the mine is open. There is a charge of $10.00 to collect up to ten pounds of minerals, and an additional charge of $1.00 per pound for each pound over that amount. Collectors must be at least thirteen. Bring a jacket or sweater and good walking shoes. Call ahead to make sure the mine is open.

There's a lot more than zinc in the north Jersey hills. The Franklin-Ogdensburg area of eastern Sussex County has yielded a greater number of species and varieties of minerals than any other location in the world—at last count, more than 340 species and 360 varieties. The Franklin minerals—the discovery of which was largely associated with nearly three centuries of zinc-mining operations that ended in 1954—are on exhibit at the ***Franklin Mineral Museum, Inc.*** Franklin's rich mineral deposits are the result of a complex series of geological events that date back a billion years and were never duplicated elsewhere, hence the occurrence in local ore deposits not only of such an incredible diversity of minerals but of thirty types discovered nowhere else on Earth. For the layperson, perhaps the most interesting facet of the museum's display is the collection of fluorescent minerals—the world's largest—exhibited under ultraviolet light, which brings out their color and luminosity.

The mineral museum also includes a replica of the interior of a zinc mine, realistic to the last detail because it is made up of actual equipment used in

We Called Him Uncle Guy

Old-timers living in the Upper Greenwood Lake area, near the border of Passaic and Sussex Counties, may remember a remarkably ingenious storekeeper named Guy Futrell. Arkansas-born, a one-time cowboy, and a chief petty officer in the U.S. Navy during World War I, Futrell came to Upper Greenwood Lake in the 1920s and built the first gas station in that then-wild region. His station, and the store he ran with his wife, Josephine, had Upper Greenwood Lake's first electric lights, run off a generator he built himself out of an old Model T. There was little Guy Futrell couldn't do, using his hands and his wits. In later life, he decided he'd like to make a violin. He read everything he could on the subject, then took a month just to fashion the necessary tools. Three months after that, he had two violins judged tonally near-perfect by a New York appraiser—a man who found it hard to believe that Futrell couldn't read a note of music.

—William Guy Scheller Jr.

the operations of the New Jersey Zinc Company in the days of active mining in the area. Under conditions such as those replicated here, miners discovered many of the rare and beautiful specimens on exhibit in the museum. Visitors can collect mineral specimens on the mine waste pile, adjacent to the museum, and test them for fluorescence.

The Welsh Mall exhibits more than 5,000 mineral specimens from around the world. Other exhibits include American Indian relics and fossils.

The Franklin Mineral Museum, Inc., Evans Street (off Route 23), Franklin, (973) 827–3481, is open weekends in March, daily April through November, Monday through Friday 10:00 A.M.–4:00 P.M., Saturday 10:00 A.M.–5:00 P.M., and Sunday 11:00 A.M.–5:00 P.M. Admission to the museum is $6.00 for adults, $3.00 for students, and $4.00 for seniors. Guided tours are offered hourly. The fee for rock collecting only is $6.00 for adults and $4.00 for children and seniors. A combination tour and collecting ticket costs $11.00 for adults and $6.00 for children and seniors. There is also a poundage fee for specimens collected.

Stokes State Forest, which runs along 12 miles of the Kittatinny Mountain Ridge, offers some excellent hiking opportunities, including a 12½-mile section of the Appalachian Trail. For a particular treat, head over to the southwestern portion and hike to the "teacup" near the bottom of Tillman Ravine. The large pothole carved into rock at the bottom of the falls is a great place to kick back, soak your weary feet, and listen to the falling waters. The forest is 5 miles north of Branchville on U.S. Highway 206, (973) 948–3820. The park office is open daily from 9:00 A.M. until 4:00 P.M. An entrance fee of $5.00

TOP ANNUAL EVENTS IN NORTHERN NEW JERSEY AND THE UPPER DELAWARE VALLEY

Note: Schedules may vary; call ahead.

Warren County Heritage Festival, Oxford; May; (908) 453–4381

U.S. Equestrian Team Festival of Champions, Gladstone; June; (908) 234–1251

Quick Chek New Jersey Festival of Ballooning, Solberg Airport, Readington; July; (800) HOT–AIR–9

New Jersey State Fair & Sussex County Farm and Horse Show, Augusta; August; (973) 948–5500

Garden State Wine Growers' Fall Festival, Waterloo Village, Stanhope; September; (908) 475–3671

Civil War Weekend at Fosterfields, Morristown; October; (973) 326–7645

Family Harvest Festival, Matarazzo Farms, Belvidere; October; (908) 475–3872

They're Probably Telling It Still

How many readers who were Boy Scouts in north Jersey during the 1960s remember the story of the H-Man? Told and retold around the tents and campfires of now-defunct Camp Altaha, on Fairview Lake in Sussex County, this tale was about a guy who lived way out in the woods, and had to travel a lot on business. To protect his family from intruders, he had iron bars installed on his windows. One night, he arrived home to find the house in flames, and his family trapped inside. He pressed up against the window bars, screaming, while a big red "H" was seared onto his chest. Of course he went mad, and he ROAMS THESE VERY WOODS. . . .

Lights out, boys.

is charged on weekdays, $10.00 on weekends and holidays from Memorial Day through Labor Day only.

As motoring families began to fan out along the nation's byways in the early years of the automotive age, an institution known as the "roadside attraction" came into existence. These attractions often took the form of small, randomly assembled zoos, many of which could still be found in the rural and suburban back roads of New Jersey as recently as twenty-five or thirty years ago. The vast majority of the roadside zoos fell victim either to development pressures or concern over the unprofessional way in which they were operated, but, fortunately, the best of the lot in New Jersey has continued to thrive: ***Space Farms Zoo and Museum,*** in Sussex, has operated for more than seventy-five years on a policy of clean surroundings, good care for animals, and public education.

Founded in 1927 by Ralph Space, Space Farms Zoo and Museum has grown under three successive generations of the Space family to comprise a 425-acre integrated operation housing more than 500 animals of more than one hundred species. The zoo and museum cover one hundred acres, and nearly all the remainder is used to grow food for the zoo's hooved animals and other herbivores. Of the land actually occupied by the zoo, as much as possible is maintained in natural-habitat condition.

Not that New Jersey is the natural habitat of all the creatures at Space Farms Zoo. There are, of course, white-tailed deer, foxes, raccoons, bobcats, black bears (several thousand are believed to roam wild in the state), snakes, and waterfowl indigenous to the area, but the Space collection also includes species such as lion, tiger, llama, yak, elk, jaguar, leopard, monkey, coatimundi, wolf, coyote, and mountain sheep.

An interesting adjunct to the zoo itself is the Space Farms museum complex, which houses an eclectic assortment of Americana: horse-drawn wagons and carriages, old cars and motorcycles, toys and dolls, Indian artifacts, firearms, and antique farm equipment.

Space Farms Zoo and Museum, Beemerville Road (Route 519), (973) 875–5800, is open daily May through October 31, 9:00 A.M.–5:00 P.M. Admission is $10.95 for adults, $6.50 for children ages three through twelve, and free for children under three; group rates are available.

If present-day cities such as Paterson and Hackensack were little more than villages surrounded by farmland in the late eighteenth century, we can well imagine the circumstances that prevailed in those days in the remote corners of Sussex County—and the hardiness of an individual such as the Reverend Elias Van Bunschooten, who was sent in 1785 by the New Jersey Synod of the Dutch Reformed Church to minister to the area's faithful. The Reverend Van Bunschooten built his Wantage Township farmhouse in 1787 and lived here until his death in 1815.

didyouknow . . . ?

- The Rabbinical College of America, the world's largest institution for the study of Hasidic Judaism, is in Morristown.

- Reports of monsters in Lake Hopatcong, New Jersey's largest lake, date back to the seventeenth century.

- Roselle was the first city in the world to be lit by incandescent lightbulbs.

The *Van Bunschooten House,* overseen by the local chapter of the Daughters of the American Revolution, contains furnishings and other artifacts characteristic not only of the minister's era but of that of later owners, the Cooper family, throughout the nineteenth century. Especially interesting is the contrast between the 1787 bedroom furnishings and the far more ponderous articles of 1860, exhibited in an adjacent room. Most important to the modern visitor, though, is the sense of perspective on time and distance that a place like this has to offer: same house, same location; 200 years ago an arduous trek from the Old Dutch towns along the Hudson, today a short scoot up Route 23.

The Elias Van Bunschooten House, 1097 Route 23, Sussex, (973) 702–0016 or (973) 875–5335, is open May 15 through October 15 or by appointment, Thursday and Saturday 1:00–4:00 P.M. Admission is $2.00 for adults and $1.00 for children. Special events include Christmas in July.

High Point State Park occupies more than 14,000 acres that touch the New York State border almost at the northernmost tip of New Jersey and also contains the state's highest peak, 1,803-foot High Point. High Point State Park represents a classic case of collaboration between private and public interest for the preservation of an outstanding natural area. Although the land that the park now occupies was part of a royal grant as far back as 1715, its remoteness ensured that it would remain pristine throughout the following two centuries. The only construction of note was an exclusive resort, the High Point Inn, built in 1888 near the shore of Lake Marcia, which was remodeled into the present structure by the Kuser family of Bernardsville, New Jersey. In 1922 Col. Anthony Kuser made a gift of some 10,000 acres—the bulk of the modern park—to the state of New Jersey.

A multiuse park, High Point is managed with an eye toward balancing backcountry preservation with the provision of ample recreational facilities. The northernmost part of the park is the 800-acre John D. Kuser Natural Area, much of which is old-growth Atlantic white cedar swamp. Just south of the natural area is the summit of High Point itself, topped with a 240-foot obelisk that affords terrific views of the Delaware Valley, the Catskill and Pocono Mountains, and the lakes and forests of the park itself. (The monument, also a gift of the Kuser family, was completed in 1930.) Dryden Kuser Natural Area's white cedar swamp is the highest elevation swamp of its type in the world; a self-guided tour brochure is available.

There are three public-access lakes within the boundaries of High Point State Park: twenty-acre Lake Marcia, at 1,600 feet the highest lake in New Jersey, has a supervised bathing beach; Lake Steenykill, west of Marcia, has a boat-launching ramp and two furnished cabins, which may be rented by family groups between May 15 and October 15; Sawmill Lake, near the center of the park, also has boat-launch facilities (only electric motors are permitted on the state park's lakes), as well as fifty campsites.

Hiking is one of the prime attractions at High Point State Park. The Maine-to-Georgia Appalachian Trail runs north and south through the length of the park (look for white blazes) and is intersected by a system of nine park trails, varying in length from ½ to 4 miles. Each trail is identified by blazes or markers of

When Sussex County Was the Wild Frontier

Swartswood Lake, the lovely centerpiece of a state park just west of Newton, owes its name to an early Sussex County settler who died in what was likely one of New Jersey's last Indian attacks. Captain Anthony Swartwout was a British officer who had served in the French and Indian War, and who in 1756 was living with his family at a homestead near the lake. In that year a party of thirteen Indians, wartime enemies of Swartwout, raided his property and killed his wife. The captain shot several of the attackers but was soon captured, whereupon he was carted off and disemboweled by the Indians.

High Point obelisk

a different color, and relative difficulty is noted in a trail guide, available at the park office.

High Point State Park, 1480 Route 23, Sussex, (973) 875–4800, is open daily throughout the year. Park entrance fees of $5.00 weekdays and $10.00 weekends and holidays are charged from Memorial Day weekend through Labor Day; there is no entrance fee the rest of the year.

Featured on Home & Garden TV's "If Walls Could Talk," **Glenwood Mill B&B**—in a 200-year-old grist mill—is one of the state's more unusual lodgings. The historic flour mill, with a refurbished 12-foot water wheel, has just two rooms and two suites. The rooms have queen beds, the suites king beds; all are furnished with antiques and have private baths, gas fireplaces, TVs, phones, and dataports. The inn is at 1860 Route 565, Glenwood; (973) 764–8660; www.glenwoodmill.com. Rates range from $130 to $225 per night.

At **Wawayanda State Park** there are 1,300 acres to explore by canoe, on mountain bike, or on foot (20 miles of the Appalachian Trail are within park limits). You can rent a canoe ($8.00 an hour, $24.00 a day) for a paddle around 255-acre Wawayanda Lake; throw in a line to fish for trout, bass, pickerel, and perch; or just explore the lake and its islands. Keep an eye out for endangered,

red-shouldered hawks if you opt for a hike to the top of Wawayanda Mountain for spectacular views of the surrounding mountains. The park, at 885 Warwick Turnpike in Hewitt, (973) 853–4462, is open mid-April through late September 6:00 A.M.–6:00 P.M. In season there's a beach with a lifeguard.

Simplicity Inn on Blueberry Point overlooks a fifty-five-acre private lake in the heart of a 450-acre estate. All of the five spacious guest rooms have lake views, and four have shared baths. Aunt Dorothy's and Uncle Herb's Room, with windows on three sides, a sitting area, and a semiprivate bath, is one of our favorites. Grandma and Grandpa's Room has a private bath, beautiful views, and access to a lovely screened-in porch. The inn has a private tennis court, rowboats and canoes for guests' use, and a hiking trail around the lake.

Rates at Simplicity Inn on Blueberry Point, 81 Otterhole Road, West Milford, (973) 697–0494, range from $115 to $135 a night plus tax and include a continental breakfast. Some rooms have shared baths. The inn is smoke free and children are welcome. Their Web site is www.siminn.com.

Up along the New York State border, at the northern tip of Passaic County, is a state park rich in historical associations. *Ringwood Manor,* the focal point of *Ringwood State Park,* was established in 1740 and produced munitions for every major armed conflict from the French and Indian War to World War I. The Ringwood iron mines operated intermittently from the 1920s until 1957.

The present structures at Ringwood Manor reflect the period from 1854 to 1936, when the Hewitt family, who operated the mines under the auspices of Cooper Hewitt and Company, used the manor and its 33,000 surrounding acres as their country estate. The manor houses an excellent collection of furnishings, Hudson River School paintings, and prints and lithographs that reflect the tastes of patriarch Abram S. Hewitt and his family. In planning the gardens at the manor, Hewitt was inspired by the classical designs used for the grounds of the Palace of Versailles. Hewitt's son, Erskine, donated Ringwood Manor to the state in 1936.

In front of the manor are twenty-six links of the chain forged to keep the British from ascending the Hudson beyond West Point during the Revolution.

A visit to Ringwood Manor is only part of the attraction of a visit to Ringwood State Park. The house is a fine place from which to head out onto a well-developed system of hiking and cross-country ski trails, some making a short loop on the immediate grounds and others heading northwest for a considerable distance into *Abram S. Hewitt State Forest.* (Detailed trail maps are available at the park office, in the manor.)

One recommended route takes you across the Ringwood River and Sloatsburg Road to Shepherd Lake (1½ miles), a nice place for swimming, fishing, and boating; it then extends another ⁹⁄₁₀ mile to *Skylands Botanical*

. . . andtheworldhas neverbeenthesame

Legendary guitarist Les Paul invented the solid-body electric guitar in Mahwah in 1940.

Garden, also part of Ringwood State Park, and formally called the New Jersey Botanical Garden at Skylands.

Skylands was sold in 1922 to Clarence McKenzie Lewis, an investment banker and trustee of the New York Botanical Garden. Determined to make Skylands a botanical showplace, he tore down an existing house and replaced it with a forty-four-room Tudor mansion (built of native granite), which features interior fixtures and architectural details imported from European châteaus and stately homes, as well as a fireplace piazza and an enormous room used only for arranging cut flowers. He hired the most prominent landscape architects of his day to design the gardens and, for thirty years, collected plants from all over the world and from New Jersey roadsides. The result is one of the finest collections of plants in the state.

In March 1984 Governor Thomas Kean designated the ninety-six acres that surround the manor house as New Jersey's official botanical garden.

Ringwood State Park, 1304 Sloatsburg Road, off Route 511, Ringwood, (973) 962–7031, is open daily all year from sunrise to sunset. Admission to the grounds is free, although a modest admission is charged for guided tours of the Ringwood Manor house and Skylands. Guided tours of the gardens (May through October) and the first floor of the manor are offered on the first Sunday afternoon of each month (except July, when tours are given on the second Sunday of the month). Major events include a May plant sale and an October Harvest Festival. For information on the gardens, call (973) 962–9534 or visit the Web site www.njbg.org.

"In our turbulent world so full of cross-currents, we have found a tiny haven; a place to give a demonstration of how life begins, continues, and, with the wonderful interaction developed eons of years ago, re-creates itself and goes on in peace and beauty." Thus May Weis described the 160-acre parcel of land in Ringwood that she and her husband, Walter, purchased in 1974 for the enjoyment of all. **The Weis Ecology Center** is a wonderful place to stroll or hike, observe nature, and learn about the northern New Jersey Highlands regions.

New Jersey Audubon Society's Weis Ecology Center, 150 Snake Den Road, Ringwood, (973) 835–2160, is open Wednesday through Sunday 8:30 A.M.–4:30 P.M. Special programs (admission charge) are held on weekends. The center also rents wooded campsites and rustic cabins by reservation only.

Hopatcong Region

The restored *Village of Waterloo* does a fine job of re-creating the character and physical environment of a bygone era—two eras, in fact: Waterloo was a lively town back in Revolutionary times, when local forges supplied armaments to Washington's troops, and it entered a whole new phase of growth and importance as a way station on the Morris Canal in the 1830s. The workaday world and domestic arrangements of both periods are brought to life here not only by the superbly restored homes, gardens, and commercial establishments open to visitors, but by working artisans and authentically costumed guides.

Restored and managed by the nonprofit Waterloo Foundation for the Arts, the village features a grist- and sawmill built in 1760 as a charcoal house; a blacksmith shop that still echoes with the clang of hammer on anvil; original towpaths of the 1831 Morris Canal; a general store that offers Waterloo-crafted textiles, pottery, wrought iron, candles, and brooms; and even a cozy tavern in which you can sit by the fire, have a tankard of ale, and pretend you are a jolly canal boatman, fortifying yourself against the elements. In all there are twenty-three restored houses and other structures on the property, including a number of antiques-furnished Victorian homes that reflect Waterloo's canal-era prosperity.

The Indian village is considered to be one of the most authentic reconstructions in the Northeast. The Lenape Village, on an island called Winakung (Place of Sassafras), faithfully re-creates the way of life of the Lenape (or Delaware) people who lived in this area more than 250 years ago.

Highlights of the village include a grove with symbols from a local Lenape petroglyph, a furnished bark longhouse whose interior replicates a trading session in 1625 between European traders and the Indians, and a native garden. There are also an Indian museum and a gift shop.

In addition to maintaining the village, the Waterloo Foundation each year sponsors the *Waterloo Festival for the Arts,* a May-to-October program of craft shows, brewfests, ethnic festivals, opera, jazz, and pop music. An admission fee is charged for some events. Check the schedule on www.waterloo village.org.

Waterloo Village, in Allamuchy State Park, Waterloo Road, Stanhope, (973) 347–0900, is open mid-May through June weekends 11:00 A.M.–5:00 P.M. Hours in July and August are Wednesday through Friday 11:00 A.M.–4:00 P.M. and weekends 11:00 A.M.–5:00 P.M. Call for fall hours. Admission is $9.00 for adults, $8.00 for seniors, and $7.00 for children ages six through fifteen; under six, free. Weekend rates may be higher if a special event is being held.

You Must Be Hooked on a Log—Your Rod's Practically Bent Double

If you're looking to catch a really big fish in New Jersey, you don't have to head for salt water. Muskellunge, the largest and feistiest members of the pike family, have been successfully established in Lake Hopatcong over the past few years, and muskies measuring more than 40 inches with a weight in excess of twenty pounds have been caught in the big lake bordered by Morris and Sussex Counties. Hopatcong muskies must be at least 36 inches long to be legal, but anglers are encouraged to release the fish no matter what their size, so that the species will continue to establish its "finhold" in the lake.

The **Whistling Swan Inn,** a 1905 Victorian B&B in Stanhope, is "for those with more refined nesting instincts." Each of the ten rooms and suites is furnished in a theme: Among them are an art deco room, an Oriental antiques room, a White Iron room, and a 1940s Swing room. All the rooms have private baths—one with two claw-foot tubs in it. Rates, from $99 to $219, include a full buffet-style breakfast. The inn is at 110 Main Street (P.O. Box 791), Stanhope 07874, (973) 347–6369; www.whistlingswaninn.com.

Waiters and waitresses in Tyrolean costumes serve up German specialties as well as continental fare at the **Black Forest Inn.** Portions tend to be large, the ambience Teutonic, and customers dress up to come to this multiroomed roadside inn at 249 Route 206, Stanhope; (973) 347–3344. Open for lunch Monday and Wednesday through Friday 11:30 A.M.–2:00 P.M., as well as for dinner Monday and Wednesday through Saturday 5:00–10:00 P.M. and Sunday 1:00–8:00 P.M.

Roadside fare doesn't get much better than at **Zinga's Corn Patch,** a popular eatery in Sparta since 1971. The sloppy joes are oozingly sloppy, the muffins are homemade, and, as to be expected from its name, the corn fritters are fresh and crunchy. After a meal, what could be better than a delicious ice-cream cone? Zinga's has twenty-one flavors to choose from. The restaurant is at 640 Lafayette Road, (973) 383–6572, and open daily for breakfast, lunch, and dinner in summer. Call for fall hours.

The Wooden Duck B&B, right across from Kittatinny Valley State Park, offers privacy, comfortable accommodations, and, in the morning, lots of home-baked goodies. Set on seventeen acres of open fields and woodlands, the inn has central air-conditioning, a double hearth fireplace, game room, and swimming pool. Each of the nine rooms and the suite has a queen-size bed, private bath, phone, TV, VCR, computer modem hookup, and writing desk.

Those wishing ultimate privacy should request a room in the Hor. Carriage House. The inn is at 140 Goodale Road, Newton; (973) 300–0 www.woodenduckinn.com. Rates for a standard double range from $110 to $190, and include a full breakfast.

Twenty-four arctic, tundra, and timber wolves make their home at the **Lakota Wolf Preserve.** Visitors view the wolves from an observation center in the middle of the preserve and learn all about them: the structure of their packs, their eating habits, and how they relate to man.

After a visit to the observation center, visitors are given a tour of the fox and bobcat compound and are then invited to use the facilities at Taylor Campground, which include swimming, hiking trails, and a picnic area, at no additional charge.

The ten-acre preserve is owned by New Jerseyan Jim Stein, Dan Bacon, and his wife, Pam. The threesome moved their preserve from Colorado, when the red tape there began to bind them too tightly, and opened their preserve in Columbia in June 1998.

The Lakota Wolf Preserve, 89 Mt. Pleasant Road, (877) SEE–WOLF (733–9653), is open year-round. The one-and-a-half-hour Wolf Watch is $15.00 for adults and $7.00 for children under twelve and is given daily at 10:30 A.M. and 4:00 P.M. Reservations are required on weekdays. No pets are allowed and credit cards are not accepted.

It doesn't taste like butter and it doesn't taste much like milk, but the buttermilk at **Hot Dog Johnny's** on Route 46, Buttzville, (908) 453–2882, is the perfect drink to wash down a couple of dogs and some homemade fries. For the more traditional, there are frosty mugs of birch beer. And it all goes down even better when you're sitting at one of the outdoor tables overlooking the Pequest River. The restaurant's hours vary, depending on the season and how busy it is, but it generally opens around 9:00 A.M. and stays open until 9:00 or 10:00 P.M. Call ahead to check.

Smell fresh-baked doughnuts? The aroma might well be wafting up from **Best's Fruit Farm** to the south. The folks at Best's have been baking dough-nuts and pies and making apple cider for more than forty-five years, but the farm is most famous for its fruits and vegetables. The gourmet shop is a wonderful place to pick up all the fixin's for a picnic. The farm is on Route 46, just outside downtown Hackettstown, (908) 852–3777. The market/bakery is open year-round, Monday through Friday 9:00 A.M.–6:30 P.M., Saturday and Sunday 9:00 A.M.–5:00 P.M. (in summer it stays open until 6:00 P.M. on Saturday). Call ahead to make sure they are open.

The first ring-necked pheasants arrived in New Jersey from the Orient in 1790. For many years—before the suburbanization of the state and the use of pesticides—they thrived, providing food for animals such as foxes, skunks, and raptors and sport for hunters who enjoy the challenge of stalking the elusive birds.

Today nine out of ten of the state's pheasants are raised at the 492-acre **Rockport Pheasant Farm,** which has, since 1963, raised more than two million of the birds. The farm, a property of the New Jersey Division of Fish, Game and Wildlife, releases approximately 50,000 birds each November on about 100,000 acres of state wildlife management areas, and it's estimated that 90 percent of them will be shot by hunters before the end of the year. The farm is subsidized by hunters who purchase pheasant/quail stamps, and it's estimated that the industry generates about $2.6 million in local income.

Visitors to the farm (which is also home to turkeys, white-tailed deer, and waterfowl) can tour the breeder yards and are welcome to bring a picnic.

The Rockport Pheasant Farm, Rockport Road (Route 629), Hackettstown, (908) 852–3461, is open daily from 7:30 A.M. to dusk.

If you're in the market for some new spurs or a frock for the next square dance, head west on Route 46 to the **Cherokee Trading Post** (973) 347–1228 in Budd Lake. The store, in operation for more than fifty years, carries a complete line of Western apparel and boots, as well as moccasins and Indian crafts and jewelry. The store is open year-round, Monday through Friday 10:00 A.M.–6:00 P.M., Saturday 10:00 A.M.–5:00 P.M., and Sunday 11:00 A.M.–5:00 P.M.

Crossed Keys, built in 1790 as a working farm, is now an elegantly restored B&B with five working fireplaces, a fishing pond/ice-skating rink, a reflecting pool, and three guest rooms, one suite, and one cottage, each furnished differently. The Sconset room, with old, wide floorboards that have the original tilt to them, has a fireplace and overlooks the gardens and meadows; the Suite has a private sitting area and is furnished with appropriate antiques. Rates range from $150 to $185 for rooms with private bath, and include a full breakfast. The inn is at 289 Pequest Road, Andover; (973) 786–6661. Their Web site is crossedKeys.com.

During the last Ice Age, the Wisconsin Glacier passed through northern New Jersey and deposited strange, massive boulders, called "erratics" by geologists. Some historians believe that Tripod Rock on Pyramid Mountain was a sacred place for the Lenni-Lenape people, and that two smaller boulders nearby were used as a calendar by early inhabitants. The 243-ton boulder was deposited by the Wisconsin glacier more than ten thousand years ago.

The 1,000-acre **Pyramid Mountain Natural Historic Area** is an excellent place for hikers and nature lovers. Rugged hills, kettle holes, and streams are home to more than 400 species of plants and wildflowers, 100 species of birds, and 30 species of mammals.

Six main hiking trails, each blazed with a different color, traverse the north/south axis of the area. Follow the white trail to Tripod Rock, which perches precariously on three smaller boulders and is one of numerous glacial erratics in the park. Nearby Bear Rock (white/blue trail) is one of the largest in the state. The Pyramid Mountain Visitor Center, 472A Boonton Avenue, Montville, (973) 334–3130, is open Wednesday through Sunday 10:00 A.M.–4:30 P.M. Trails are open year-round from sunrise to sunset. There are guided hikes most Saturdays and Sundays. To get to Pyramid Mountain Natural Historic Area from I–287, take exit 44A at Main Street in Montville. Turn right on Boonton Avenue (County Route 511) and head north 4 miles to the entrance, on the left.

Did you know that when a baby ostrich is born it weighs about three pounds? Or that ostriches take three years to reach maturity? Or that when they're scared, rather than sticking their heads in the sand, they can run up to 55 miles per hour? Or that the ungainly African birds make the ***Flower Place*** one of New Jersey's most unusual family attractions?

At the Flower Place, the ostriches are outside in pens, while a rainbow palette of fresh flower arrangements is artfully displayed inside the 1865 barn, which is also chock-full of baskets as well as figurines made by proprietor Jun A. Omata from natural materials such as dried leaves, twigs, feathers, wood bark, and mushrooms. Upstairs the walls are decorated with tapestries and original paintings by resident artist R. D. Walker, and there's a fine collection of Oriental antiques and art and handcrafted silver jewelry.

The Flower Place, 53 Sarepta Road, Belvidere, (908) 475–1446, is open Tuesday through Sunday 9:00 A.M.–6:00 P.M.

Any time of the year is a good time to visit ***Matarazzo Farms,*** but in fall, when you can pick your own pumpkins and apples and sample the fresh-pressed apple cider, the 392-acre farm is extra special. ***Four Sisters Winery,*** on the grounds of the farm, gives free tastings all year and complimentary tours on weekends. If you really like getting into the act, ask the winery about its grape-stomping parties. The farm and winery are on Route 519, 10 Doe Hollow Lane, Belvidere. For information on the market, call (908) 475–3671.

If you've ever wondered about the origins of those hatchery trout you fish for in spring, a visit to the ***Pequest Trout Hatchery and Natural Resource Education Center*** should answer all your questions. The Pequest facility, located 9 miles west of Hackettstown, has, since its opening in 1982, produced more than 600,000 brook, brown, and rainbow trout per year for distribution in New Jersey's lakes and streams. It takes eighteen months for the hatchery to raise a fish to stocking size, and the job involves careful maintenance of water temperature and aeration, feeding, and disease-prevention measures. The early stages of the operation, in which brood fish spawn and eggs are incubated and

The Four Sisters Winery offers tours,
tastings, and even grape stomping.

hatched, are conducted in closed quarters inaccessible to visitors, but anyone can watch the growing trout through windows in the nursery building and in the mile of outdoor concrete raceways on the Pequest premises.

On the hatchery grounds, the Natural Resource Education Center houses exhibits that explain riverine ecology, with specific emphasis on the life cycle of trout—including a display tank that approximates a cross section of a typical trout stream. Videos and self-guided tours of the hatchery complete the educational experience. Special programs are offered year-round and are listed in the center's *Budding Naturalist* brochure.

The Pequest Trout Hatchery and Natural Resource Education Center, 605 Pequest Road, off Route 46 near I–80 (exit 19), Oxford, (908) 637–4125, is open daily except holidays, throughout the year, 10:00 A.M.–4:00 P.M. Admission is free.

From ashwaganda to yucca, **Well-Sweep Herb Farm** showcases and sells one of the largest selections of herbs in the country, exhibiting them along with a large collection of perennials in a natural setting. There's also a formal educational display herb garden, as well as medicinal, perennial, English cottage, rock,

and vegetable gardens. Among the herbs: thirty-six types of basils, sixty different lavenders, eighty varieties of thyme, and one hundred varieties of scented
geraniums. The biggest selection—when weather cooperates—is available
around May 15, but there's lots to see and buy year-round, and the fields, with
flowers drying, are particularly magnificent during July and August.

Well-Sweep Herb Farm, 205 Mt. Bethel Road, Port Murray, (908)
852–5390, is open Monday through Saturday 9:00 A.M.–5:00 P.M., closed Sundays
and holidays. From January through March, call ahead to make sure they'll
be open.

Morris-Warren Hills

The gracious 1770s **Stewart Inn B&B** is a stone manor house on sixteen acres
of lawns, woods, stream, and pasture. There are five rooms and suites, each
with a private bath; three have fireplaces. There's a swimming pool, trout
stream, barn, outbuildings, and farm animals. A full breakfast is included in the
B&B's rates, which run from $95 to $135 per night, double occupancy. The inn
is at 708 South Main Street (mailing address: Box 571, R.D. 1), Stewartsville
08886; (908) 479–6060; www.stewartinnnj.com.

Since the early 1700s the town of Chester has been a magnet for travelers.
The first white settlers established farms and shops on the Black River, along
paths the native Lenni-Lenape had carved out. By 1771 a weekly stagecoach
ran from Jersey City to Chester's (then known as Black River) Crossroads. In
the early 1800s the road was improved: Washington Turnpike (Route 240) ran
through town, and the Brick Hotel opened to serve weary travelers.

Chester really became a boomtown in 1867, when iron ore was discovered
along Main Street. Unfortunately, twenty-five years later, the ore ran out, and
Chester quickly became a ghost town. In the 1950s a local family opened a
restaurant at The Crossroads called Larison's Turkey Farm Inn (sadly, now
closed), which began to draw tourists back to the area.

As tourists began to return to Chester, residents opened shops along the
historic Main Street to attract them. They were attracted, and today downtown
Chester is thriving. Baseball fans may want to pause for a moment in front of
the **Emporium Shop** at 71 Main Street. The house was once home to Billie
Dee's Store, which sold newspapers and candy. Billie Dee was also a baseball
pitcher and is credited with having invented the curveball when his finger got
caught in the covering of a ball. **Taylor's Ice Cream Parlor,** in the 1876
Centennial Building, is a great place for a light snack. The Brick Hotel is now
the **Publick House** and still rents rooms ($65–$95 with private bath and continental breakfast) and serves lunch and dinner daily. Call (908) 879–6878.

Before you head toward Morristown, go a mile in the other direction toward Long Valley to visit **Cooper Gristmill** on Route 513, one of the few waterpowered mills still operating in New Jersey. Built in 1826 on the site of a pre-Revolutionary mill, it was restored in the 1970s by the Morris County Park System. The mill is open May through October weekends 10:00 A.M. to 5:00 P.M., and July and August Friday through Tuesday. Tours run every half hour, with the last at 3:45 P.M. Admission is $3.00 adults, $2.00 seniors, $1.00 children ages six to sixteen; (908) 879–5463.

Heading back east we come to Morristown, perhaps best known to visitors for its National Historic Site that relates to the Continental army's encampments in 1776–77 and 1779–80. The more than two centuries that have passed since Washington and his men camped here have seen the surrounding countryside change from farms to still-growing suburbs, with one important exception. This is **Fosterfields,** a "living historical farm" maintained as an example of what agriculture was like in New Jersey one hundred years ago.

The 200-acre tract that became Fosterfields had been cultivated for a century or more by 1852, when Paul Revere's grandson, Lt. Joseph Warren Revere, bought the land and built his country seat, The Willows, here. There have been only two private owners of Fosterfields since Revere: Charles Foster, who bought the property in 1881, and his daughter, Caroline Rose Foster, who inherited it in 1927 and lived here until her death in 1979 at the age of 102. Near the end of her long life, Miss Foster donated her farm to the Morris County Park Commission, which maintains it, using much the same farming techniques her father employed in the late 1800s. Everything is authentic—

A Forgotten Canal

Much of the Delaware and Raritan Canal, which slices across the Garden State at its narrowest part, has been preserved as a park waterway. But the more northerly Morris Canal, which once had its western terminus at Phillipsburg, is gone and largely forgotten.

The Morris Canal reached from Newark Bay to the Delaware River, ascending from sea level to an altitude of 914 feet at Lake Hopatcong, then dropping to 760 feet at the Delaware—all via a system of twenty-three inclined planes. Completed in 1831 at a cost of nearly $3 million, it could accommodate canal boats weighing up to twenty-five tons. But like many other waterways dug during America's golden age of canal building, the Morris Canal soon fell prey to competition from the newer and faster railroads. The Lehigh Valley Railroad leased the canal in 1871 and prevailed upon the state to take it over in 1903. Twenty-one years later it was destroyed, by state order.

tools, plows, and harvesting equipment, and, of course, the horses that turned the wheels of farms and much of civilization itself four generations ago.

In addition to following the self-guided trail through the farm or taking one of the guided tours offered on Sundays at 2:30 P.M., visitors to Fosterfields are encouraged to participate in a busy schedule of workshops and demonstrations that emphasize old-time agricultural, crafts, and home-economics techniques. The Willows, the Gothic Revival mansion on the site, is open for tours April through October, Thursday through Sunday 1:00–4:00 P.M. The last tour begins at 3:30 P.M., and there is an additional fee of $1.00 for the tour.

Fosterfields Living Historical Farm, Route 24 and Kahdena Road, Morris Township, (973) 326–7645, is open April through October, Wednesday through Saturday (and holidays) 10:00 A.M.–5:00 P.M., Sunday noon–5:00 P.M. Admission is $5.00 for adults, $4.00 for seniors, and $3.00 for children ages six through sixteen; under six, free.

Another gem of the Morris County Park Commission is the 127-acre **Frelinghuysen Arboretum,** surrounding the stately colonial revival mansion that houses the commission's offices. All the trees in the arboretum are identified by species, and among the numerous trails that crisscross the property is a natural path for the blind, with signs in braille. The Frelinghuysen Arboretum is especially beautiful in springtime, when azaleas, rhododendrons, roses, and spring bulbs bloom in profusion, but cross-country skiers should also keep the trails in mind for fine winter sport.

The Frelinghuysen Arboretum, on East Hanover Avenue near Whippany Road, Morris Township, (973) 326–7600, is open daily during daylight hours; closed Thanksgiving, Christmas, and New Year's Days. Admission is free.

Historic Speedwell recalls the lives and work of a family that played an important part in the transformation of the United States from an agricultural to an industrial nation in the nineteenth century. Stephen Vail was the owner of the thriving Speedwell Iron Works, a cast-iron foundry powered by the fast-running Whippany River. One of the most important commissions of the Speedwell works in the early 1800s was for the iron machinery used in the SS *Savannah,* the first steamship to cross the Atlantic Ocean.

While attending New York University, Vail's son, Alfred, met Samuel F. B. Morse, who had come to demonstrate a rudimentary apparatus he had devised for sending electromagnetically generated signals over wires. Alfred offered Morse financial backing and helped perfect the device at Speedwell. On January 6, 1838, Alfred sent the first message, "A patient waiter is no loser," on a working model of the improved telegraph. The more famous "first" telegraph message, Morse's own "What hath God wrought," was transmitted to Vail at Baltimore six years later over an improved apparatus featuring a register that

The first message transmitted by Morse code was sent years before Morse's more famous "What hath God wrought."

recorded the dots and dashes of Morse code on a strip of paper. That machinery, too, was built by Vail at Speedwell.

Today, Speedwell enjoys designation as a National Historic Site. Structures open to visitors at Speedwell include Vail House itself, restored to its 1840s appearance; the 1829 building where the first public demonstration of the telegraph was made on January 11, 1838; and the granary, housing exhibits of antique tools and vehicles. In addition to these original structures, the Speedwell property is the site of three eighteenth- and early-nineteenth-century houses moved here from Morristown in the 1960s.

Historic Speedwell, 333 Speedwell Avenue, Morristown, (973) 540–0211, is open from April through October, Wednesday through Saturday 10:00 A.M.–5:00 P.M., Sunday noon–5:00 P.M. Admission is $4.00 for adults, $3.00 for senior citizens, and $2.00 for children ages six through sixteen. Tours of the Vail House are offered Thursday and Sunday.

If you don't mind using your feet to get off the beaten path, Morris County offers some excellent options.

The ***Farney Highlands Trail*** system in Jefferson and Rockaway Townships encompasses the Four Birds Trail, an isolated, 19³⁄₁₀-mile segment that crosses only one paved road. "Four birds" refers to environments found along the trail: wild turkey in the forests, red-tailed hawk near the cliffs, osprey on the shores of the lake, and, in the marshes, great blue heron. The trail is a great place for migratory bird-watching in the fall. To reach the southern trailhead, take Route 513 north from Route 80 in Rockaway Township, and, after 2¾ miles, turn right onto Sunnyside Road. Look for white blazes about 150 feet down on the left. The northern section of the trail is on land owned by the Newark Watershed Conservation and Development Cooperation. Call (973) 697–2850 for a hiking and parking permit.

Head over to Morris County's **Mount Hope Historical Park** to see remains of the county's twentieth-century iron mines. Pick up a trail guide at the parking lot and then meander along 3 miles of trails that wind past historic sites, including numerous subsidence pits (large holes created by abandoned mine shafts). Keep an eye open for chunks of magnetite iron ore—small, black, somewhat rectangular rocks. To reach the park, take I–80 to exit 35 north toward Mount Hope. After ½ mile, turn left onto Richard Mine Road, then turn right onto Coburn Road after 7/10 mile. When the name of the road changes to Teabo Road, watch for the parking lot after another 7/10 mile.

For maps and information on all of Morris County's parks, call (973) 326–7600 weekdays. Maps are available at the Hagarty Education Center at the Frelinghuysen Arboretum.

Gustav Stickley, the foremost American spokesperson for the Arts and Crafts Movement, was a proponent of "a fine plainness" in art and the art of living. He incorporated his philosophy of building in harmony with the environment by using natural materials when he built his log home at **Craftsman Farms** circa 1908–10. As he explained in his magazine, *The Craftsman,* in November 1911: "There are elements of intrinsic beauty in the simplification of

Fort Nonsense

Morristown is rich in relics of the days when New Jersey was the "Cockpit of the Revolution." On the grounds of Morristown National Historical Park are the Ford Mansion, twice Washington's winter headquarters, and the site of the troop encampment at Jockey Hollow. A lesser-known Revolutionary War site on the park's grounds is Fort Nonsense, marked by an earthworks reconstruction on Morristown's Mount Kemble. Why the irreverent name? The fort, constructed in 1777 under George Washington's orders, was never used except for storage of supplies. As the years wore on, locals came to suspect that the Commander had built it only to keep his men busy during a long winter bivouac. So they named it Fort Nonsense, in what was perhaps the only instance of that word being connected with the decidedly no-nonsense Father of His Country.

The Log House at Craftsman Farms

a house built on the log cabin idea. First, there is the bare beauty of the logs themselves with their long lines and firm curves. Then there is the open charm felt of the structural features that are not hidden under plaster and ornament, but are clearly revealed, a charm felt in Japanese architecture. . . . The quiet rhythmic monotone of the wall of logs fills one with the rustic peace of a secluded nook in the woods."

Stickley dreamed of establishing a farm school for boys at his "Garden of Eden," but his dream began to fade as the tastes of the American people moved away from the clean, strong lines of Craftsman furniture toward revival of early American and other styles. The dream died in 1915, when he filed for bankruptcy. In spite of these failures, he was a visionary, whose philosophy of art and architecture helped people make the transition from the overwrought interiors of the Victorian Age to the modern decorative arts to come.

Twenty-six acres of the 650-acre tract that originally made up Craftsman Farms have been declared a National Historic Landmark. The landmark is owned by the Township of Parsippany-Troy Hills and is operated by The Craftsman Farms Foundation, which is restoring the interior of the house and the gardens as they were in Stickley's time. Many of his original pieces of Mission furniture and comparable period Stickley pieces are on display to show how the house would have looked in his day.

The interior of the Main Log House at the Stickley Museum at Craftsman Farms, on Route 10 West and Manor Lane, Parsippany (mailing address: Box 5, Morris Plains 07950), (973) 540–1165, is open April through mid-November, Wednesday through Friday noon–3:00 P.M. and Saturday and Sunday 11:00 A.M.– 4:00 P.M. (The last tour starts at 3:15 P.M.) Throughout the season there are a variety of special events, including brown-bag lunch lectures and holiday programs the first three weekends in December. The grounds are open from dawn to dusk. Admission is $7.00 for adults, $4.00 for children under six. Call for a calendar.

Among the exhibits at *Imagine That!!!,* a children's discovery museum with more than fifty hands-on activities, is a space shuttle experience and a veterinarian pet center. Some of the old favorites include a science discoveries room, gravity maze, dance studio, and the cockpit of a real Piper airplane. In the TV newsroom, kids can write, produce, and direct their own television news show.

Imagine That!!! is at 4 Vreeland Road in Florham Park; (973) 966–8000. The museum is open daily 10:00 A.M. to 5:30 P.M. Admission is $7.99 for children and $4.99 for adults. One adult must accompany every four children.

Places to Stay in Northern New Jersey and the Upper Delaware Valley

The Bernards Inn
27 Mine Brook Road,
Bernardsville;
(888) 766–0002 or
(908) 766–0002;
fax (908) 766–4604;
www.bernardsinn.com.
Expensive.

Chestnut Hill on the Delaware
63 Church Street,
P.O. Box N, Milford;
(908) 995–9761 or
(888) 333–2242;
www.chestnuthillnj.com.
Moderate–expensive.

Inn at Millrace Pond
313 Johnsonburg Road,
Box 359, Hope;
(800) 746–6467 or
(908) 459–4884;
fax (908) 459–5276;
www.innatmillracepond.com.
Moderate.

Inn at Panther Valley
Route 517, Box 183,
Allamuchy;
(908) 852–6000;
fax (908) 850–1503;
www.panthervalleyinn.com.
Moderate–expensive.

Olde Mill Inn
225 Route 202,
exit 30B (Route 287),
Basking Ridge;
(800) 585–4461 or
(908) 221–1100;
fax (908) 221–1560;
www.oldemillinn.com.
Moderate–expensive.

Somerset Hills Hotel
200 Liberty Corner Road,
Warren;
(908) 647–6700;
fax (908) 647–8053;
www.shh.com.
Moderate.

The Woolverton Inn
6 Woolverton Road,
Stockton;
(888) AN–INN–4U or
(609) 397–0802 or
(888) 264–6648;
fax (609) 397–0987;
www.woolvertoninn.com.
Moderate–expensive.

Places to Eat in Northern New Jersey and the Upper Delaware Valley

Arthur's Tavern
700 Spedwell Avenue,
Morris Plains;
(973) 455–9705
Complimentary garlic pickles, hot peppers, pickled tomatoes, and homemade sauerkraut set the tone for a large selection of burgers, sandwiches and salads, and the famous bet-you-can't-finish twenty-four-ounce Delmonico steak (or, for the true *fresser,* "the double" forty-eight-ounce), all to be washed down with liter mugs of cold draft beer. Save room for homemade cheesecake. Lunch and dinner daily. Also in Hoboken, Emerson, and North Brunswick. Inexpensive–moderate.

Cloves

61 International Drive,
Budd Lake;
(973) 347–9290
Indian cuisine includes classic vindaloos (from mild to beyond hot), curries, and papadam. Lunch and dinner daily. Inexpensive–moderate.

Good Times

Route 31, Oxford;
(908) 453–2833
A laid-back atmosphere and a menu with everything from pizza to pasta to escargo and seared salmon with wild mushrooms make this restaurant a popular choice for families. Dinner Tuesday through Sunday. Moderate–expensive.

The Grand Cafe

42 Washington Street,
Morristown;
(973) 540–9444
For more than twenty years this sophisticated restaurant with its tuxedoed waiters has set the bar for classic French cuisine in the area. Dishes are prepared with a deft touch bordering on the *nouvelle,* but no calories are spared in the fabulous homemade desserts. Lunch Monday through Friday, dinner Monday through Saturday. Expensive.

Il Capriccio

633 Route 10, Whippany;
(973) 884–9175
Piano music, a courtyard with fountains, and candlelight set the mood for a romantic evening of fine Italian dining. The menu is extensive, with classics such as tortellini with walnuts and gorgonzola, and buffalo mozzarella with fresh tomato. There's an excellent wine list

and a fine selection of grappas. Lunch Monday through Friday, dinner Monday through Saturday. Expensive.

Jasper

810 Route 46 West,
Parsippany;
(973) 334–6088
Classic Chinese dishes include the house special Peking duck, and steamed striped bass. Lunch and dinner daily. Moderate.

Perryville Inn

167 Perryville Road,
Perryville;
(908) 730–9500
While the ambience at the inn is early American, the menu is quite contemporary. Choose from specialties such as lobster ravioli, corn and shrimp bisque, and a tender rib eye in a Roquefort cheese crust. Lunch Tuesday through Friday, dinner Tuesday through Sunday. Expensive.

Pierre's Bistro & Wine Bar

955 Mount Kemble Avenue, Route 202,
Harding Township;
(973) 425–1212
All of the bistro favorites are here—from Provençal fish soup to duck confit. Although there's a fine wine list, Tuesday evenings customers are invited to bring along their favorite bottle of wine (no corkage fee). The lunch buffet ($14.95) is a most satisfying affair. Open for lunch and dinner Tuesday through Sunday. Moderate.

The Rail

350 East Main Street,
Bound Brook;
(732) 748–7245
Nightly specials, live bands,

and karaoke in a renovated hundred-year-old railroad station now a T-stop. Sports fans will love the wall-to-wall TVs; those looking for a bargain turn out for the inexpensive steak dinners offered Tuesday through Sunday. Lunch and dinner daily. Bar open until 2:00 A.M. Inexpensive.

Rattlesnake Ranch Cafe

Foodtown Shopping Center,
559 East Main Street,
Denville;
(973) 586–3800
The eclectic menu includes blackened catfish, fried alligator, and barbecued baby back ribs; the margaritas are enormous; and on Tuesday one kid eats free with every adult entree. Lunch and dinner daily. Moderate.

Restaurant Latour

Crystal Springs Country Club, Route 94, Hamburg;
(973) 827–0548
An intimate dining room, spectacular views, and a superb wine list complement the fine contemporary American menu. Look for appetizers such as quail "lollipops" and lobster bisque, and a terrific dry-aged steak and mustard-crusted rack of lamb. Dinner Thursday through Sunday. Expensive.

Scalini Fedeli

63 Main Street, Chatham;
(973) 701–9200
Well-prepared Northern Italian food with a French flair served in a romantic room with vaulted ceilings and soft lighting. The menu is fixed price, and includes treats such as mushroom napoleon, ravioli stuffed with ricotta, spinach and white

SELECTED REGIONAL INFORMATION CENTERS, CHAMBERS OF COMMERCE, AND VISITOR CENTERS IN NORTHERN NEW JERSEY AND THE UPPER DELAWARE VALLEY

Parsippany Area Chamber of Commerce
12–14 North Beverwyck Road,
Lake Hiawatha 07034
(973) 402–6400
www.njpacc.org

Skylands Tourism Council
360 Grove Street, Bridgewater 08807
(908) 725–1582
www.skylandstourism.org

truffles, and braised lamb shanks. Lunch Monday to Friday, dinner Monday to Saturday. Expensive.

Other Attractions in Northern New Jersey and the Upper Delaware Valley

Acorn Hall
68 Morris Avenue,
Morristown;
(973) 267–3465

Blue Army of Our Lady of Fatima and the Immaculate Heart of Mary Shrine
Mountain View Road,
Washington;
(908) 213–2223

Boonton Historic District
210 Main Street,
Boonton;
(973) 402–8840

Bull's Island Recreation Area
2185 Daniel Bray Highway
(Route 29),
Stockton;
(609) 397–2949

Cross Estate Gardens
Leddel Road,
Bernardsville;
(973) 539–2016

Gallery One Main
1 Main Street,
High Bridge;
(908) 638–3838

The Meadows Foundation, Inc.
1289 Easton Avenue,
Somerset;
(732) 828–7418

Middlebrook Winter Encampment of Washington's Army
Middlebrook Road,
Bridgewater;
(908) 722–2124

Millbrook Village
Old Mine Road, Millbrook;
(908) 841–9531

Rudolf W. Van der Goot Rose Garden
156 Mettler's Road,
East Millstone;
(732) 873-2459

Van Campen Inn
Old Mine Road,
Walpack Center;
(973) 729–7392

Whippany Railway Museum
1 Railroad Plaza, Route 10,
Whippany;
(973) 887–8177

Central New Jersey

The central swath of New Jersey constitutes the narrowest portion of this wasp-waisted state. From the mouth of the Raritan River at South Amboy to the Delaware River at Trenton is barely 35 miles—no wonder this is the crossroads of New Jersey, the place chosen for early New York–to–Philadelphia transportation enterprises such as the Delaware and Raritan Canal and the Camden and Amboy Railroad of the 1830s. More than fifty years before these technological marvels were undertaken, George Washington led his troops westward across Central Jersey in a successful attempt to escape the British threat in New York. Crossing the Delaware near Trenton (a state park commemorates the event today), he struck back at the British and Hessians in one of history's great surprise attacks. In our own day the central corridor of New Jersey is where the famous New Jersey Turnpike makes its dash from the northeastern to the southwestern part of the state.

Central New Jersey, however, is not just a place of comings and goings. Here, at Trenton, is the state capital; here, too, are two of America's finest universities, Rutgers (in New Brunswick) and Princeton. Old industries, like china and glass, and new ones, like electronics and refining, have found Central Jersey a place conducive to growth.

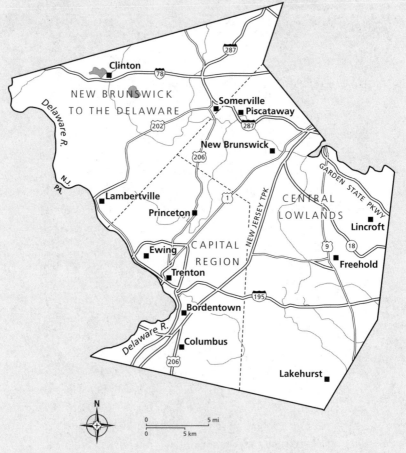

Clinton

287

78

NEW BRUNSWICK
TO THE DELAWARE

Somerville
Piscataway

202

287

New Brunswick

206

Delaware R.

N.J.

PA.

Lambertville

Princeton

1

NEW JERSEY TPK

CENTRAL
LOWLANDS

GARDEN STATE PKWY

Lincroft

9

18

CAPITAL
REGION

Ewing

Freehold

Trenton

Bordentown

195

Delaware R.

Columbus

206

Lakehurst

N

0 5 mi
0 5 km

All such boundaries are imprecise, but we might say that Central New Jersey begins where the state's northern uplands give way to the gently rolling hills of Somerset County horse country, and it extends south almost to the edges of the Pine Barrens. The western border is, of course, the Delaware River. On the east is the coastal plain, but because the Jersey Shore has such a distinct character of its own, we'll save it for a later chapter.

Note: The orientation in this chapter is east to west, from New Brunswick to the Delaware River; then south, through the Capital Region; and, finally, counter-clockwise as we move back north to the Raritan Valley of the Central Lowlands.

New Brunswick to the Delaware

When **Mead Hall** at **Drew University** was damaged by fire in August 1989, the administration determined to salvage some good from the disaster. They decided to restore the 1830s Gibbons family mansion with as much historic precision as possible. The building is now a period piece: The wallpaper and flooring duplicate the originals, and a number of original marble fireplaces were uncovered in the restoration.

Mead Hall at Drew University, Madison, (973) 408–3000, houses the president's and executive offices and is used for meetings and student seminars.

CENTRAL NEW JERSEY'S TOP PICKS

Museum of Early Trades and Crafts	Old Barracks Museum
Great Swamp	"Little Italy"
Red Mill Museum Village	Kuser Farm Mansion
Flemington Cut Glass Company	Bordentown
Black River and Western Railroad	Bellevue
Delaware and Raritan Canal State Park	Naval Air Engineering Station
Lambertville	Historic Allaire Village
Howell Living History Farm	New Jersey Vietnam Veterans' Memorial
Drumthwacket	Zimmerli Art Museum
The Art Museum of Princeton University	Hutcheson Memorial Forest

It is open Monday through Friday 9:00 A.M.–5:00 P.M., except during holidays and long holiday weekends. There is no admission charge.

Fortunately not all the physical remains of earlier times had to be restored from ashes. Many of the everyday objects associated with life in the seventeenth and eighteenth centuries simply collected dust in attics, cellars, and barns, and if they stayed out of the way of zealous spring cleaners, they survived into our own age to be treasured as antiques. The preservation of these artifacts, particularly those associated with the world of work, is the mission of the *Museum of Early Trades and Crafts* in Madison.

The heart of the museum's holdings is the Edgar Law Land collection of eighteenth- and nineteenth-century tools and products that pertain to New Jersey homes, farms, trades, and shop crafts. The museum interprets a time when most New Jerseyans lived on farms or in country villages. The collection encompasses both common and unique everyday products of the home, from horn spoons to bobbin-lace pillows, as well as the tools of carpenters, coopers, tinsmiths, masons, cobblers, wheelwrights, bookbinders, and stonecutters plus unusual lens-making tools and early medical equipment.

Exhibits, many of which feature hands-on discovery areas, include a re-created colonial kitchen, shoemaker's shop, one-room schoolhouse, and changing displays. The museum also offers educational programs for people of all ages, including school programs, adult tours, and special programs every Saturday throughout the school year.

The museum, a nonprofit organization founded in 1970, is housed in the former James Library building, which was built in 1900. The building is listed

A New Jersey Lord

The comfortable residential suburb of Stirling, which lies just south of the Great Swamp National Wildlife Refuge, is named after an American-born aristocrat named William Alexander. An American aristocrat? Yes—and not just in the figurative sense of wealth and power, which Alexander also enjoyed. Born in New York, and owner of a magnificent estate in Basking Ridge, New Jersey, Alexander was a direct descendant of the Scottish earls of Stirling.

Despite his noble rank, Lord Stirling was an active and effective participant on the American side in the Revolution. He commanded New Jersey's first body of Continental troops and was soon elevated to the rank of general. He executed a daring strategic retreat at the Battle of Long Island, captured a British supply ship off Sandy Hook, and brilliantly commanded American artillery at the Battle of Monmouth. With Stirling's untimely death at Albany before the war's end, George Washington lost a good friend and a valuable commander—a man Washington always called "my lord."

AUTHORS' FAVORITE ATTRACTIONS IN CENTRAL NEW JERSEY

The Art Museum of Princeton University

Great Swamp

Hunterdon County Courthouse

New Jersey State Police Museum and Learning Center

New Jersey Vietnam Veterans' Memorial

Old Barracks Museum

on the National Register of Historic Places as an excellent example of the Richardson Romanesque style. It features stained-glass windows, stenciling, a glass-floor gallery, and an 1899 Seth Thomas tower clock.

The Museum of Early Trades and Crafts, Main Street and Green Village Road, (973) 377–2982, is open year-round Tuesday through Saturday 10:00 A.M.–4:00 P.M., Sunday noon–5:00 P.M. Admission is $3.50 for adults and $2.00 for seniors and children six and older.

There is one part of New Jersey, just 26 miles west of Times Square, that has changed very little, if at all, since the days when coopers made barrels and wheelwrights wrought wheels. The *Great Swamp* has, in fact, changed hardly at all over the past few thousand years. It isn't going to change during the foreseeable future either, because this more-than-7,400-acre tract of wetland and forest is protected as a national wildlife refuge.

The stories of how the swamp came to be and how it came to be saved are equally interesting. At one time the land occupied by the swamp—and a good deal more of what was to become north-central New Jersey—was covered by a 200-foot-deep lake, fed by meltwater from the receding Wisconsin Ice Sheet of 10,000 years ago. This vast inland sea, called Lake Passaic by modern geologists, did not drain off until the retreating ice had uncovered a gap at Little Falls, through which water could pour downstream to the Atlantic. The bottom of Lake Passaic, however, never dried out completely. Its understructure of dense clay was a poor absorber of water, and wetlands were created along a long swath of North Jersey, extending from the Great Swamp to Fairfield's Great Piece Meadow. Three centuries of development around the fringes of the swamp failed to result in any permanent penetration of its deepest recesses. In the 1950s it was still left to wood ducks and bitterns, to fox, otter, and muskrat.

In 1959, however, the death knell of the swamp was very nearly sounded, in the form of a report from the Port Authority of New York and New Jersey that favored the vast wetland as the site for a proposed jetport. Projects like this had traditionally been viewed as the triumph of civilization over "wasteland," but this time a substantial portion of the citizenry of the surrounding towns did not agree. They banded together to form the Great Swamp Committee and set about raising the necessary funds to buy the threatened land and present it to the U.S. Department of Interior for use as a refuge. The initial 3,000-acre tract was so dedicated in 1964, and the property in federal hands has since more than doubled. Eighty percent of the swamp is now protected, more than 3,600 acres of it as wilderness, free from motorized traffic and permanent construction.

The *Great Swamp Outdoor Education Center* in Chatham is an excellent place to begin your visit. The center, open daily from 9:00 A.M. to 4:30 P.M., provides an introduction to the geology and ecology of the area. A wheelchair-accessible boardwalk trail and an observation blind are here as well. The center is at 247 Southern Boulevard; (973) 635–6629.

A wildlife observation center, with observation blinds, trails, and rest rooms that are handicap accessible, borders the management and wilderness sectors of the property. A system of 8½ miles of marked trails extends through the wilderness. Maps are available at the headquarters, as are checklists of the bird, reptile, amphibian, and mammal species, as well as common wildflowers that have been documented here.

The Great Swamp National Wildlife Refuge headquarters is located at 152 Pleasant Plains Road (exit 30A off I–287), Basking Ridge, (973) 425–1222, and is open daily throughout the year. The south gate of the refuge, on Pleasant Plains Road, is closed between dusk and 8:00 A.M.

The Bernards Inn has long had a reputation for superb cuisine: *Gourmet* magazine consistently honors it as "one of America's top tables." Served in a beautifully restored, elegant Mission-style building, the cuisine is described as progressive American, and chef Edward Stone utilizes classic French techniques to create such delicacies as warm lobster salad with avocado and mango, and pan-seared medallions of Cervena venison with pink peppercorn mashed potatoes and roasted beet jus. To truly sample his creativity, opt for the five-course tasting menu ($75 without wine, $110 with a selection of wines), served Monday through Friday evenings and Saturday after 8:00 P.M.

There are twenty guest rooms at the four-star, four-diamond inn; prices for a double range from $150 to $215, with a lovely continental breakfast.

The Bernards Inn, 27 Mine Brook Road (Route 202), Bernardsville, (888) 766–0002, www.bernardsinn.com, is open for lunch Monday through Friday and dinner nightly. Jackets are requested.

One of the state's finest seafood restaurants is in the tiny, inland town of Gladstone. The aquarium in *Opah Grille* ("Opah" is a Hawaiian moonfish) sets the mood for the menu, a blending of old favorites prepared with an unexpected touch, and more unusual dishes. Traditional crabcakes are served on a bed of shredded jicama; steamed mussels come in a lemongrass-flavored Thai broth; and scrod is baked in a *panko* (Japanese bread crumb) crust. Mondays are lobster nights: For $21.95 diners can feast on lobster bisque, salad, and lobster (get there early to avoid disappointment). Entrees are in the $20 range, and there are several "landlubber" choices.

Opah Grille, 12 Lackawanna Avenue, Gladstone, (908) 781–1888, is open for lunch Monday through Friday, dinner nightly.

One of the premier rock gardens in the East has been "growing" since it was first conceived in the late 1930s. The **Leonard J. Buck Garden,** nestled in a thirty-three-acre wooded stream valley, is actually a series of alpine and woodland gardens.

Tucked among rock outcroppings are a bewildering variety of rare and exotic rock garden plants, all placed to appear as if they were occurring naturally. Leafy trails connecting the outcroppings are lined with wildflowers. A profusion of heaths and heathers, all varieties of *Calluna* and *Erica,* flourish in a raised peninsula bed at the entrance to the visitor center.

On a slope behind the center is the F. Gordon Foster Hardy Fern Collection, which includes Christmas and northern maidenhair ferns, rare fern species such as the tiny rusty woodsia, and painted and autumn ferns from Japan.

Although Buck Garden's peak bloom period occurs in spring, there are splashes of color—or at least a welcome green—almost every week of the year. The garden is maintained by the Somerset County Park Commission, which also oversees the Colonial Park Arboretum and its magnificent Rudolf W. van der Goot Rose Garden, with more than 3,000 roses of more than 200 varieties.

The Leonard J. Buck Garden, 11 Layton Road, Far Hills, is open Monday through Friday 10:00 A.M.–4:00 P.M., Saturday 10:00 A.M.–5:00 P.M., and Sunday noon–5:00 P.M.; closed on weekends and major holidays from December through March. A $3.00 per person donation is requested ($1.00 for seniors). For information on the garden or the arboretum, call the park commission at (908) 234–2677.

It's rumored that when chefs want a night out, they head to **Ryland Inn** for French/American cuisine prepared by owner-chef Craig Shelton. The restaurant, in a restored late-eighteenth-century home, features creations such as sautéed softshell crabs with vegetables a la grecque and roasted baby lamb with oven-dried tomatoes, artichokes, and basil. Diners can choose from tasting menus ranging in price from $90 to $120 per person (without wine), or an a la carte menu whose entrees range in price from $36 to $48. The Ryland Inn is on Route 22W in Whitehouse, (908) 534–4011, and serves dinner nightly. Jackets are required at dinner. A classic bistro menu is served in the piano bar lounge

passwithcare

In 1904 it cost $30,767 to erect the **Riegelsville Bridge,** which spans the Delaware River between New Jersey and Pennsylvania. The 577-foot-long wire-rope suspension bridge is just 16 feet wide—a tight squeeze for two SUVs passing each other. But even if your letters of transit aren't in order, you can get a fine view without leaving New Jersey.

Sunday through Friday (excluding holidays) beginning at 5:30 P.M. Reservations not accepted for parties under five in the lounge. Before or after dinner, be sure to take a stroll through the restaurant's fifty acres of woods, meadows, and gardens: Don't miss a visit to the herb and vegetable gardens. Nondiners are also invited to enjoy the grounds.

Like Waterloo Village, Fosterfields, and the Museum of Early Trades and Crafts, *Red Mill Museum Village* provides a glimpse into a domestic past that was, historically, just the day before yesterday but seems, in technological terms, as remote as the Middle Ages. Located on the South Branch of the Raritan River just north of I–78, the National Historic Site centers on what was formerly the most important building in these parts: the 1810 Red Mill, in which waterpower at one time ground grain, flaxseed, limestone, graphite, and talc. Today the mill exhibits suggest the rural life of the nineteenth- through early-twentieth-century periods in the Delaware Valley. In many ways things didn't change that much on the farms and in backcountry villages through that long stretch of time.

The "village" that clusters near the Red Mill is a string of period structures, tucked neatly between the river and the 150-foot limestone cliffs that provided much of the mill's work. Here are an old general store/post office, a one-room schoolhouse, a log cabin, a blacksmith shop, and wagon sheds. Unique to this museum are the remains of Mulligan's lime quarry, including office, dynamite shed, lime kilns, and stone crusher.

If you are in the Clinton area July and/or August, look into the museum's Concerts in the Park program. Each week the natural outdoor amphitheater, created by the cliffs near the mill, is the site for jazz, folk, ethnic, or old-time music.

The Red Mill Museum Village's Hunterdon Historical Museum, 56 Main Street, Clinton, (908) 735–4101, is open early April through mid-October, Tuesday through Saturday 10:00 A.M.–4:00 P.M., Sunday noon–5:00 P.M. (last admission tickets are sold one hour before closing). Admission is $6.00 for adults, $5.00 for senior citizens, and $4.00 for children ages six through twelve.

The *Hunterdon Museum of Art,* housed in a nineteenth-century stone gristmill, which is on the National Register of Historic Places, is Hunterdon County's visual arts center. Galleries feature works by local and internationally renowned artists. The Anne Steel Marsh collection includes more than 350 contemporary prints by artists such as Ben Shahn, Salvador Dalí, and Edward Coker. The sales gallery features handcrafted items by regional artists. The museum is at 7 Lower Center Street, Clinton, (908) 735–8415. Exhibits and the gift shop are open Tuesday through Sunday 11:00 A.M.–5:00 P.M. There is a suggested donation of $3.00.

The Ship Inn, an authentic British pub and New Jersey's first brewpub, has fourteen British draft ales and hard cider on tap, as well as a great selection of single-malt whiskies. The cuisine is from England, Ireland, Scotland, and Wales. The inn, at 61 Bridge Street, Milford, (908) 995–0188 or (800) NJ1–ALES, is open daily for lunch and dinner. Entertainment, including music from the British Isles as well as soft rock and blues, is offered throughout the year. Check their Web site, www.shipinn.com, for a listing.

Local produce and products—including hand-picked wild mushrooms—are staples at the **Frenchtown Inn,** which also does its own smoking and sausage making. The restaurant, in an 1805 restored building that was formerly a hotel, serves French/American fare. Menu offerings include Atlantic salmon, roast rack of lamb, and duck. (The inn's Grill Inn and Bistro offers casual dining, a similar menu, and lower prices. It is open Tuesday through Friday 5:00–9:00 P.M., and Sunday 3:00–8:00 P.M.) The Frenchtown Inn is at 7 Bridge Street, Frenchtown; (908) 996–3300. It's open for lunch Tuesday through Saturday noon–2:00 P.M.; for dinner Tuesday through Friday 6:00–9:00 P.M., Saturday 5:30–9:30 P.M., and Sunday 5:00–8:00 P.M.; for Sunday brunch, noon–2:15 P.M. The inn is closed Monday.

TOP ANNUAL EVENTS IN CENTRAL NEW JERSEY

Note: Schedules may vary; call ahead.

New Jersey Flower and Garden Show, Somerset; February; (732) 919–7660

Shad Festival, Lambertville; April; (609) 397–0055

American Indian Arts Festival, Westampton; May; (609) 261–4747

Heritage Days, Trenton; June; (609) 777–1770

Annual Battle of Monmouth, Manalapan; June; (732) 462–9616

Oceanfest, Long Branch; July; (732) 222–0400

St. Ann's Italian Street Festival, Hoboken; July; (201) 659–1116

Hambletonian, Long Meadowlands Racetrack, East Rutherford; August; (201) 935–8500

George Washington Crossing the Delaware, Washington Crossing State Park, Titusville; December 25; (609) 737–0623

The hand-carved decoys of sixty-plus carvers from across the country, along with a huge collection of original wildlife art, are on display at ***Decoys & Wildlife Gallery,*** 55 Bridge Street, Frenchtown; (908) 996–6501. They're open daily 10:00 A.M.–6:00 P.M. or anytime by appointment.

Before you leave Frenchtown, stop at ***Revelations Sacred Antiquities,*** 43A Bridge Street, which sells an excellent collection of European religious paintings and sculptures. Nearby, the ***Mendham Gallery*** at 33 Bridge Street, exhibits crafts of more than one hundred American artists. Stop for lunch or dinner at the ***Cocina del Sol,*** at 10 Bridge Street, for freshly prepared California-style Mexican fare. Bring your own beer or wine and cash—credit cards are not accepted.

The town of Flemington, with its many factory-outlet stores, has become a haven for shoppers. One of the most popular continues to be ***Flemington Cut Glass Company,*** the oldest maker of hand-cut crystal and glass in the country. For almost one hundred years, this Delaware Valley firm has developed its own patterns and done hand cutting and polishing of glassware on its Flemington premises. As interesting as the glass-cutting operation is to watch, it's a fair bet that most visitors to Flemington come to purchase glassware in display rooms, advertised by the firm as holding the largest selection in the world. In addition to its own merchandise, Flemington sells first-quality products, seconds, and closeouts by manufacturers such as Riedel and Schott-Zwiesel. Flemington Glass Company, 156 Main Street, (908) 782–3017 or (800) 990–8666, is open 10:00 A.M.–5:30 P.M. daily. All you need for admission is a burning urge to shop.

The Martians Landed Here

". . . straddling the Pulaski Skyway . . . evident objective New York City . . . now in sight above the Palisades . . . five great machines . . . wading the Hudson like a man wading a brook."

It was the Martians, and they had landed in New Jersey. The occasion, of course, was Orson Welles's famous radio dramatization of H. G. Wells's *War of the Worlds* on the night before Halloween 1938. Although Welles introduced the story as fiction, his setting of the action in actual New Jersey and New York locations and his use of "live" news bulletins as a narrative device caused listeners who tuned in just a few minutes into the broadcast to believe that alien invaders were really on the march.

For his Martian landing place, Welles chose Grover's Mill, New Jersey, a tiny hamlet in West Windsor Township, near Princeton. Today, a plaque in Grover's Mill's Van Nest Park commemorates the great scare with a depiction of a Martian attack vehicle, Welles at the microphone, and a family gathered around their radio.

In 1935 the eyes of the world were on the town of Flemington when Bruno Richard Hauptmann, accused of kidnapping and killing the baby of Charles and Anne Morrow Lindbergh, was put on trial in the **Hunterdon County Courthouse** at the corner of Main and Court Streets. Reporters stayed across the street at the Union Hotel (now a restaurant). At the end of the "Trial of the Century," which lasted six weeks, Hauptmann was found guilty and was executed on April 3, 1936, at Trenton State Prison. Over several weekends each year, semiprofessional actors re-create the trial in the courthouse, using dialogue taken directly from the transcripts. Call (908) 782–2610 for dates and/or reservations.

At **Northlandz,** the Great American Railway—the world's largest miniature railway—has 125 trains that scoot along 8 miles of track through a miniaturized landscape of 35-foot mountains, 40-foot bridges, and handcrafted cities and villages. At one point a triple-spiral, triple-track trestle bridge provides a route for three trains through desert canyons. Also here is a ninety-four-room mansion at the Doll Museum, complete with indoor swimming pool and ballroom; it exhibits more than 150 dolls from around the world. In the American Music Hall a magnificent 2,000-pipe organ rocks the walls of the 250-seat theater several times a day. Snacks are served in the Club Car Cafe.

The sixteen-acre attraction is the culmination of a project begun in 1972 by Bruce Williams Zaccagnino. It's at 495 Route 202 in Flemington, (908) 782–4022, and is open daily, weekdays 10:30 A.M.–4:00 P.M. and weekends and holidays 10:00 A.M.–6:00 P.M. Admission is $13.75 for adults, $12.50 for seniors, $9.75 for children ages two through twelve, free under two.

An enduring American icon is the steam locomotive. It's been more than fifty years since diesels began to outnumber steamers on the nation's railroads, and four decades have passed since the iron horse became extinct in regular United States commercial operation. Still, we can't let go of steam. A recently published guide to rail museums and tourist railroads listed nearly ninety operations that run regularly scheduled or special steam-powered trains. Two of them are right here in New Jersey—one in Allaire State Park (which we'll get to later) and another headquartered in the small central-western New Jersey town of Ringoes. This is the **Black River and Western Railroad,** which offers a one-hour ride between Ringoes and Flemington along a former branch of the Pennsylvania Railroad.

Weekdays from mid-April through December and Fridays in July and August the BR&WRR operates vintage 1920s steam coaches with antique diesel locomotives that depart from Ringoes or Flemington and journey through the rolling West Jersey farm country. Beginning in 2006 the company hopes to be able to have their 1937 Alco 2-8-0 locomotive up and operating. They're looking for members (and volunteers) to join the Black River Railroad Historical Trust to help restore equipment more quickly.

The company also offers hot-air balloon rides. Excursions last approximately one hour and range in price from $400 for two to $650 for four.

For the latest schedule and fare information, contact the Black River and Western Railroad, Route 12 and Stangl Road, P.O. Box 200, Ringoes 08551, (908) 782–9600, or check their Web site: www.brwrr.com.

In 1933 lyricist Lorenz Hart and composer Richard Rodgers visited *The Stockton Inn.* Inspired by the inn and its environs, they wrote "There's a Small Hotel with a Wishing Well." Rodgers and Hart weren't the only artists inspired by the inn, built as a private residence in 1710. Kurt Wiese, illustrator of the original book *Bambi,* painted murals on the dining-room walls. Bandleader Paul Whiteman kept a regular table at the inn, which came to be known as "Colligan's" for the Colligan family who owned it, and signed off his radio and TV shows by announcing he was going to dinner at "Ma Colligan's." A table favored by Dorothy Parker, Robert Benchley, S. J. Perelman, and friends became known as The Algonquin Roundtable, in honor of their New York City meeting place.

The "Small Hotel with a Wishing Well" is still a popular meeting spot for lunch and dinner. Cuisine is contemporary American, and meals are served in the dining room or in The Garden—complete with waterfalls and trout pond. Dinner entrees run between $24 and $34; a lighter menu is served in the tavern.

Overnight guests can choose from a variety of accommodations, including a suite with gas fireplace in the main inn, a loft with fireplace in the 1832 Wagon House, or a suite with a queen-size canopy bed and fireplace in the 1850 Federal House. Rates range from $80 (weekdays) to $170 (weekends).

The Stockton Inn, One Main Street, Route 29, Stockton, (609) 397–1250, www.stocktoninn.com, is open for lunch daily and dinner nightly.

Built in the late 1700s, the elegant *Woolverton Inn,* just a mile from the Delaware Canal and River, stands graciously amid ten acres of century-old oak and apple trees. Eight of the inn's thirteen rooms and cottages are in the three-story 1792 stone manor house. All have private baths and air-conditioning; two have working fireplaces, and three have Jacuzzi tubs. Genuine feather beds are available. The lovely veranda is a wonderful place to rock away idle hours; the elegantly appointed, fireplaced living room a charming spot for tea on a cold winter day. The innkeepers serve a full country breakfast and afternoon tea and will provide lunch and/or dinner on request.

The Woolverton Inn is at 6 Woolverton Road, Stockton; (888) 264–6648 or (609) 397–0802; www.woolvertoninn.com. Room rates, which include breakfast, range from $130 to $425. There is a two-night minimum stay on weekends.

You have to go a long way in New Jersey to drive through a covered bridge—to Sergeantsville, in fact. The ***Green Sergeants Bridge*** on Route 604 is the only covered bridge on a public road in the state. Built in 1872, it was scheduled to be demolished in the 1950s, but a group of citizens banded together and saved it. The 73-foot-8-inch wooden bridge over the Wickecheoke Creek is on its original abutments. For more information call (609) 397–3240.

Before the great days of railroads, canals were king. A hundred and seventy years ago, when the first toylike locomotives were beginning to chuff and sputter along weak and uneven track, it was considered a tremendous advantage to be able to ship freight along the slow, smooth canals, rather than over the treacherous carriage roads of the day—thus the enthusiasm with which New Jerseyans greeted the opening of the Delaware and Raritan Canal in 1834.

From the day it opened, the Delaware and Raritan Canal was one of America's busiest waterways. Along its 44-mile length between Trenton and New Brunswick, coal traveled east from Pennsylvania to New York, finished goods were sent west from the great metropolis, and New Jersey produce was shipped beyond the valleys where it was grown to help boost the agricultural fame of the "garden" state. The canal became so much a part of the fabric of life in New Jersey that even though it last showed a profit in 1892, it remained open to traffic for another forty years before finally succumbing to the highways and railroads.

A 44-mile canal makes a mighty big white elephant. After the D&R was closed to barge traffic, it was used to channel water for farm irrigation and for industrial and residential use. During this period the canal began to attract recreational users; the old towpaths, along which draft animals at one time pulled the barges, made ideal hiking trails, and fishing and boating were easy along such a long, calm stretch of water, with only fourteen locks between Trenton and New Brunswick. Eventually the state legislature responded to what had been a de facto recreational use pattern and created the ***Delaware and Raritan Canal State Park.***

The D&R Canal State Park is probably the only such entity in America that is 60 miles long and, for most of that length, only 25 yards across. In addition to those portions of the route that were never filled in (sections near Bordentown and New Brunswick), the park includes the 22-mile feeder channel that extends along the east bank of the Delaware from Bulls Island to Trenton.

There are two centers for visitors in the D&R Canal State Park: near Blackwells Mills, off Route 27 southeast of New Brunswick; and at Bulls Island, on the Delaware north of Lambertville. The Blackwells Mills site is the location of the main park office and information center, whereas Bulls Island has seventy seasonal campsites, half of which may be reserved. (Contact Bulls Island

Area, 2185 Daniel Bray Highway, Stockton 08559, 609–397–2949.) are welcome throughout the park, as long as no gasoline engines d. Information on privately operated canoe-rental services is available adquarters or by mail. Park headquarters can also supply details on the approximately fifty park access points, about half of which offer parking.

Delaware and Raritan Canal State Park, Route 29 (mailing address: 625 Canal Road, Somerset 08873), (609) 397–2949, is open throughout the year. Contact the park superintendent at the above address regarding camping season and regulations.

There are big doings in **Lambertville** during the last full weekend in April. Each year the town hosts the Shad Festival—a nationally recognized event that features artists, crafters, and the environment. Through shad-hauling and fish-tagging demonstrations, the festival helps focus on the importance of keeping the Delaware River clean. The aroma of cooked shad permeates the town as street vendors serve it up barbecued and fried, and down by the river the boat club and chamber of commerce host grilled shad dinners Sunday afternoon. Tickets for the dinners sell out quickly. For reservations call (609) 397–0055. Their Web site is www.lambertville.org.

If your appetite tends toward shopping, more than one hundred dealers sell their wares at the **Lambertville Antique Market,** 1864 River Road, (609) 397–0456, Wednesday, Saturday, and Sunday.

De Anna's, at 54 North Franklin Street in Lambertville, specializes in home-made pastas and sauces. The restaurant does not allow smoking except on the seasonal patio. It serves delicious food and is open for dinner Tuesday through Sunday. Reservations are recommended on weekends; call (609) 397–8957.

For dining al fresco, **Hamilton's Grill Room** at 8 Coryell Street serves contemporary Mediterranean fare prepared on an open grill. Dinner is served

A California Connection

Picturesque little Lambertville, with its upscale bistros, inns, and galleries, has been linked with New Hope, Pennsylvania, ever since Samuel Coryell began running his ferry across the Delaware River in 1732. More than a century later, the little town made a connection with history across a much greater distance. James Marshall, a descendant of Declaration of Independence signer John Hart, was born in Lambertville and lived in the Marshall family's brick house, which still stands at 60 Bridge Street. While supervising the building of Sutter's Mill in northern California in 1848, Marshall discovered the nuggets that set off the fabled gold rush of the following year.

Marshall, by the way, died broke.

The Delaware and Raritan Canal

nightly both indoors and on an outdoor patio along the Delaware Canal, and features grilled meats and seafood. For reservations call (609) 397–4343.

Lambertville Station serves American cuisine in the town's restored Victorian train station. Specialties include shrimp amandine, pan-blackened swordfish, and fine aged beef; from January to March the chefs serve up special wild-game dishes. The restaurant is on Bridge Street at the Delaware River, Lambertville, (609) 397–8300. Lunch is served Monday through Saturday, dinner nightly, and brunch, with an optional buffet in the Riverside Ballroom, every Sunday. The Station Pub serves lighter fare and offers live music Friday and Saturday evenings.

Next door, each of the forty-five rooms at *The Inn at Lambertville Station* is uniquely decorated with antiques from throughout the world. It's a perfect spot for those who like the charm of a B&B but the amenities of a small luxury hotel. Rates range from $120 to $300 and continental breakfast is delivered to your room. The inn is at 11 Bridge Street, Lambertville; call (609) 397–4400 or, from out of state, (800) 524–1091. The Web site is www.lambertvillestation.com.

The four-diamond *Lambertville House,* a National Historic Inn built in 1812, was once a stagecoach stop serving U.S. presidents and dignitaries traveling between Philadelphia and New York. Today the beautifully restored inn, with its imposing facade of quarried stone etched with wrought-iron balustrades, welcomes guests looking for gracious accommodations. The twenty-six large, elegantly appointed rooms and suites are furnished with antiques and period reproductions, and all have jetted tubs. Twenty-three have gas fireplaces. Many have balconies overlooking the courtyard or town. The inn is at 32 Bridge Street, Lambertville; (609) 397–0200 or (888) 867–8859; www.lambertvillehouse.com. Rates range from $200 to $385 and include a continental-plus breakfast.

Capital Region

The 130-acre **Howell Living History Farm** has been a working farm for 200 years and is being restored to operate like a typical New Jersey family farm circa 1900. Special programs throughout the year are planned around the actual seasonal activities of a working farm. A self-guided tour for visitors includes thirty points of interest, including a sheep barn, a chicken house, a wagon house, and an icehouse. There's even a genuine outhouse! Special hands-on programs for groups are offered throughout the year.

Howell Living History Farm, 101 Hunter Road, Titusville, (609) 737–3299, is open for self-guided tours Tuesday through Friday from 10:00 A.M.–4:00 P.M. February through November, and from April through November it is also open Saturday 10:00 A.M.–4:00 P.M. and Sunday noon–4:00 P.M. Admission is free.

Dosai (rice and lentil crepes), *machli ke dikke* (marinated, charbroiled swordfish chunks), and *dhaba gosht* (broiled chunks of marinated lamb) are just a few house specialties at the highly acclaimed **Passage to India.** The restaurant, in the Lawrence Shopping Center, 2495 Route 1 and Texas Avenue, Lawrenceville, (609) 637–0800, is open for lunch and dinner Tuesday through Sunday. An all-vegetarian, all-appetizer buffet is served Wednesday evening, and a lunch buffet is served Tuesday through Sunday.

The town of Princeton is forever secondary in the public mind to the great institution that it harbors—Princeton University, New Jersey's entry in the Ivy League—but there is more to Princeton than its university, as a ride down Stockton Street (Route 206) will show. Here are two magnificent mansions that have been the official residence of the governors of New Jersey.

Historic **Morven,** the older of the two mansions, was, for more than 200 years, the home of the Stockton family. Richard Stockton, signer of the Declaration of Independence, built his original house here in 1701 on land he purchased from Philadelphia's founder, William Penn. The present structure, recently restored, is an agglomeration of additions to that early home, most of them added in the mid-eighteenth century, when the Georgian style predominated. The mansion and elegant gardens, located on Stockton Street at Liberty Place, are open to visitors for house tours Wednesday through Friday from 11:00

A.M.–3:00 P.M. and weekends noon–4:00 P.M. A tour and tea is offered Wednesday. Admission is $5.00 for adults and $4.00 for seniors and students. Children under eight and strollers are not permitted. For more information call (609) 683–4495.

The present executive mansion is **Drumthwacket,** a mile past Morven on Stockton Street. Drumthwacket is a stately Greek Revival structure, with six great central pillars, looking for all the world like an antebellum Southern mansion transported to the Delaware Valley. Drumthwacket was built in 1835 by Charles Olden, who later became governor of New Jersey. His building was the original central, columned portion; the wings were added by a later owner in the 1890s. Drumthwacket is open to the public on Wednesday for tours beginning at noon by reservation. A $5.00 donation is requested. For information call (609) 683–0057 or check www.drumthwacket.org.

The permanent collection of ***The Art Museum of Princeton University*** ranges from ancient to contemporary art and concentrates geographically on the Mediterranean regions, Western Europe, China, the United States, and Latin America. There is an outstanding collection of Greek and Roman antiquities, including Roman mosaics from Princeton University's excavations in Antioch.

An ancient Chinese sculpture, circa A.D. 1250, on display at Princeton's Art Museum.

The collection of Western European paintings includes outstanding examples from the early Renaissance through the nineteenth century. Among the greatest strengths are Chinese art, with significant holdings in bronzes, tomb figures, and paintings; and pre-Columbian art, with remarkable examples of the art of the Maya. The museum has important collections of old-master prints and a comprehensive collection of original photographs. Princeton University's John B. Putnam Jr. Memorial Collection of twentieth-century sculpture, located throughout the campus, includes works by such modern masters as Henry Moore, Alexander Calder, Pablo Picasso, and Jacques Lipchitz.

The Art Museum of Princeton University, McCormick Hall, Nassau Street, (609) 258–3788, is open Tuesday through Saturday 10:00 A.M.–5:00 P.M. and Sunday 1:00–5:00 P.M. The museum is closed on major holidays. Admission is free.

Behind Palmer Square, near the public library, is **Princeton Cemetery,** final resting place of notables, including Aaron Burr, Grover Cleveland, and Jonathan Edwards. Pick up a map at the superintendent's house near the entrance. The cemetery, 29 Greenview Avenue, is always open. For information call (609) 924–1369.

Stop in at the **Nassau Inn**'s Yankee Doodle Tap Room for a drink, a bite, or just to see Norman Rockwell's 13-foot-long mural, *Yankee Doodle Dandy.* The inn, which has been accommodating weary travelers since 1756, is at 10 Palmer Square, Princeton; (609) 921–7500.

The whole family will enjoy a trip to **Terhune Orchards** at 330 Cold Soil Road in Princeton; (609) 924–2310. There are berries, cherries, and apples to pick, fresh-baked goodies to munch on, fresh produce to buy, and lots of old farm equipment for the kids to climb on. Visitors are encouraged to bring along a picnic lunch. The orchard is open Monday through Friday 9:00 A.M.–7:00 P.M. and weekends 9:00 A.M.–6:00 P.M. Call for information on special events or check the Web site at www.terhuneorchards.com.

Trenton, the capital of New Jersey, was in 1776 a tiny village of no more than one hundred houses, important chiefly as the head of navigation on the

A Brief Presidential Term

Reverend Jonathan Edwards, the famed Congregationalist minister whose fiery sermon "Sinners in the Hands of an Angry God" terrified the faithful when he delivered it from his pulpit in Northampton, Massachusetts, left New England in 1757 to take up the presidency of Princeton University, then known as the College of New Jersey. Just two weeks after arriving at Princeton, however, Edwards died of smallpox, which he contracted after participating in an early experiment with inoculation.

Elmer Always Leaves Flowers

Yes, Virginia, there was an Elsie the Cow. Her real name was You'll Do Lobelia, and she was a star of the Borden Company's milking exhibit at the 1939 New York World's Fair. "Elsie" had been Borden's cartoon mascot for several years, and when the exhibit opened, so many visitors asked "Which cow is Elsie?" that Y. D. Lobelia—a doe-eyed cutie of a cow—was picked to carry the famous name.

"Elsie" began touring the country, but her career as Borden spokescow was tragically cut short when she suffered fatal injuries in a traffic accident in 1941. She was buried on a farm in Plainsboro, New Jersey, where you can see her gravestone (moved from its original site, which is now part of a housing development) near the Plainsboro Museum on Plainsboro Road.

Delaware River. Since Christmas of that year, however, it has loomed inestimably larger in American history, because of George Washington's crossing of the ice-clogged Delaware and defeat of Great Britain's Hessian mercenaries in the Battle of Trenton.

Tradition holds that at the time of the battle, Hessians were quartered in an eighteen-year-old stone building located near the spot where the New Jersey State House stands today. After having survived many uses and a few dates with the wrecker's ball, this venerable structure survives today as the *Old Barracks Museum.*

The Old Barracks were built in 1758 to house British troops fighting in the French and Indian War. Formerly troops who were waiting out the winter for the next season's campaign had been billeted among New Jersey townspeople and farmers, but popular dissatisfaction with this practice (a resentment against being forced to quarter troops later made it into our Bill of Rights) led to the construction of army housing at five New Jersey locations. Rented out for other purposes by the legislature during the interim between the French and Indian and Revolutionary Wars, the barracks were activated again by the British when the rebellion broke out. When the war was over, the New Jersey legislature sold the barracks to private investors, who began fixing them up for use as civilian housing—one of the earliest instances of a type of "condo conversion" in a former institutional building. Throughout the nineteenth century the barracks and officers' quarters served one purpose after another, from tenements to schools to a home for widows. What remained of the complex (a portion was torn down in 1792) was finally purchased for preservation between 1902 and 1914, first by private groups and later by the state. The demolished section was rebuilt, the entire structure restored to its original appearance inside and out, and the Old Barracks Museum came into being.

Today's visitor to the Old Barracks is offered a rare view of what a soldier's life was like 200 years ago. Each of twenty-two 16-by-23-foot rooms, with their fireplaces (one to a room) and single doors, was home to up to fourteen men. Life in the nearby officers' quarters was, needless to say, a shade more pleasant.

Visitors meet role players in eighteenth-century dress, who portray Revolutionary War–era soldiers and camp women. In addition there's an orientation exhibit with a video introduction, changing historical exhibits, displays of original firearms, and dioramas of the Battle of Trenton. That battle is reenacted the Saturday after Christmas.

The Old Barracks Museum, Barrack Street, Trenton, (609) 396–1776 or, on weekends, (609) 777–3599, is open daily 10:00 A.M.–5:00 P.M. Admission is $6.00 for adults, $5.00 for senior citizens and students.

Just minutes from Trenton's State House is a section of town called Chambersburg. Nicknamed *"Little Italy,"* it's a mecca for lovers of Italian food: Within one square mile there are numerous Italian restaurants—Amici Milano, Chianti's, Marsilio's, Rossi's—each with its own ambience and specialties. Perhaps the best way to choose is to wander about and inhale the wonderful aromas. For a brochure and map of Chambersburg and its restaurants, call (800) THE–BURG (in New Jersey only) or the Trenton Convention and Visitors Bureau at (609) 777–1770, or visit www.trentonnj.com.

Artifacts Gallery is a browser's dream—a treasure trove of antique and contemporary posters and prints, postcards, maps, sculpture, ephemera, collec-

A Depression-Era Experiment

Located about 20 miles east of Trenton, the town of Roosevelt was founded in 1935 as a community called Jersey Homesteads. Incorporating a women's clothing factory and a forty-acre farm, the settlement would provide a new home for garment workers previously confined to the tenements of New York and Philadelphia. Launched with both government and private funds, the community was to be an experiment in cooperative ownership of factory, farm, and stores, with an equal distribution of profits. New housing was built, and attractive mortgage terms offered.

The Homesteads' manufacturing and agricultural ventures met with little success; within a few years the community was opened to everyone and the cooperative scheme abandoned. Renamed after the death of President Franklin Roosevelt in 1945, the little town evolved into an ordinary suburban community. But many of the severe, International-style homes and public buildings remain, reminders of a certain vision of the future that found appeal during the Depression's darkest days.

tibles, and memorabilia. The gallery is at 1025 South Broad Street, (609) 599–9081; open Tuesday through Friday 9:00 A.M.–6:00 P.M., Sa 10:00 A.M.–4:00 P.M.

In September 1921, 120 recruits reported to Sea Girt and began training under the watchful eye of Col. H. Norman Schwarzkopf, Stormin' Norman's father. Eighty-one passed the rigorous course and became New Jersey's first state troopers. Their story and many others—including a fascinating, in-depth exhibit on the Lindbergh kidnapping—are told at the ***New Jersey State Police Museum and Learning Center.***

Several of the exhibits here are interactive. In the Criminal Investigation area, visitors help a detective search a crime scene for evidence, analyze bullets and fibers under a microscope, and examine fingerprints. Part of the museum is housed in a 1934 log cabin that was originally used as a dormitory and class-room for new recruits. It now houses a transportation exhibit that includes a 1921 Harley Davidson motorcycle, a 1930 Buick State Police touring car, and a present-day cruiser car in which visitors can sit, activate the light bar, and listen to recordings of actual radio transmissions.

The New Jersey State Police Museum and Learning Center, River Road (Route 175), West Trenton, (609) 882–2000, ext. 6400, is open Monday through Saturday 10:00 A.M.–4:00 P.M. Admission is free.

Fred and Theresa Kuser began construction of their magnificent Queen Anne country home in 1888. They spared no expense. In addition to the man-sion, a laundry house, barn, coachman's house, chicken house, windmill, shower house, and corncrib were constructed, as well as one of the finest clay tennis courts in New Jersey. Four years later the family finally sat down to its first dinner at ***Kuser Farm Mansion.***

A tour of the mansion includes a visit to the Delft Bedroom, whose fireplace has more than one hundred different delft tiles, and the Kuser Farm Theatre/ Dining Room and Projection Room (the family helped finance the Fox Film Corporation, which later became 20th Century Fox). The intricately carved

No Doubt It Was a Diner-Saur

New Jersey has two state animals: the horse and *Hadrosaurus foulkii*, a large dinosaur whose remains were found in the town of Haddonfield many years ago. Traces and skeletons of dinosaurs and other fossil animals have been uncovered at Fort Lee, and dinosaur tracks were found in the Triassic rock of the Palisades during construction of the George Washington Bridge. A hadrosaur model is on display at the State Museum in Trenton.

mansion was executed by German craftspersons on
Ɡer Brewery in New York City. (Mrs. Kuser was the

ꞩion, 2090 Greenwood Avenue, Hamilton, (609) 890–
1:00 A.M.–3:00 P.M. February through April; Thursday
–3:00 P.M. May through November; and in December
(call for information). The mansion is closed for the
month of January. Last tour is at 2:00 P.M. Admission is free.

The thirty-five-acre *Grounds for Sculpture,* on the site of the former
New Jersey State Fairgrounds, showcases works by American and internationally known artists. Permanent pieces by artists such as Magdalena
Abakanowicz, Marisol, and Anthony Caro and special exhibitions are displayed
in two museums and on the lovely grounds. The gazebo overlooking the lotus
pond is a delightful place to enjoy a box lunch: it is open noon–6:00 P.M.
weather permitting. The Cafe, in the Domestic Arts Building, is open 10:00
A.M.–4:00 P.M. The upscale restaurant, Rat's, serves contemporary global cuisine
and is open for lunch Tuesday through Saturday and for dinner Tuesday
through Sunday. Sunday brunch is served 11:30 A.M.–1:00 P.M.

The Grounds for Sculpture, 18 Fairgrounds Road, Hamilton, (609)
586–0616, is open year-round, Tuesday through Sunday 10:00 A.M.–6:00 P.M.
November through March, and 10:00 A.M.–8:00 P.M. from April through October.
Admission prices vary throughout the week; call ahead for rates. The Web site,
www.groundsforsculpture.org lists ongoing events.

Bordentown, on the Delaware River just south of Trenton, is one of the
oldest settlements of central New Jersey. The primary thrust of colonization in
this part of the state was from the south (along the river) rather than from the
New York Harbor area, as it was in the northern counties; consequently, the
ethnic and cultural influences were English rather than Dutch and owed much
to the Quaker society of early Philadelphia. The first settler of Bordentown was

babyit'strenton

Trenton, New Jersey's capital, is one of
the few cities to have had its motto featured in a major motion picture. In the
1983 John Sayles film *Baby It's You,* the
legend "Trenton Makes. The World Takes"
can be seen proudly emblazoned on one
of the city's bridges.

a Quaker shoemaker, Thomas
Farnsworth, who arrived here
from Burlington, New Jersey, in
1682. Farnsworth's property—it
eventually totaled some 548
acres—was to form the core of
the present-day community, and
on it stand Bordentown's most
important historic structures.
Principal among these is *Bellevue,* also known as the *Gilder*

House after its long association with the Gilder family of distinguished soldiers, authors, and musicians. Most likely built in the late 1780s and owned by the Gilders from the mid-nineteenth century until presented to the city of Bordentown in 1935, Bellevue

landho!

It is believed that the first white man to see the New Jersey shore was the Florentine navigator Giovanni da Verrazano, who sailed up the Atlantic Coast in 1524.

is an expansive old home that demonstrates the organic growth of American practical architecture in the years immediately before and after 1800.

Three of the ground-floor rooms and four upper rooms of the Gilder House have been furnished by the Bordentown Historical Society with period furnishings and artwork. Among the most interesting are several pieces once owned by Emperor Napoleon's brother, Joseph Bonaparte, who, as deposed king of Naples and Spain, spent twenty years of comfortable exile at his Bordentown estate.

Bellevue, the Gilder House, on Crosswicks Street (near Route 130), (609) 298–1740, is open for tours by special arrangement. For information contact the Bordentown Historical Society, 13 Crosswicks Street (P.O. Box 182), Bordentown 08505. Also of interest in town is the country's first public school and Thomas Paine's home and statue. The society also offers a self-guided walking tour that encompasses fifty-nine historic sites in town.

Within a block of the Gilder House is the ***Clara Barton School,*** a Bordentown landmark associated with the early career of the woman who was to found the American Red Cross. Barton's later humanitarian accomplishments tend to obscure the fact that she was instrumental in launching the concept of public education in New Jersey.

Before she came to Bordentown in 1852, the state's schools were mostly operated by religious institutions; those that were not generally assessed each student a fee that not everyone could afford. The only alternative was the poorly run, state-supported system of "pauper schools," usually conducted in an ill-trained teacher's home. In the year Clara Barton arrived, not one of Bordentown's seven schools occupied a town-owned building.

Clara Barton badgered the Bordentown school committee into reopening the old school building long used by the Quakers and other religious groups and briefly operated as a town school in 1839. In May 1852 she began teaching a class of six students; within a week the school's enrollment was fifty-five. By the following year there were three Bordentown schools, 600 pupils, and eight teachers. The town—and the state—needed no further convincing that a modern system of centralized public education could succeed in New Jersey as it was

Never Mind the Meat Loaf— Order a Whole Diner

Although diners originated in New England—in Providence, Rhode Island, to be exact—they reached the height of their mid-twentieth-century fame in the Garden State. Great diners were manufactured in New Jersey by companies named O'Mahony, Mountain View, Fodero, and Silk City. Today only one diner builder remains. Kullmann Industries in Lebanon, New Jersey, specializes in prefabricated modular buildings ranging from banks to schools to prisons—but they'll still be happy to custom-build you a diner, as they've been doing since Samuel Kullmann founded the company in Newark in 1927.

succeeding in Barton's native New England. Unfortunately Clara Barton wasn't around Bordentown for long to savor her triumph. Sidelined from teaching by the temporary failure of her voice, she was replaced by a new school principal.

Clara Barton's original schoolhouse in Bordentown was acquired by the city in 1920; it has since been restored to its original (at the time of her teaching) appearance. Located on Crosswicks Street near Farnsworth Avenue, it may be visited by arrangement with the Bordentown Historical Society. For details contact the Bordentown Historical Society at the address and telephone number listed above.

It's hard to stand out in a state that has the informal title of "Diner Capital of the World," but *Mastoris* does just that. Of course, with seating for 650, calling this local institution a diner may be stretching things a bit. But sure enough, at the core of the sprawling red-brick building is a 1968 Kullmann-manufactured diner.

The family-owned restaurant has grown like topsy since it opened in 1927 with just twelve stools. Today there are four separate dining rooms (including the fireplaced Lexington Room), a bakery, and a cocktail lounge. And the extensive menu includes everything from standard diner fare to prime lamb chops with mint jelly and sautéed jumbo shrimp. Don't fill up on the complimentary basket of the restaurant's trademark cinnamon and cheese breads: The portions here are huge!

Even with all those seats, Mastoris fills up quickly on a busy Saturday night, so be sure to make a reservation well in advance. It's at 144 Route 130 and the junction of Route 206, Bordentown; (609) 298–4650. Open Sunday through Thursday 5:00 A.M.–1:00 A.M., Friday and Saturday until 2:00 A.M.

Speaking of diners, aficionados will want to check out the Web site www .njdiners.com.

Burlington lies farther south along the river than Bordentown, and is older still. English Quakers arrived here as early as 1677; the settlement was incorporated as a township in 1693 and granted a city charter by King George II in 1734. By the time of the Revolution, Burlington was a center for pottery making and shipbuilding, and it enjoyed the status of a sea-trading port because of its easy river access to the open ocean.

Despite the fact that Burlington was chosen as the place where the New Jersey State Constitution would be written in 1776, the little city harbored a fair number of Tory sympathizers. One of them, a lawyer and mayor of Burlington, was John Lawrence. Lawrence left the United States for Canada at the close of the Revolution, but before he departed, his son James was born at what is now known as the ***Lawrence House*** on High Street. James Lawrence's politics turned out to be quite a bit different from those of his father, as did his profession. Originally intended by his father to study law, young Lawrence was back in Burlington studying navigation by 1796 and two years later was a midshipman in the U.S. Navy. One year into the war with Great Britain, he was captain of the USS *Chesapeake*. It was during the *Chesapeake*'s losing engagement with the British ship *Shannon* that Captain Lawrence was mortally wounded, but before he died he uttered five of the most famous words in U.S. naval history: "Don't give up the ship!"

It isn't often that two Americans notable in entirely different fields turn out to have been born in adjacent houses, but this block of High Street in Burlington offers just such a coincidence. In 1798 the ***Cooper House,*** now the

Cooper House

headquarters of the Burlington County Historical Society, was the birthplace of James Cooper (he added the middle name Fenimore as an adult) and his home for thirteen months before his parents packed up their large brood and headed for the upstate New York haunts with which the novelist became associated through works such as *The Deerslayer* and *The Last of the Mohicans.* He is remembered today, in the house that bears his name, with a collection of his works and an assortment of associated items. The house also contains a Bonaparte Room, furnished with items once belonging to Napoleon's brother Joseph Bonaparte during his Bordentown sojourn.

The oldest of the three houses that make up the Burlington County Historical Society's High Street Complex is the *Bard-Howe House,* built about 1743. Among the antiques on display at the house is a signed clock, built by the accomplished local silversmith and clockmaker Isaac Pearson.

The Lawrence House is at 459 High Street, the Cooper House at 457, and the Bard-Howe House at 453. The houses are open Tuesday through Saturday 1:00–5:00 P.M. For information contact the Burlington County Historical Society, 451 High Street, Burlington 08016; (609) 386–4773. The society's *Corson-Poley Center* exhibits an excellent collection of quilts, tall case clocks, and samplers, as well as examples of the J. H. Birch Company's jinrikishas (rickshaws).

Everything from antiques to vintage clothing to wallpaper is on sale at flea market prices at the *Columbus Farmers' Market,* 2919 Route 206 South; (609) 267–0400. Fresh flowers are for sale along Flower Row, and produce and fish mongers hawk their wares along Produce Row. The indoor market is open Thursday, Friday, and Sunday from 8:00 A.M.–8:00 P.M.; the outdoor vendors set up booths Thursday, Saturday, and Sunday from 7:00 A.M.–2:00 P.M.

Head on Route 524 toward Clarksburg to *Horse Park of New Jersey at Stone Tavern, Inc.,* the state's first major horse-show grounds. Activities here begin in late March and continue just about every weekend from May through October. Call for a calendar of events, (609) 259–0170; check www.horseparkof newjersey.com; or write to P.O. Box 419, Cream Ridge 08514.

Central Lowlands

Webbs' Mill Bog Cedar Swamp in the 27,298-acre Greenwood Wildlife Management Area is one of the few places in the state to hear—and possibly see—the endangered Pine Barrens tree frog, a tiny, bright green frog with lavender stripes. The best time to hear one is in the evening during the months of May and June. A boardwalk and trail run over a bog that's home to the delicate pitcher plant and rare curly grass ferns. The area is also home to the endangered timber rattlesnake: Although meetings are rare, if you do encounter one, just back away quietly. The swamp environment is a fragile one; be sure to stay on the boardwalk and trails.

Webbs' Mill Bog Cedar Swamp is on County 539 south of Whiting. For more information contact the New Jersey Division of Fish, Game and Wildlife, CN 400, Trenton 08625; (609) 292–2965.

After observing Germany's successful military use of zeppelins in World War I, the United States established the Lakehurst Naval Air Station and began making its own airships, or dirigibles. The popularity of dirigibles peaked in 1936, after the *Hindenburg* had completed ten successful commercial round-trips from Europe to Lakehurst, but the romance ended the following year when the dirigible burned while landing at Lakehurst. Lakehurst Naval Air Station is now the ***Naval Air Engineering Station,*** and both the memorial plaque for the *Hindenburg* and Historic Hangar #1 (the site of the first international airport) are on the center's grounds. The Navy Lakehurst Historical Society offers a free tour on the second and fourth Saturday of the month beginning at 10:00 A.M. Pre-registration is required, and must be done at least two weeks in advance. The tour includes the Information Center, Historic Hangar #1, the Air Park, and the crash site marker. For a schedule call (732) 818–7520.

The Naval Air Engineering Station is on Route 547 (north of Route 70).

Nick Demartino doesn't charge people to dream—they're free to wander through ***Golden Classics,*** where more than 150 exotic, classic, and antique autos are on display. The showroom, at 1165 Route 88 West, Lakewood 08701, (732) 370–2323, is open Monday through Saturday 9:00 A.M.–6:00 P.M.

A trip back up the Delaware Valley to Trenton and due east across central New Jersey on I–195 will take you to ***Historic Allaire Village*** in ***Allaire State***

Up in Flames

The town of Lakehurst, long the site of the U.S. Navy's Naval Air Engineering Station, has played a prominent role in the development of lighter-than-air flight. But it wasn't an American airship that figured in Lakehurst's most famous event—it was the German luxury passenger dirigible *Hindenburg,* which used the facility as a landing field in 1936 and 1937. On May 6, 1937, the *Hindenburg* caught fire while approaching her mooring mast. The hydrogen-filled craft was quickly consumed in flames, and thirty-six people were killed. The disaster marked the end of lighter-than-air transatlantic passenger service, even though airships filled with helium instead of hydrogen would have been impervious to fire and explosion. In the days of the *Hindenburg,* the United States controlled world supplies of helium, which was considered a strategic material and was withheld from the Nazi German regime. In a way, those thirty-six unlucky airship travelers were among the first victims of the gathering storm of World War II.

Park. Allaire Village was a company town, back in the days when the mining and smelting of bog iron was big business in these parts. James P. Allaire, a New York City brass founder, came here in 1822 to exploit this resource by means of an integrated mining, smelting, and forging operation. Within fifteen years he had created an entire community around his "Howell Works," with 400 employees, a free school, and even a stagecoach to Red Bank. Allaire's workers lived in substantial brick row houses, among the first examples of company housing in the United States. Some of the products they turned out were kitchenware, stoves, screws, and flatirons.

The iron industry, however, was not destined to become a long-standing New Jersey staple. Once discovered, Pennsylvania anthracite coal became a cheaper fuel than local charcoal for smelting, and eventually large deposits of iron ore from the north-central Midwest made the mining of bog iron obsolete. After 1850 the village of Allaire became a ghost town. The fact that its buildings remain is due partly to the solidity of their brick construction and partly to the wise acquisition of the town and its environment by newspaperman Arthur Brisbane early in the last century. For many years Monmouth County's Boy Scout organization used several of the buildings as headquarters and helped with restoration projects. In 1941 Brisbane's widow gave the village and much of the surrounding land to the state for use as a park, and restoration efforts continued. Putting an abandoned town back in shape after so long a period of disuse is a big job. Preservation and interpretation of the site continues under the direction of Allaire Village, Inc.

Among the sites to visit at Allaire today are the old carpenter and blacksmith shops, general store, and bakery; workers' houses and foreman's cottage; enameling furnace and casting-house stack; and the picturesque millpond (children only are allowed to fish).

As if a historic village weren't enough to make Allaire unique among New Jersey state parks, this is also the home of the ***Pine Creek Railroad.*** The steam-powered and diesel trains are operated by the New Jersey Museum of Transportation, and the rides last ten minutes.

Allaire State Park, on Route 524 (off I–195 exit 31B, and off Garden State Parkway exit 98), (732) 938–2371, is open daily year-round from dawn to dusk. An admission fee of $5.00 adults and $2.00 for ages six to twelve is charged only on weekends and holidays from Memorial Day through Labor Day. Historic Allaire Village buildings are open Wednesday through Sunday during that period 11:00 A.M.–5:00 P.M. From Labor Day through November, and in May, the buildings are open weekends only from 10:00 A.M.–4:00 P.M. For museum information call (732) 938–2253. There is a separate charge of $3.00 (ages four and over) for rides on the Pine Creek Railroad, which runs weekends from May to October noon–4:00 P.M. For railroad information call (732) 938–5524.

If it has ever gobbled, it's most likely sold at **Hinck's Turkey Farm,** 1414 Atlantic Avenue, Wall; (732) 223–5622. You can buy a fresh turkey, or opt for one oven-ready or already cooked. And there's turkey soup, turkey sandwiches, turkey potpies, and, well, you get the idea. There's also a zoo to amuse the kids. The stand is open weekdays 9:00 A.M.–7:00 P.M., weekends 9:00 A.M.–6:00 P.M.

do-si-do

In 1983 the square dance was designated the official American Folk Dance of the state of New Jersey.

Collingwood Park Auction and Flea Market, with more than 600 indoor and outdoor tables, is a bargain hunter's paradise. Don't miss the antiques auction held Saturday nights in summer (preview starts at 3:00 P.M., bidding begins at 5:00 P.M.). There's also a slew of vendors selling fresh produce, flowers, baked goods, and food. The market is on Routes 33 and 34 (just ½ mile west of the Collingwood Circle) in Farmingdale; (732) 938–7941. The inside is open Friday 11:00 A.M.–7:00 P.M., Saturday 9:00 A.M.–7:00 P.M., and Sunday 9:00 A.M.–5:00 P.M. The outside is open 7:30 A.M.–4:00 P.M. A shrub auction begins at 6:00 P.M. on Saturday.

Slightly to the northwest of Allaire is a state park dedicated in commemoration not of the long-term production of iron, but the short-term exchange of lead—in the form of musket balls. **Monmouth Battlefield State Park** came into being on June 28, 1978, the 200th anniversary of the Battle of Monmouth. The struggle that took place on that June day in 1778 was the longest of the entire Revolution, and the only one in which both supreme commanders— George Washington and Sir Harry Clinton—were involved against each other.

Among the tales of valor that emerged from the smoke and dust of Monmouth, one of the most enduring is that of Molly Pitcher. While her husband fought with the Continental army as a member of a cannon crew, Molly Pitcher carried water to thirsty soldiers during the heat of battle; when her husband was wounded, she herself took his place with the artillerymen. No one has been able to find exactly where Molly's well was, but just for the sake of heroic tradition, if not accuracy, a reproduction has been set up on Route 522 in the 1,520-acre park. Other park features include a visitor center and a marked footpath through the battlefield.

Another important park attraction is the **Craig House,** a 1710 farmstead occupied at the time of the battle by the family of John Craig, paymaster for the local patriot militia. Craig fought at the Battle of Monmouth, and his wife, children, and two slaves left their home when it was apparent that the British were approaching the vicinity. The enemy found Mrs. Craig's silver (hidden in the bottom of the well, which is the first place we would look if we were pillaging enemy territory), and used the house to treat their wounded. The place survived the battle intact and has now been restored to its Revolutionary-era appearance. The four-room Craig House, with its massive kitchen hearth and three smaller fireplaces, offers a good look at how eighteenth-century women lived when they weren't fighting off His Majesty's army or throwing their silver down the well.

Also on the grounds is the 1745 Rhea-Applegate House, whose exterior has been restored. It's the oldest standing two-story Dutch-crafted farmhouse in the state.

Monmouth Battlefield State Park, accessible via Route 9 or Route 33, is at 347 Freehold-Englishtown Road in Menalapan, (732) 462–9616, and is open daily during daylight hours. The visitor center is just off Business Route 33 in Manalapan and is open daily 8:00 A.M.–4:00 P.M. The Craig House is open Sunday 12:30–4:00 P.M. from April through November. There is no admission fee. The Battle of Monmouth is reenacted on the fourth weekend of each June.

You never know what you'll find at the **Monmouth Museum,** founded in 1963 as a "Museum of Ideas." Exhibitions on art, science, nature, culture, and history change constantly. Art and artifacts for the exhibits are borrowed from the nation's leading museums, galleries, and private collections. Kids can participate in a variety of hands-on activities at the Becker Children's Wing, where changing exhibitions complement the curriculum of the local schools.

Monmouth Museum, Brookdale Community College, Newman Springs Road, P.O. Box 359, Lincroft 07738, (732) 747–2266, is open Tuesday through Sunday; call for hours. Admission is $5.00. Children two and under are free.

There are 366 polished black granite panels arranged in a circle at the **New Jersey Vietnam Veterans' Memorial**—one for each day of the year. Engraved on the dated panels are the names of the 1,555 New Jersey soldiers, marines, sailors, and airmen killed or reported missing in action on each date. At the center of the memorial, under a red oak tree, three large bronze statues represent the more than 80,000 New Jerseyans who served in Southeast Asia. The 10,000-square-foot Vietnam Era Educational Center, dedicated in 1998, is "devoted solely to gaining an understanding of the violent conflict in Southeast Asia and the surrounding political strife in America." A historic timeline chronicles the events of the era, documenting both activity in Vietnam and in the United States. Eyewitness accounts—letters and other written material—give visitors an idea of the war's emotional toll on those directly involved. Oral histories of those who lived through the Vietnam War era, including a protester and a mother whose son was killed, bring the war even closer to home. There's also a resource center, which houses information on New Jerseyans killed in Vietnam as well as information on all those in the state who served in the armed forces from 1959 to 1975.

The New Jersey Vietnam Era Educational Center is at 1 Memorial Lane, Holmdel; (800) 648–8387 or (732) 335–0033. The center is open Tuesday through Saturday 10:00 A.M.–4:00 P.M. Admission is $4.00 for adults, $2.00 for senior citizens and students, and free for children ten and under. Veterans and active military personnel are admitted free. The memorial is open at all times.

Chef/owner/wunderkind Nicholas Harary and his wife, Melissa, have been operating **Nicholas** to rave reviews since it opened in early 2001, and they don't seem to be slowing down. Reservations are a must: This is *the* in place for fine American cuisine with a French flair. Diners have a choice of two- to four-course prix fixe ($38 to $75) dinners (including a vegetarian menu) that change with the seasons. A recent menu included as appetizers chilled white almond gazpacho and morel mushroom ragout, and as entrees pan-roasted cod and braised suckling pig. The house special cheese-tasting course ($5.00 surcharge), with four or more artisan cheeses, is a highlight and a good dessert option (although there is a fine choice here, also, including peach upside down cake). The wine list includes a fine selection of dessert wines, many available by the glass and half bottle.

Nicholas, 160 Route 35, Middletown, near Red Bank, (732) 345–9977, is open for dinner Tuesday through Sunday. Smoking is not allowed.

Bruce Springsteen fans will want to walk or drive by two of the homes in **Freehold** where he lived in his early years. The rock and roll legend lived at 39½ Institute Street from the age of six to thirteen, and at 68 South Street when he was fourteen. Pick up a *Walking Tour Guide* at the Western Monmouth Chamber of Commerce, 17 Broad Street; (632) 462–2123.

Until such time as Paterson renames its East Side after Allen Ginsberg or Rutherford comes through with a William Carlos Williams neighborhood, Matawan will remain the only New Jersey community with a section named after an American poet. The poet is Philip Freneau, known as the "Poet of the American Revolution" because of his biting anti-British satirical verse. Freneau lived on an estate called Mount Pleasant in Middletown Point, as Matawan was then called. After his house burned down in 1818, he spent his last fourteen years with relatives near Freehold. Having been out drinking in Freehold village one December night in 1832, the eighty-year-old poet got lost while walking home and died of exposure in a bog. He was buried in the family plot on his old estate, in what is now the built-up Freneau section of Matawan. The **Freneau Gravesite,** which may still be visited, is at the end of a short, tree-lined drive on the left side of Route 79, about a mile south of

Freneau Center. The grave is marked by a marble shaft, which stands within a small fenced enclosure.

If you're a collector of vintage clothing, jewelry, or other aged collectibles, be sure to visit the **Freehold Antique Gallery,** 2 Monmouth Avenue; (732) 462–7900. If you're an aficionado of more recent vintages, the **Jackson Outlet Village,** 537 Monmouth Avenue, (732) 833–0503, just up the road, has more than seventy outlet stores.

For yet another kind of vintage collection, the **Metz Bicycle Museum** exhibits a fine assortment of early cycles, including quadricycles, "boneshakers," and a "Zimmy" built by Freehold native Arthur Zimmerman, who won many bicycle races in the late 1800s. It's at 54 West Main Street, Freehold; (732) 467–7363. Call Mr. Metz to set up an appointment.

Ready for some great barbecue? Make a pit stop at **Big Ed's Barbecue,** 174 State Highway No. 54, Old Bridge; (732) 583–2626. The restaurant, whose ambience evokes that of a roadhouse deep in South Carolina, serves up great baby back ribs, pulled pork, beef brisket, and barbecued chicken. They're open for lunch daily at 11:30 A.M., and Monday through Thursday until 10:00 P.M., Friday and Saturday until 11:00 P.M., and Sunday until 9:00 P.M.

The Jane Voorhees **Zimmerli Art Museum** on the New Brunswick campus of Rutgers University houses the school's collection of more than 35,000 works of art. The art museum's major concentrations are in nineteenth-century French graphics, Russian and Soviet art, twentieth-century American art, and contemporary American printmaking. The collection also includes ancient art and European art of the fifteenth through nineteenth centuries, pre-Columbian ceramics, and designs for American stained glass. The Zimmerli incorporates the International Center for Japonisme and presents related art in the Kusakabe-Griffis Japonisme Gallery. A special gallery features the extensive

The Name Game

Rutgers, New Jersey's state university, was chartered in 1766 and ranks as the eighth oldest institution of higher learning in the British American colonies. But the university, which has its main campus in New Brunswick, wasn't always called Rutgers. It was originally called Queen's College, in honor of George III's consort Queen Charlotte, and was renamed in 1825 after a prosperous local citizen, Col. Henry Rutgers. Hoping that the colonel would come to the aid of the financially strapped college, the administration effected the name change in his honor before actually receiving a contribution. Rutgers did loosen his purse strings, eventually donating more than $5,000 to the school.

Rutgers Collection of Illustrations for Children's Literature. At the entry level of the modern museum building are special exhibition galleries, the George Riabov Collection of Russian Art, a cafe, and a gift shop; works from the permanent collection are exhibited on the lower level.

The Zimmerli Art Museum, Rutgers University, George and Hamilton Streets, (732) 932–7237, is open weekdays except Monday 10:00 A.M.–4:30 P.M., and on weekends noon–5:00 P.M. The museum is closed on major holidays, Mondays, and all of August. There is an admission fee of $3.00 for adults; children under eighteen are admitted free. The first Sunday of each month there is no admission fee.

"Life is uncertain. Eat dessert first!" cautions the menu at **Old Man Rafferty's.** To make sure you heed the warning, Rafferty's offers more than four dozen sweets from which to choose. The restaurant, near Rutgers University, also serves moderately priced steaks, sandwiches, salads, and a terrific selection of wines and beers. Old Man Rafferty's, 106 Albany Street, New Brunswick, (732) 846–6153, is open Monday through Thursday 11:30 A.M.–11:00 P.M., Friday and Saturday 11:30 A.M.–midnight, and Sunday noon–midnight. There is also another Rafferty's at 284 Route 206 in Hillsborough; (908) 904–9731.

In East Millstone there is a tract of natural land that is a good deal smaller than the Great Swamp but no less remarkable for having survived in primeval condition right down into our own time. This is the **Hutcheson Memorial Forest,** 400 acres of woods and fields maintained by the Department of Ecology, Evolution, and Natural Resources at Rutgers University.

At the core of the Hutcheson tract (it's named after William L. Hutcheson, a past president of the United Brotherhood of Carpenters and Joiners, which was instrumental in securing the forest preservation) is sixty-four-acre Mettler's Woods, believed to be the only uncut upland forest in New Jersey. *Uncut* means that throughout three and a half centuries, while the vast forests of the ever more populous Northeast fell for cordwood, for buildings, and to clear land for agriculture, this tiny tract escaped the axe. This is not to say that the elements haven't taken their toll; fire, wind, and insects interfere in the lives of all primeval forests. But there has never been any timber harvesting or soil cultivation here. The living white oak trees in Mettler's Woods average 235 years in age, whereas some of the trees that have died within the past twenty years have been up to 350 years old.

Mettler's Woods is surrounded by more than 300 acres of younger forest, consisting of second growth over land that was previously cultivated and logged. This adjacent forest helps researchers understand the difference between untouched climax growth and the far more prevalent reestablished forest; also, it provides a welcome buffer for the primeval woods within.

The Hutcheson Memorial Forest is open to visitors on select Sundays throughout the year, by scheduled tour by Rutgers University faculty only. Reservations aren't necessary for individuals and groups smaller than ten, and tours last from an hour to two hours. For schedules and directions to the forest, call (732) 932–3388. There is no charge for individual tours.

When former Rutgers University basketball player Darius Griffin and his wife, Mary, lived and traveled throughout South Africa for several years they learned to appreciate African art. They established a network of artisans, and returned home to open *Port Africa,* a gallery/cultural and education center/salon.

All of the wood and stone carvings, wall hangings, clothing, and drums and masks are original and one-of-a-kind. The gallery also hosts cultural events, including poetry slams and drum circles, and offers remedial classes to children and young adults. There's also an upscale natural hair salon.

Port Africa, 4945 Stelton Road, South Plainfield, (908) 222–1152 or (888) 8–AFRICA, is open Monday through Saturday 10:00 A.M.–8:00 P.M. and Sunday noon–6:00 P.M. Check the Web site www.portafrica.com for a listing of events.

The aptly named *Pillars of Plainfield,* a restored Georgian Revival mansion, boasts—count 'em—fourteen pillars surrounding its front porch. Set on an acre of land in the town's Van Wyck Brooks Historic District, the house is surrounded by wildflowers, flowering trees, rhododendrons, and azaleas. A circular staircase winds up three stories to a stained-glass skylight and leads to six beautifully furnished rooms, each with private bath (one has a fireplace). Refreshments, including wine and home-baked cookies, are served hearthside in the Music Room each afternoon and evening.

Rooms at the Pillars, 922 Central Avenue, Plainfield, (888) PILLARS, www.pillars2.com, range in price from $114 to $250 a night. The innkeepers' cairn terrier presides over the mansion.

Places to Stay in Central New Jersey

Cabbage Rose Inn
162 Main Street,
Flemington;
(908) 788–0247
Moderate.

Holly Thorn House
143 Readington Road,
White House Station;
(908) 534–1616;
hollythornhouse.com.
Moderate.

Hyatt Regency New Brunswick
2 Albany Street,
New Brunswick;
(732) 873–1234
Moderate–expensive.

Hyatt Regency Princeton
102 Carnegie Center,
Princeton;
(800) 233–1234 or
(609) 987–1234;
fax (609) 987–2584
Moderate–expensive.

Jerica Hill Inn
96 Broad Street,
Flemington;
(908) 782–8234
Moderate.

Main Street Manor
194 Main Street,
Flemington;
(908) 782–4928;
mainstreetmanor.com.
Moderate.

Martin Coryell House B&B
111 North Union Street,
Lambertville;
(609) 397–8981;
www.martincoryellhouse.com.
Moderate–expensive.

The National Hotel
31 Race Street,
Frenchtown;
(908) 996–4871;
frenchtownnational.com.
Moderate.

Riverside Victorian B&B
66 Leigh Street,
Clinton;
(908) 238–0400;
www.lanierbb.com.
Moderate.

Seven Springs Farm B&B
14 Perryville Road,
Pittstown;
(908) 735–7675;
www.sevenspringsfarm
bandbnj.com.
Moderate.

Places to Eat in Central New Jersey

Bombay Grill and Bistro
371 George Street,
New Brunswick;
(732) 248–7474
The lunch buffet is a great bargain, and gives those unfamiliar with North Indian Muglai cuisine an opportunity to sample a wide variety of dishes. Vegetarian and nonvegetarian selections. Lunch and dinner daily. Inexpensive–moderate.

Giovanni's
300 Old Croton Road,
Flemington;
(908) 806–0722
Northern Italian cuisine, an oak bar, and an outdoor patio with a waterfall— Giovanni's has everything one looks for in an unpretentious, family-friendly restaurant. Lunch Tuesday through Friday, dinner Tuesday through Sunday. Moderate–expensive.

The Grain House Restaurant
225 Route 202,
Basking Ridge;
(908) 221–1150
American country inn fare, including a bountiful Sunday brunch buffet, adjacent to the 1768 Old Mill Inn. Lunch and dinner daily; Sunday brunch. Moderate–expensive.

Hamilton's Grill Room
8 Coryell Street,
Lambertville;
(609) 397–4343
Bring along a bottle of your favorite wine, grab a seat on the outdoor patio (the street is closed to traffic), and pick and choose from the fabulous raw bar or from the menu, which features fish, steak, and veal dishes. Dinner nightly. Moderate–expensive.

Lawrenceville Inn
2691 Main Street,
Lawrenceville;
(609) 219–1900
Headquartered in an 1892 farmhouse, the restaurant offers an imaginative and eclectic menu, with dishes such as tuna tartare, Arctic char ravioli, and smoked squab. Lunch Monday, Wednesday through Friday, dinner Wednesday through Monday. Expensive.

Makeda Ethiopian Restaurant
338 George Street,
New Brunswick;
(732) 545–5115
Opt for a meal served in the traditional, communal style, or in the more formal, candlelit dining room where dishes are served European style. Live reggae, salsa, and calypso music Friday and Saturday evenings. Lunch Monday through Saturday, dinner nightly. Moderate.

Meemah
The Shoppes at Colonial Village, Highway 27,
Edison;
(732) 906–2223
This informal eatery offers both Chinese and Malaysian dishes, with specialties such as roast duck and Malaysian satays. Bring along your own beer, particularly if you order your dishes hot and spicy. Lunch and dinner Tuesday through Sunday. Inexpensive–moderate.

Ram's Head Inn
9 West White Horse Pike,
Galloway;
(609) 652–1700
Chicken pot pie, roast duck, and baby rack of lamb are among traditional American favorites in this cozy, candlelit dining room. Opt for a seat by the fireplace. Lunch Tuesday through Friday, dinner Tuesday through Sunday. Expensive.

Stage Left
5 Livingston Avenue,
New Brunswick;
(732) 828–4444;
www.stageleft.com.
Contemporary American
fare with an accent on prime
beef and fresh seafood, and
an outstanding wine list.
Lunch Friday, dinner nightly.
Expensive.

Tropea Ristorante
Routes 202/206,
Bridgewater Manor;
(908) 658–3000
Regional Italian specialties
include capellini crabcake
and lamb chops over
roasted eggplant. Dinner
Tuesday through Saturday.
Moderate.

Other Attractions in Central New Jersey

The Benjamin Temple House
27 Federal City Road,
Ewing;
(609) 530–1220

Beverly National Cemetery
Bridgeboro Road,
Beverly;
(609) 877–5460

Englishtown Auction
90 Wilson Avenue,
Englishtown;
(732) 446–9644
Open-air flea market

Garden State Discovery Museum
2040 North Springdale
Road, Cherry Hill;
(856) 424–1233

Heritage Glass Museum
25 East High Street,
Glassboro;
(856) 881–7468

Lakehurst Historical Society Museum
Old Street John's Church,
300 Center Street,
Lakehurst;
(732) 657–8864

Lawrence Township Historic Sites
Lawrence;
(609) 844–7000

SELECTED REGIONAL INFORMATION CENTERS, CHAMBERS OF COMMERCE, AND VISITOR CENTERS IN CENTRAL NEW JERSEY

Cherry Hill Regional Chamber of Commerce
1060 Kings Highway North,
Suite 200, Cherry Hill 08034
(856) 667–1600
www.cherryhillregional.com

Greater Bordentown Chamber of Commerce
P.O. Box 65, Bordentown 08505
(609) 298–7774

Regional Chamber of Commerce Princeton
9 Vandercenter Avenue,
Princeton 08542
(609) 924–1776
www.princetonchamber.org

Trenton Convention and Visitors Bureau
Lafayette and Barrack Streets,
Trenton 08608
(609) 777–1770
www.trentonnj.com

Longstreet Farm
Holmdel Park,
Longstreet Road,
Holmdel;
(732) 946–3758

New Jersey State Museum
P.O. Box 530,
205 West State Street,
Trenton;
(609) 292–6464
Closed for renovations;
scheduled to reopen in 2006.

Red Bank Battlefield
100 Hessian Avenue,
National Park;
(856) 853–5120

Smithville Mansion
803 Smithville Road,
P.O. Box 6000,
Easthampton;
(609) 265–5068

State House
125 West State Street,
Trenton;
(609) 633–2709

Washington Crossing State Park
355 Washington Crossing–
Pennington Road
(Route 546),
Titusville;
(609) 737–0623

The Shore

At one time or another, nearly everybody in New Jersey has gone "down the Shore." Little kids have enjoyed the rides at Asbury Park (now, sadly, a memory), and big kids have cruised the boardwalk at Seaside Heights; the rich have gone to Deal and Allenhurst, whereas the not-so-rich take their sun at Lavallette or Ortley Beach. Methodists flock to camp meeting at teetotaling Ocean Grove, high rollers hit the blackjack tables at "A.C.," and surfers search for the perfect Jersey wave at—where else?—Surf City (there were never "two girls for every boy" there, regardless of what the song said). And some people are even discovering what savvy summer travelers knew a hundred years ago, by heading for the Victorian guest houses of Cape May as an alternative to four-figure weekends on certain New England islands. For that matter even a fair number of people who *aren't* from the Garden State go to the Jersey Shore (and not just Atlantic City) simply because it is one of the finest ocean beaches in the world's temperate zones, period.

So what can there be to learn about the Shore? Plenty, if you want to come in out of the sun for a bit and look behind the slot machines and sausage-and-pepper stands. The Jersey Shore has a rich history of settlers, shipwrecks, lighthouses,

THE SHORE

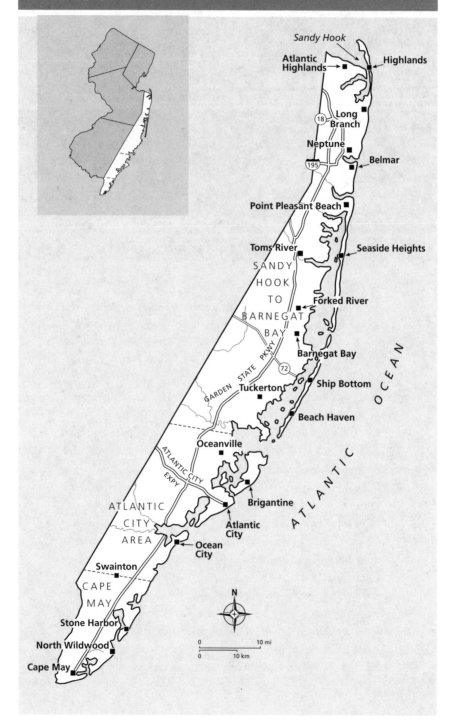

Sandy Hook

Atlantic
Highlands ← ■   ■ → Highlands

18

Long
Branch

Neptune ■

195   ■ → Belmar

Point Pleasant Beach ■

Toms River ■   ■ → Seaside Heights

SANDY
HOOK
TO   ■ → Forked River
BARNEGAT
BAY

GARDEN STATE PKWY   72
                           ■ ↗ Barnegat Bay

Tuckerton   ■ Ship Bottom

                           ■ → Beach Haven

Oceanville ■

ATLANTIC CITY
EXPY
                           ■ ↗ Brigantine

ATLANTIC
CITY   Atlantic
AREA   City

                 ■ → Ocean
                     City

Swainton ■

CAPE
MAY

Stone Harbor ■

North Wildwood ■

Cape May ■

ATLANTIC OCEAN

N

0   10 mi
0   10 km

and naval engagements. There's also the land itself—barrier dunes, salt marshes, and a holly forest. Much of the region would surprise even a lifelong visitor. Like the urban northeastern corner of New Jersey, the Shore is a part of the state that people think they know and few really try to discover.

Note: The orientation in this chapter is from north to south; from Sandy Hook to Barnegat Bay, through the Atlantic City area, and down to Cape May.

Sandy Hook to Barnegat Bay

The northernmost reach of the Jersey Shore proper is the curving finger of land called *Sandy Hook.* Saved from development for nearly two centuries because of its status as a federal military reserve, Sandy Hook is now a unit of the *Gateway National Recreation Area,* other sections of which occupy shoreline stretches of Staten Island and Long Island.

The oldest structure on Sandy Hook is the 1764 *Sandy Hook Light- house,* visible 19 miles out at sea. The United States government acquired all

THE SHORE'S TOP PICKS

Gateway National Recreation Area (Sandy Hook)	Marine Mammal Stranding Center and Sea Life Museum
Twin Lights	Lucy the Elephant
Ocean Grove	Somers Mansion
Co-op Seafood	Ocean City Historical Museum
Floyd L. Moreland Historic Dentzel/Looff Carousel	Stone Harbor Bird Sanctuary
	The Wetlands Institute
Maritime Museum	Leaming's Run Gardens and Colonial Farm
Popcorn Park Zoo	
Albert Music Hall	Cape May County Zoo
Green Gables Restaurant & Inn	Cape May
Edwin B. Forsythe National Wildlife Refuge	Emlen Physick Estate
	Cape May Lighthouse
Tuckerton Seaport	Angel of the Sea
Noyes Museum of Art	

of Sandy Hook in 1817, and the first permanent fort construction started in 1859. But construction was suspended eight years later and the fort was never completed. In 1895 shore batteries and attendant facilities were officially named **Fort Hancock.** The fort was deactivated in 1974, and, as surplus government property, it became part of Gateway.

Although a number of the Fort Hancock buildings have been adaptively reused and incorporated into Gateway's interpretive program, most of Sandy Hook is of interest because of the natural environment. The areas along the eastern Atlantic Ocean face of the peninsula are mostly primary and secondary dunes, but you don't have to go very far inland to find dense thickets of bayberry, beach plum, and even random clumps of prickly pear cactus (there's also poison ivy, so be careful). The most unusual aspect of Sandy Hook, to most first-time visitors, is the holly forest. Holly does well in sandy soil, and its leaves are tough enough to withstand salt breezes.

The **Gateway Sandy Hook Unit Visitors Center** is located on Spermaceti Cove (2 miles beyond the entrance gate) in a building that at one time housed the all-important U.S. Life Saving Service. Maps of all the area's self-guided nature trails are available here, as are details of organized programs and guided nature and history tours.

Behind the visitor center is **Sandy Hook Museum.** Formerly a guardhouse and jail, this 1899 structure houses exhibits concentrating on the history of America's oldest operating lighthouse, which stands only a few yards away.

The Sandy Hook Unit of Gateway National Recreation Area, off Route 36, Highlands, (732) 872–5970, is open daily throughout the year during daylight hours. The visitor center is open daily 10:00 A.M.–5:00 P.M.; closed Thanksgiving, Christmas, and New Year's Day.

The museum is open weekends 1:00–5:00 P.M. throughout the year and daily during July and August. There is a fee of $10 per car from Memorial Day weekend through Labor Day; a season pass is available for $50, and seniors are admitted for half price. The visitor center and Fort Hancock parking area are free.

Sandy Hook is also home to **Gunnison Beach,** the state's only "naturist" facility, and it's a very popular spot on a fine summer day, when thousands of sunbathers park in lot G and head for the dunes. Clothing is optional, but most folks are there for a full complement of rays. A word of caution: Don't strip until you're officially at Gunnison; you have to walk past a "suit required" beach to get there.

As you approach Sandy Hook from the mainland, it's impossible not to notice the massive stone towers of a double lighthouse that dominate the bluff of the Highlands. These are **Twin Lights** of the **Navesink Lighthouse Historic**

Site, decommissioned in 1949 and now maintained as a New Jersey state park.

Twin Lights was once one of the five major lighthouse installations that dotted the dangerous 127-mile-long New Jersey coast. Built in 1862 to replace a pair of stone light towers that had stood on the Highlands since 1828, the north and south towers of Navesink each held beacons to inform mariners of the approach to land.

thestateshell

In 1995 the knobbed whelk, also known as *Busycon carica* or the conch shell, was designated the official state shell. The large, pear-shaped, yellowish gray shell can be found along the state's beaches.

The south tower held a light of the "first order," indicating simply that land-fall was at hand. The north tower was equipped with a "second-order" light, indicating a headland and the approach to a bay—in this case, the lower bay of New York Harbor. As a first-order light, the south-tower installation was always the brighter of the two, and in 1898 it became the brightest in the United States. The Statue of Liberty is traditionally regarded as the first sight of America for passengers on incoming ships, but to any seaman or traveler who approached the coast at night, Twin Lights on the Navesink heralded the New World.

Although a small blinking beacon is still lit in the north tower between dusk and dawn, the south tower is dark. Its giant Fresnel lens, at one time so blindingly powerful that the west-facing windows of the tower had to be paneled over lest the entire countryside be floodlit, is on exhibit today at ground level, in what was formerly the lighthouse's power-generating station. The clockwork mechanism that operated the light is also on exhibit.

A visit to the ***Twin Lights Museum*** will reveal more than lighthouse technology. Here also are collections of memorabilia that relate to the Life Saving Service and to the work of Guglielmo Marconi, inventor of wireless telegraphy.

AUTHORS' FAVORITE ATTRACTIONS AT THE SHORE

Cape May	Marine Mammal Stranding Center and Sea Life Museum
Leaming's Run Gardens and Colonial Farm	Ocean Grove
Lucy the Elephant	Popcorn Park Zoo
	Tuckerton Seaport

It was at Navesink, in 1899, that Marconi gave his first demonstrations of wireless transmission. In September he reported on the progress of Spanish-American War hero Admiral Dewey's triumphal fleet off the Jersey coast; a month later, his wireless wizardry allowed the *New York Herald* to receive instantaneous news of the America's Cup races near Sandy Hook.

Before or after visiting the museum, climb the sixty-four steps to the top of the north tower, 246 feet above sea level. (The north tower is open during museum hours; the south tower only occasionally.)

Twin Lights of Navesink Lighthouse Historic Site, Lighthouse Road (off Route 36), Highlands, (732) 872–1814, is open Labor Day to Memorial Day, Wednesday through Sunday 10:00 A.M.–5:00 P.M.; Memorial Day to Labor Day, open daily 10:00 A.M.–5:00 P.M. The grounds are open 9:00 A.M. until sunset. The building opens at 10:00 A.M. Admission is free.

Want to visit Manhattan without sitting for hours in traffic and worrying about where to park the car? Hop aboard the ***Seastreak America, Inc.***: It makes trips daily from South Amboy, Atlantic Highlands, and Highlands (weekends from Highlands only) to Pier 11 (Wall Street) and East Thirty-fourth Street in Manhattan. The round-trip fares for adults range from $28 to $37, with special rates for children under twelve; under five, free. For information call (800) BOAT RIDE or write to Seastreak America, Inc., Two First Avenue, Atlantic Highlands 07716. For their schedule, check the Web site www.seastreakusa.com.

The Rocky Point section of 736-acre ***Hartshorne Woods Park,*** (732) 842-4000, has 3 miles of paved paths closed to cars—a perfect spot to bike or hike. There's also fine fishing in the Navesink River, and horseback riding. The park's 11 miles of trails are popular with mountain bikers. There are two entrances: off Navesink Road and off Portland Road, in Atlantic Highlands. The park is open daily 8:00 A.M. to dusk, and admission is free. For information contact Monmouth County Park System, 805 Newman Springs Road, Lincroft 07738; (732) 872–2670.

Hidden Ponds

Mention Sandy Hook and most people will think of the long stretch of sandy shoreline that defines the narrow peninsula's Atlantic side. But five freshwater ponds lie within the boundaries of the Sandy Hook portion of Gateway National Recreation Area. One was so well concealed by surrounding thickets of beach plum and bayberry that its existence was only revealed when aerial photos of the area were first taken. The ponds were created when freshwater gradually supplanted seawater that had rushed into inland hollows during storms.

The often long wait for a table at **Doris & Ed's** gives credibility to its reputation as one of the Shore's best seafood restaurants since it opened in 1978. Although dress is casual, this isn't a casual fish house. In addition to fried seafood platters, the kitchen turns out finely prepared specialties such as bouillabaisse, tuna carpaccio, and lobster stuffed with fresh lump crabmeat. There's also a large selection of oysters from around the world, an excellent wine list, and plenty of choices for meat eaters. Doris & Ed's, 348 Shore Drive, Highlands, (732) 872–1565, is open for dinner Tuesday through Sunday from 5:00 P.M. (opens Sunday at 3:00 P.M.) in July and August; from September through June, open Wednesday through Sunday; closed December through late February. Reservations are recommended.

With its many night clubs and cafes, it's astonishing to think that Asbury Park was originally conceived in the 1870s as a temperance resort. The seaside town is enjoying a rebirth after some rather rough years in the 1970s and 1980s: On the Boardwalk, Convention Hall and the former vaudeville Paramount Theater have been restored and are once again hosting events.

No matter what the town does to gain recognition in days ahead, however, to Bruce Springsteen fans Asbury Park will always be the place that "the Boss" got his start. He began performing at the **Stone Pony** on Ocean Avenue and Second Street, and to this day the club is a premier destination for music lovers in search of the Asbury Sound—and of a glimpse of Springsteen, who shows up here occasionally to jam. Even when he's not in town, though, it's a great place to hear top-rate music.

Serious music fans should get a copy of the second edition of *Rock and Roll Tour of the Jersey Shore,* by lifelong New Jersey residents Stan Goldstein and Jean Mikle, who for many years ran walking tours of the area. The 146-page book includes information on more than 200 locations of historical rock-'n'-roll sites in Monmouth, Ocean, and Middlesex Counties, including many Bruce-related sites. The book retails for $25 and can be ordered at www.backstreets.com.

And speaking of celebrities, hop over to **Mom's Kitchen** on 1129 Fifth Avenue in Neptune for some good, reasonably priced Italian food and an occasional glimpse of local hero Jack Nicholson, who sometimes returns to his hometown for some of the good home cooking Mom's has served since 1945. It's open Wednesday through Monday for lunch and dinner. Telephone (732) 775–4823 for information.

Next door to Asbury Park is an entire town entered on the National Register of Historic Places. **Ocean Grove,** which has one of the largest assemblages of authentic Victorian architecture in the United States, was founded in 1869 for The Ocean Grove Camp Meeting Association by Dr. William B. Osborn. He

The Chain Had to Go

Ocean Grove has always taken its origins as a Methodist camp meeting town seriously—to this day, not one establishment in the community possesses a liquor license. But another tradition connected with Ocean Grove's maintenance of a quiet, sedate atmosphere had to be abandoned a couple of decades ago, when a New Jersey court ruled that the town could no longer stretch a chain across the only road leading in and out of the place on Sundays. The reason for the chain? Ocean Grove prohibited driving within its precincts on the Sabbath.

chose this one square mile because it had the highest beach and the best grove of trees around—and no mosquitoes.

When the first camp meeting was held in 1870, the faithful erected tents in which to live. Camp meetings are still held every summer, and today 114 tent structures ring the 6,000-seat Great Auditorium in Auditorium Square. Each July the Historical Society of Ocean Grove includes one or two of the tents on the tour it offers (which also includes seven Victorian houses). Contact the Historical Society of Ocean Grove, P.O. Box 446, 50 Pitman Avenue, Ocean Grove 07756, (732) 774–1869. Events are held in the auditorium throughout the summer months. For information on organ recitals, call (800) 773–0097, or visit www.oceangrove.org.

Don't miss a visit to **Centennial Cottage,** a completely restored and furnished vacation home built in 1874, also operated by the Historical Society of Ocean Grove, at the corner of Central Avenue and McClintock Street. Call for hours.

If your idea of an elegant getaway includes oceanfront accommodations and superb Italian/Mediterranean cuisine, make a reservation at **The Majestic Hotel** at 19 Main Avenue, Ocean Grove; (732) 775–6100; www.ogmajestic.com. The Victorian hotel, open year-round, offers airy rooms and suites.

The 1870s Victorian **Manchester Inn** at 25 Ocean Pathway in Ocean Grove, (732) 775–0616, has rooms with ocean views, as well as the **Secret Garden Restaurant,** which serves a popular Sunday jazz brunch and also breakfast and dinner Monday through Saturday, and dinner Sunday. London broil is a house specialty, and al fresco dining is available. The restaurant is open from Memorial Day to Labor Day; the inn is open year-round. Rates begin at $59 for a room with a shared bath, and go up to $230 for a suite. Their Web site is www.themanchesterinn.com.

"Say Good Morning to the Atlantic from almost every room" advertises **Cashelmara Inn.** And indeed, most of the twelve rooms and two suites (all with private baths) at the landmark mansion have fabulous unobstructed water views. They feature antique furnishings, gas log fireplaces, air-conditioning, and refrigerators, and the rates include a full country breakfast, admission to the inn's Grand Victorian Movie Theater, and beach badges.

Cashelmara Inn, 22 Lakeside Avenue, Avon-by-the-Sea, (800) 821–2976, www.cashelmara.com, is open year-round. Rates range from $95 to $357.

After several moves, *Thompson's Fish & Chips* has found a new home at 617 10th Avenue in Belmar; (732) 556–9200. But Arthur Ostrom assures devotees of his mother's—Doris's—fish and chips that the recipe hasn't changed. He still makes coleslaw the way his grandmother, Florence, did (and still won't reveal the recipe), and he has kept the same simple menu, which also features fried and broiled fish and homemade New England and Manhattan chowders.

Entrees range from $5.95 for a single meat pie to $17.95 for the Fisherman's Platter, with shrimp, scallops, fried clams, stuffed shrimp, and fish. The Fish and Chips Platter is $12.95. The restaurant is open in summer Sunday noon–8:30 P.M., Monday through Thursday 4:00 P.M.–9:00 P.M., and Friday and Saturday noon–9:30 P.M., closed Tuesday in the fall, and Monday and Tuesday in winter.

Down the road apiece in Spring Lake is another splendid Victorian B&B— the *Normandy Inn.* Built as a private residence in 1888, the oceanfront inn

TOP ANNUAL EVENTS AT THE SHORE

Note: Schedules may vary; call ahead.

World Series of Birding, Cape May; April; (609) 884–2736

New Jersey Seafood Festival, Belmar; June; (800) 523–2587

New Jersey State Ice Cream Festival, Toms River; July; (732) 341–8738

Ocean Fest, Long Branch; July; (732) 222–0400

New Jersey Offshore Powerboat Race, Point Pleasant Beach; August; (732) 899–2424

Street Rod Weekend, Ocean City; September; (609) 525–9300

Clownfest, Seaside Heights; September; (732) 741–4459

Wings 'n Water Festival, Wetlands Institute, Stone Harbor; September; (609) 368–1211

Old Time Barnegat Bay Decoy and Gunning Show, Tuckerton; September; (609) 971–3085

Victorian Week, Cape May; October; (609) 884–5404

Chowderfest, Long Beach Island; October; (609) 494–7211

Cape May Jazz Festival, Cape May; November; (609) 884–7277

anunexpectedport ofcall

On September 8, 1934, the liner *Morro Castle* caught fire off the New Jersey coast on the return leg of a New York to Havana cruise. The blaze took the lives of 134 passengers and crew, and left the powerless ship to the mercy of the waves and wind. The smoldering hulk soon grounded only a few hundred yards off the beach at Asbury Park, where it became a macabre tourist attraction for several months before being towed away and scrapped.

serves guests a huge country breakfast and then lends them bicycles so that they can work off the calories with a ride on the town's boardwalk. The inn is at 21 Tuttle Avenue, Spring Lake; (732) 449–7172 or (800) 449–1888; www.normandyinn.com. Rates range from $225 to $295.

To learn about the state's Citizen Soldiers and the contributions they've made to the state and the nation, drop in at the *National Guard Militia Museum of New Jersey,* Sea Girt Avenue, Sea Girt; (732) 974–5966. The museum exhibits a large selection of artifacts and memorabilia pertaining to the militia and National Guard. The museum is open Tuesday, Thursday, Saturday, and Sunday 10:00 A.M.–3:00 P.M. Call for winter hours. Donations are most welcome. There is also a fine library on the premises.

Up to ten million pounds of fresh fish a year are caught by fishermen from Point Pleasant Beach, making it the third largest fishing port in New Jersey. The best place to sample the wares is at the eighteen-member retail market/takeout restaurant *Co-op Seafood,* which serves up some of the freshest and most delicious fare on the coast. House specials include shrimp scampi, fish and fries, and the combination plate—a medley of crab cakes, fish fillets, ocean scallops, and shrimp. The Co-op offers a free tour of the facility, which includes a trip to the docks to watch the unloading of the day's catch. The tour lasts forty-five minutes to an hour, and reservations are required. Co-op Seafood, 57 Inlet Drive, Point Pleasant Beach, (732) 899–2211, is open year-round: winter months, 9:30 A.M.–6:00 P.M., closed Mondays; summer months, open weekdays 9:00 A.M.–7:00 P.M., weekends 9:00 A.M.–9:00 P.M. Tours are offered between 10:00 A.M. and 1:00 P.M., but call ahead.

Wednesday evenings in summer, pack a picnic and a chair and head down to *Jenkinson's Pavilion* at Point Pleasant Beach for the free live classical and Broadway summer concerts, which begin at 7:30 P.M. For the best seats, get there before 5:00 P.M. Call (732) 892–0600 or visit www.jenkinsons.com for information. There is an admission fee to the beach: weekdays, adults $5.50, weekends $6.50; ages five to eleven $1.50, under five free. There are chair and umbrella rentals; a bathouse is available at an additional charge.

The family-owned ***Anchor and Palette Art Gallery,*** a Bay Head institution for more than twenty-five years, exhibits and sells the works of New Jersey artists who specialize in Jersey Shore art. Most summer Sundays from 11:00 A.M. to 2:00 P.M., the gallery hosts demonstrations and "meet-the-artist" gatherings. It's at 45 Mount Street, (732) 892–7776, and it is open daily.

South of Point Pleasant there are, in effect, two Jersey shores—the narrow strip of barrier beach that actually faces the Atlantic, and the marshy inner shore that fronts the Intracoastal Waterway and Barnegat Bay. The beach resorts are clustered out on the sandy ocean shore. Head south along the beach road, Route 35, to Seaside Heights' Casino Pier for a ride on one of the country's finest hand-carved wooden carousels. The ***Floyd L. Moreland Historic Dentzel/Looff Carousel,*** more than ninety years old, is one of approximately 130 carousels left in the United States—and the number is diminishing rapidly, as each year some are destroyed by the elements and others are dismantled and sold off to collectors and museums. Music at the Seaside Heights carousel is provided by New Jersey's only continuously operating Wurlitzer Military Band Organ, which plays by means of a pneumatic system generated by leather bellows. The notes are activated by perforated music rolls like those of a player piano. The fifty-eight animals—thirty-six of which move up and down—were carved by William Dentzel and Charles Looff. Fifteen of the eighteen paintings on the "header," at the top of the center casings, are the original ones.

The Carousel at Casino Pier, Seaside Heights, (732) 793–6489 or (800) 830–8374, is open daily during summer, 10:00 A.M.–midnight, and on weekends and holidays all year from noon until early evening. A small fee is charged for rides.

Early Resort Development

New Jersey has long been famous for its 120-mile-long ocean shoreline—but the seashore, where Indians fished and harvested salt from dried tidal pools, was one of the last places early colonists cared to settle. The barrier beach islands offered few decent harbors, and the mosquitoes were ferocious.

The story of Lavalette, a popular middle-class resort community with a steady year-round population, is typical. Developers started making their pitch in the 1870s, issuing a prospectus that praised the local crabbing and bluefishing. The promoters used a nineteenth-century version of today's condo timeshare come-on: They'd charter a train to Toms River, 7 miles away on the mainland, hire a sailing yacht, and bring prospects across Barnegat Bay for a picnic on the Lavalette beach. After 1881 the railroad extended across the bay right into Lavalette, and the resort boom began in earnest.

If all that spinning around has given you an appetite, stroll along the boardwalk to **Maruca's Pizza** for a slice of Dom and Joe's famous pie, and chase it down with a couple of saltwater taffies from the **Berkeley Sweet and Taffy Shop.**

There are few more beautiful—and uncrowded—spots to be on an early morning than **Island Beach State Park,** a 3,002-acre paradise of white, sandy beach, windswept dunes, wetlands, sea grass, and nature trails that stretches for 10 miles between the ocean and Barnegat Bay. For a wonderful view of Barnegat Light, across Barnegat Inlet at the northern tip of Long Beach Island, drive to the end of the island, and hike for 1½ miles to the southern tip of the peninsula.

During the summer, naturalists lead canoe and kayak trips through the tidal marshes to observe nesting ospreys, falcons, and shorebirds. Be sure to reserve a spot well in advance. For a bird's-eye view of the state's largest osprey colony, which thrives on the Sedge Islands—marshy masses of land in Barnegat Bay—park at lot A20 and hike a short distance to the Spizzle Creek Bird Observation Blind. The park is a horticulturist's as well as an ornithologist's dream: More than 300 plants have been identified here, and the grounds include the state's largest expanses of beach heather. Dog lovers and their canine companions are welcome to romp in the surf at any time of the year here. Just stay clear of the adjacent people-bathing beaches.

Island Beach State Park, Route 35 (mailing address: P.O. Box 37, Seaside Park 08752), (732) 793–0506, is open daily year-round. From Memorial Day to Labor Day, admission is $6.00 per vehicle Monday through Friday; $10.00 on weekends and holidays. The rest of the year admission is $5.00 per vehicle.

Back on the mainland in Toms River is a museum dedicated to the preservation of New Jersey's maritime heritage, with emphasis on the Barnegat Bay area. A number of boat types were developed and built in the area to allow fishermen access to the area's shallow estuaries and bays. The **Maritime Museum,** operated by Toms River Seaport Society, displays a number of these craft, including the *Sheldrake,* a 12-foot "sneakbox," in which the late F. Slade Dale cruised from Bay Head to New York and then on to Florida in 1925 (the Barnegat Bay Sneakbox, named for its ability to sneak up quietly on waterfowl, was invented by Hazelton Seaman of West Creek; historians credit the sneakbox as possibly the only boat designed in the United States without any Old World ancestors). The museum's growing collection, which now numbers thirty, includes a lifesaving surf rowboat, a Barnegat Bay garvey, and a Hankins rowing skiff. The two-story museum, headquartered in an 1868 carriage house, also displays numerous artifacts associated with the area's maritime history.

The Maritime Museum, on the corner of Hooper Avenue and Water Street, Toms River, (732) 349–9209, is open Tuesday, Thursday, and Saturday 10:00 A.M.–2:00 P.M. Donations are welcome.

If your interests tend to the celestial, visit the **Robert J. Novins Planetarium** at Ocean County College. The planetarium, one of the largest in New Jersey, offers a number of programs, including Mars Quest, Wonderful Sky, and seasonal programs. Fridays at 9:00 P.M. (weather permitting), free observing sessions are offered. Wonderful Sky is recommended for children ages seven and under.

The Robert J. Novins Planetarium, Ocean County College, College Drive, Toms River, (732) 255–0342 for recorded information, (732) 255–0343 weekdays for general information, is open all year. Call for hours and ticket prices or visit the Web site: www.ocean.edu/campus/planetarium/index.htm. Children under six are not admitted to main features. Tickets go on sale at the door about half an hour before show time.

It's 5:00 A.M.; you've been up most of the night watching for shooting stars and are famished. Head on over to the **Toms River Diner** on Route 31, (732) 929–0440—it's open twenty-four hours a day.

The **Popcorn Park Zoo** in Forked River is the only institution of its kind in the United States. Popcorn Park was founded in 1977 by the Associated Humane Societies for the express purpose of taking in wild animals no longer able to fend for themselves due to age, infirmity, injury, or abuse by humans. Within a few years, however, the zoo's managers realized that their mission should be extended to domestic and exotic animals in distress, and so it was. Today's Popcorn Park Zoo is the home of last resort for all manner of creatures, from abandoned Easter chicks and rabbits to lions, tigers, mountain lions, bears—even an elephant—that were confined and abused by the shady operators of roadside animal shows and fly-by-night "circuses." All the creatures at Popcorn Park have one thing in common: They very likely would not have made it were it not for the zoo's open-door policy and expert care and for the kindness of those who brought them to this unique facility. What would have become of Marlboro, the goat, left for dead after a bizarre cult ritual; of Hawkeye, the rhesus monkey, found loose at Newark Airport after escaping from a contingent of monkeys bound for a research lab; or Rowdy, the three-legged raccoon?

Popcorn Park Zoo offers spacious, clean accommodations for its animals, and tamer species are allowed to wander freely on the grounds as much as possible. The zoo is situated on the eastern fringes of the New Jersey Pine Barrens, and landscaping is deliberately minimal—a natural scrub-forest environment prevails.

Popcorn Park Zoo, Humane Way at Lacey Road, (609) 693–1900, is open daily 11:00 A.M.–5:00 P.M. Admission is $4.25 for adults, $3.00 for children under twelve and senior citizens.

Forked River is home to another classic Jersey diner—the **Forked River Diner** on Route 9. It's open daily 5:00 A.M.–3:00 P.M., except Christmas Day.

More than thirty years ago, a handful of musicians began to gather every Saturday night in the secluded deer camp of Joe and George Albert in the Waretown pinelands to play music. Known as the "Home Place," it became known as *the* place to go to hear down-home music. The "pickin' pineys" have changed venue several times over the years, but the "Sounds of the Jersey Pines" still ring out every Saturday night, and the pinelands musical heritage lives on.

In 1997 the Pinelands Cultural Society, formed around the original members, completed construction of a 6,000-square-foot building. The air-conditioned, 350-seat **Albert Music Hall** is now the site of year-round Saturday night concerts featuring country, bluegrass, and folk music. There are also special Sunday shows.

The Albert Music Hall is at 125 Wells Mill Road (Route 532), Waretown. Concerts begin at 7:30 P.M. (doors open at 6:30 P.M.) and end at 11:30 P.M. Admission is $5.00 for adults and $1.00 for children under twelve. For more information contact the Pinelands Cultural Society, P.O. Box 657, Waretown 08758; (609) 971–1593; www.alberthall.org.

Have a yen for some coconut-cluster toasted marshmallow? Milk pecan patties? Double-dipped chocolate mints? **Stutz Candy Company** has been making a wide variety of candies for almost sixty years. The 2,000-square-foot factory at Fourteenth Street and Long Beach Boulevard, Ship Bottom, (609) 494–5303, is open year-round, off-season 10:00 A.M.–6:00 P.M. daily; in-season 9:00 A.M.–10:30 P.M. daily. (Don't miss the cherry vanilla fudge!)

Newarkies and Rah-Rahs

Along the boardwalks of the Jersey Shore in the 1960s, you could tell who was who by the clothes they wore. Among teenagers, there were two basic casts of characters: the Newarkies and the Rah-rahs. The Newarkies mostly came from the cities of North Jersey (hence the name), while the Rah-rahs were suburban kids. Newarkies hit the boardwalk wearing tight black pants, black shoes, and strap T-shirts. Rah-rahs wore white denim cutoffs, anything they could find that was made of madras, and sandals or—on formal occasions—penny loafers with no socks. They also surfed, or pretended they did. Newarkies, as well as we can recall, just hung out.

Miniature Golf Tournament

Every summer Thursday morning at 9:30 sharp, dozens of the Jersey Shore's fiercest golf competitors gather at Bill Burr's Flamingo Golf, on the Boulevard in Ship Bottom. A tradition "for more than twenty years," according to one volunteer scorekeeper, Burr's weekly miniature golf tournaments draw kids and adults alike. It's a microcosm of the Masters, with a slew of goofy obstacles that put Augusta National's ponds, bunkers, and azaleas to shame.

The Flamingo is serious about its little tournament: The summer's winners to date are always posted on a board near the entrance. The players are no less devoted, talking about their birdies and eagles and critical putts, and even dropping the occasional remark about their prowess on the full-size links . . . which is where you won't find them on Thursday mornings.

The folks at **ALO** (Alliance for a Living Ocean) are dedicated to promoting clean water and a healthy coastal environment, and they believe that their best weapon is an educated and active public. So they host programs that give everyone a chance to get involved. Among them are the Inherit the Earth trips to environmental points of interest, including the Marine Mammal Stranding Center, the Wetlands Institute, Whitesbog Village.

Other programs include three-hour trolley tours of Long Beach Island (adults $10, children five and under, free); Stories-by-the-Sea for kids ages three to seven (free); Twilight at the Bay, hour-long programs of music, games, and entertainment (free); and Inlet Lore, which includes beach walks and tours around Barnegat Inlet and Lighthouse Park (free).

For information contact the ALO, 2007 Long Beach Boulevard, North Beach Haven 08008, (609) 492-0222, or check their Web site: www.livingocean.org.

The new owners of the **_Green Gables Inn & Restaurant_** plan to make a great place even more spectacular. Stephen and Sondra Beninati bought the inn in September 2005, and immediately started renovating the nineteenth-century Victorian inn's six rooms and dining area. Among the plans—a secluded and romantic al fresco dining area, and private baths in all rooms. The best news is that the Beninatis will continue Aldolfo de' Martino and Rita Rapella's tradition of serving outstanding prix fixe menus; in addition, they'll add an a la carte menu and offer Sunday brunch. The inn is at 212 Centre Street, Beach Haven; (609) 492–3553; www.ibnet.com/greengables.

Indulge your sweet tooth with a treat at the **_Country Kettle._** The sweet shop has been making hand-whipped fudge for more than forty years, and it sells twenty-six flavors, including an incredible Oreo crunch. Visitors can watch

Red Flag's Up—Ladies off the Beach!

Surf City, on Long Beach Island, was one of the first New Jersey Shore communities to feature resort hotels. At the "Mansion of Health," which flourished as early as the 1820s, men and women guests were assigned separate bathing times on the hotel's beachfront. A red flag was the signal for men to use the beach, and a white flag meant it was the ladies' turn. The system was vital for maintaining propriety and decorum—in those days, men swam nude at the Jersey Shore.

the candy being made in Beach Haven, at Ninth and Bay Avenue, (888) 524–3834. The shop is open daily mid-May through mid-October, and on weekends until New Year's and from President's Day until mid-May. There's also a shop in Surf City at Twentieth Street and the Boulevard.

If you don't mind singing for your banana split, ***Showplace Ice Cream Parlor*** has a treat for you. The waitstaff are also professional performers, and serve up show and cabaret tunes along with huge, gooey sundaes. All are named for shows, hence creations such as the Peter Pan—peanut butter ice cream, hot fudge, walnuts, whipped cream, and a cherry. But even in an ice cream parlor there's room for ham: customers are invited—even urged—to participate. The parlor, at 202 Centre Street in Beach Haven, (609) 492–0018, is open from 6:00 P.M. until midnight from Memorial Day weekend (weekends only in early June) until Labor Day. Arrive by 11:00 P.M. for the full show. The take-out window is open from noon until midnight July through Labor Day. Rainy day matinees are performed at 1:00, 2:00, and 3:00 P.M.

The three-story fake windmill on Ocean and Brighton Avenues in Long Beach isn't just another fast-food joint; it's part of a restaurant dynasty whose underpinnings are the humble hot dog. The wiener lovers' mecca opened here in 1963 and was bought by Leo and Edward Levine in 1976. Since then, the Levine family has opened up eleven more ***Windmill Restaurants*** (only the original has a windmill) throughout the state, and all together the restaurants fry up more than 832,000 dogs each year. The chain sells other goodies, including fresh burgers and rib-eye steaks, but the four-ounce Sabrett dogs (Sabrett's headquarters are in East Rutherford)—with a side of cheese fries—are the local favorite.

Be sure to bring along a cooler . . . or at least an appetite . . . when you visit ***Mario's Italian Market*** in Surf City. The aroma alone is worth a visit, but don't stop there: Load up with cheeses, pastries, cold cuts, fresh baked breads, homemade soups, olives, and the market's special stuffed mushrooms and fried ravioli. The shop is at 1905 Long Beach Boulevard; (609) 361–2500.

One more lighthouse: This one is **Barnegat Light,** in **Barnegat Light-house State Park,** at the northern tip of Long Beach Island. "Old Barney," as shore residents call their now-extinguished beacon, was built in 1858 to replace an 1834 lighthouse that toppled during a flood. This time the government didn't fool around: Project engineer Gen. George Gordon Meade, later famous as the Union Commander at Gettysburg, supervised the construction of a 168-foot tower, with brick walls that are 10 feet thick at the bottom and taper to an 18-inch thickness at the top. The illumination source was a five-ton Fresnel lens rotated smoothly on a bed of bronze rollers by a mechanism that resembled the innards of a giant grandfather clock. Every four minutes the beacon rotated, and lives and shipping were saved from the sands of Barnegat Beach.

Barnegat Light came to the end of its usefulness even earlier than Twin Lights at Navesink. The great structure was replaced by a lightship anchored off-shore in 1927, but its dismantling was prevented by public sentiment and, prob-ably, the fact that nothing short of a full-scale naval bombardment could have taken it down. So it survives as the focal point of a lovely state park that offers some of the Jersey Shore's best swimming, surf casting, and birding, not to men-tion sightseeing. Anyone who cares to mount the lighthouse's 217 steps, when the building is open, will be rewarded by a panoramic view of Barnegat Bay, the barrier beaches and the distant mainland, and the vast sweep of the Atlantic.

One of New Jersey's last remnants of maritime forest—predominantly black cherry, eastern red cedar, and American holly—is in the park, making it a popular stopover for migrating birds.

Improving the Plovers' Odds

Within sight of the casino towers of Atlantic City, there are low, sandy wilderness islands that hardly anyone ever visits. Some, in fact, are absolutely off-limits—they're managed as part of the Edwin B. Forsythe National Wildlife Refuge as breeding grounds for endangered bird species, most notably the piping plover. Plovers nest on the ground, where their eggs and newly hatched chicks are in danger not only from human intrusion, but from the predations of foxes, raccoons, and other creatures of the barrier beach islands. Refuge personnel erect mesh enclosures over the plovers' nests, designed to allow the parent birds and their chicks access, while keeping predators out.

We visited one such island, with a government biologist as our guide, and can report that the plovers have on their side a far better deterrent to unauthorized human visitors than mere warning signs. In the summer the biting greenhead flies are so thick on these islands that our pens began to melt from the volume of repellent we were forced to use.

"Old Barney," a historic lighthouse in
Barnegat Lighthouse State Park

Barnegat Lighthouse State Park, Broadway, Barnegat Light, (609) 494–2016, is open all year. The lighthouse is open daily. It is also open some evenings in the summer. Call for specific times. There is a $1.00 fee for admission to the lighthouse between Memorial Day and Labor Day.

Atlantic City Area

Star Route 72 is the only way on and off Long Beach Island, of which Barnegat Lighthouse State Park forms the northern tip. Right after you turn right at the town of Ship Bottom and head back toward the mainland on Route 72, you'll pass the Barnegat Division of the *Edwin B. Forsythe National Wildlife Refuge.* The crowning achievement in the struggle to keep the wetlands of the

Jersey Shore from yielding entirely to development, as well as a vital link in the fragile chain of stopover areas in the Atlantic Flyway used by migratory birds, the refuge offers a refreshingly different coastal experience for human visitors, too. Although there are at this time no developed facilities for visitor use at the smaller Barnegat Division of the 40,000-acre refuge, the Brigantine Division, just across Reeds and Absecon Bays from Atlantic City, has a fine 8-mile auto-tour route and two short interpretive nature trails.

If you'd like to take the self-guided 8-mile auto tour of the Brigantine Division of the refuge, plan on spending about an hour and a half. The tour begins at the division headquarters on Great Creek Road, off Route 9 at Oceanville, and makes a loop back to the starting point. Be sure to pick up a checklist of the refuge's bird species (more than 200 have been identified) at headquarters.

Headquarters of the Brigantine Division of the Edwin B. Forsythe National Wildlife Refuge is P.O. Box 72, Oceanville 08231 (for location, see above); (609) 652–1665. The refuge, auto route, and nature trails are open daily, all year, from sunrise to sunset. Admission is $4.00 per noncommercial vehicle; $2.00 for bicyclists and pedestrians.

Tuckerton Seaport is a living museum carved out of what has been a working seaport village and shipbuilding center since colonial times. The seaport, under the auspices of Barnegat Bay Decoy and Baymen's Museum, Inc., is dedicated to preserving the rich traditions and heritage of the New Jersey Shore region.

Buildings and exhibits include the re-created Tucker's Island Light, which houses a museum devoted to the history of the state's lighthouses and the U.S. Life Saving Service; a sea captain's home; a 1930s houseboat; a decoy-carving shop; and the Perrine Boat Works, where the world-renowned Barnegat Bay Sneakboxes are still built to this day.

The Jacques Cousteau National Estuarine Research Center's Visitor Center, now located on the upper level of the Tuckerton Yacht Club,

By the Sea

New Jersey's 127 miles of white sandy beaches offer some of the finest swimming in the East. And like much of the state, they're a study in contrasts, ranging from the crowded, carnival atmosphere at Wildwood to the laid-back, genteel scene along the strand at Cape May. The prize for the most surreal bathing experience has to go to the beach at Atlantic City. The people who bustle along the boardwalk from one high-rise casino to another seem to exist in another dimension from that of the bathers romping on the uncrowded beaches just a few feet away.

offers a virtual tour of the 110,000-acre tract in southern New Jersey that encompass the Pinelands, Great Bay, Barrier Islands, and ocean ecosystems.

Boardwalks on the forty-acre site wind past boatbuilders, decoy carvers, clammers, oystermen, and baymen and -women at work. In the Hunting Shanty, now a visitor center, there are decoys by area carvers including the renowned H. V. Shourds, who carved more than 3,500 shorebird decoys before he died in 1920. The *Rainbow II* excursion boat cruises to Beach Haven in July and August.

Tuckerton Seaport, 120 West Main Street, (609) 296–8868, is open daily during the summer 10:00 A.M.–5:00 P.M. Winter hours are Wednesday through Sunday 11:00 A.M.–4:00 P.M. Closed Thanksgiving, Christmas, and New Year's Day. Admission is $6.00 for adults, $4.00 for seniors, and $3.00 for ages six to seventeen. Children under five are admitted free.

Adjacent to the Forsythe National Wildlife Refuge, overlooking Lily Lake, is the ***Noyes Museum of Art,*** which features a collection of nineteenth- and twentieth-century American folk art from the mid-Atlantic region. The Noyes Museum is the result of the interest, vision, and resources of two individuals—Fred W. Noyes Jr. and his late wife, Ethel Marie. Mr. and Mrs. Noyes, antiques dealers and developers of the nearby Towne of Historic Smithville restoration, became interested during the mid-1970s in establishing a museum of American arts and crafts.

Approximately 200 North American decoys are a major exhibit at the museum. The carving of decoys, at one time an indigenous cottage industry on the Jersey Shore, is now recognized as an important branch of folk art. In addition to the Noyes decoy collection, the museum exhibits its collection of contemporary American art and crafts and mounts twelve to fifteen exhibitions annually. It also features special exhibitions of works by leading regional artists. Special "Meet the Artist" days are scheduled to coincide with the special exhibitions.

The Noyes Museum, Lily Lake Road, Oceanville, (609) 652–8848, is open Tuesday through Saturday 10:00 A.M.–4:30 P.M. and Sunday noon–5:00 P.M. Admission is $4.00 for adults, $3.00 for senior citizens, $2.00 for full-time stu-

Inventing Las Vegas East

The modern era in Atlantic City dates to the opening of the Resorts, Inc., casino on Memorial Day weekend in 1978, a year and a half after New Jersey voters approved a ballot referendum allowing casino gambling. The move was a response to years of declining fortunes at the old oceanside resort city, which had given the world saltwater taffy and Miss America, but had fallen on hard times in the postwar era as vacationers found they could fly inexpensively to more distant and exotic retreats.

North American decoys, on display
at the Noyes Museum of Art

dents, and free for children under twelve. Admission is free to all every Friday; donations welcome.

More than sixty boutiques and specialty shops are housed in several historic buildings at ***The Towne of Historic Smithville,*** a lovely spot with cobblestone and brick paths, a pond with paddleboats and ducks, and a carousel and train on ***The Village Greene*** (general information, 609–748–6160). Visitors can sample some of South Jersey's finest wines and champagnes at the outlet store for ***Tomasello Winery*** (609–652–2320) and pick up some Betty Boop and Elvis memorabilia at ***Celebrity Collectibles*** (609–652–8110). ***Brownstone Puppet Theater & Museum,*** (609) 652–5750, houses puppets from around the world. Among the restaurants is the lakefront, gracious 1787 ***Historic Smithville Inn*** (lunch, dinner, and Sunday brunch 609–652–7777). Numerous events are hosted throughout the year, including May and Oktoberfests. Call (609) 652–7777 or check www.smithvillenj.com for more

averylongwire

The western terminus of the world's first fiber-optic transatlantic cable is in Tuckerton.

information. *The Colonial Inn,* on the Village Greene, (609) 748–8999, offers elegant overnight lodging. Their Web site is www.colonialinnsmithville.com.

You have to go through Atlantic City to get to the Marine Mammal Stranding Center in Brigantine (see directions below), and it's only a 1-block detour off the main route to the *White House Sub Shop* at 2301 Arctic Avenue; (609) 345–8599. The "Home of Submarines" is hardly undiscovered: Their sign advertises OVER 15 MILLION SOLD and the restaurant is a favorite stop for visiting celebrities. The sandwiches are huge and delicious (unless you're positively ravenous, share one or buy a half). The shop is open Monday through Thursday 10:00 A.M.–11:00 P.M., Friday and Saturday 10:00 A.M.–midnight, and Sunday 11:00 A.M.–10:00 P.M.

After you've eaten, follow signs for Trump Castle Casino and State Marina to the Brigantine Bridge (between Harrah's and Trump Castle) into Brigantine. The *Marine Mammal Stranding Center and Sea Life Museum* is on the left, 2 miles past the bridge. Since its founding in 1978, this private, nonprofit center has responded to more than 1,000 calls about stranded whales, dolphins, seals, and sea turtles that washed ashore on New Jersey beaches. The animals are brought to the center for rehabilitation and eventual release.

The museum offers visitors a glimpse into New Jersey's undersea world. Displays and an aquarium focus on local marine life. At the center there are observation and closed-circuit television areas, where visitors can watch marine mammals exercising or receiving treatment. The center also conducts dolphin-watching cruises, where groups can see wildlife in natural surroundings and learn about the local/regional ecosystem.

The Marine Mammal Stranding Center and Sea Life Museum is in Brigantine (mailing address: P.O. Box 773, Brigantine 08203), (609) 266–0538. The center is open daily from Memorial Day to Labor Day. Off-season, the schedule varies; check their Web site: www.mmsc.org. There is a suggested donation of $1.00.

One of the Jersey Shore's greatest pieces of folk art—and far and away the largest—stands just south of Atlantic City at Margate City. She's *Lucy the Elephant,* a ninety-ton folly, left over from the great age of American looniness.

At one time giant walk-in animals and other outsize curiosities were not at all uncommon on America's roadways. Especially after the automobile caught on, entrepreneurs just naturally assumed that travelers would want to stop for coffee in a shop shaped like a coffeepot or buy a dressed duck for dinner from a vendor in a huge cement duck (we kid you not—just such a monster fowl was saved not long ago by preservationists on Long Island).

James V. Lafferty wasn't selling elephants when, in 1881, he built Lucy on the sands of South Beach in what was then South Atlantic City; he was trying to develop a resort. Since he couldn't use free DVD players as a come-on in those days, he decided to construct an elephant that everyone would want to come and see.

Lucy is a six-story wonder. Made out of sheet metal over a wooden frame, she has 20-foot-long legs, a 38-foot-long body, and a covered howdah on her back to serve as an observation deck. Inside were spiral staircases (they ran up Lucy's hind legs) and a restaurant. If having lunch in the belly of an elephant didn't make you want to buy one of Lafferty's house lots, well, you were just against progress.

Lafferty sold Lucy in 1887 to local hoteliers Sophie and John Gertzen. They made her the namesake and an annex of their Elephant Hotel, and even after the hotel closed and John Gertzen passed away, his widow kept the elephant open. Unfortunately, by the time Mrs. Gertzen died in 1963, Lucy was creaky in her bones and shabby in her outward appearance, and officials with no sense of humor had her condemned.

Just in the nick of time, Lucy was saved by—what else?—a Save Lucy Committee. The state declared her a historic site, and a movable site at that. In 1970 she was transported to her present location.

Lucy the Elephant, a National Historic Landmark, stands on the beach at 9200 Atlantic Avenue in Margate City. She is open 10:00 A.M.–8:00 P.M. Monday through Saturday and 10:00 A.M.–5:00 P.M. Sunday from mid-June through Labor Day. Call for off-season hours (closed in January). A tour of Lucy begins with a ten-minute video on her history, continues with a guided tour through various rooms filled with artifacts and photographs, and ends at the top in Lucy's howdah, which affords a fabulous ocean view. Admission is $4.00 for

Atlantic City Facts

In Atlantic City . . .

- The year-round population numbers fewer than 38,000, but more than 30 million people visit each year.
- When the first casino opened in 1978, the line of people waiting to get in wrapped all the way around the building.
- Saltwater taffy got its name after a candy store on the boardwalk was flooded during a storm.
- The first boardwalk was built in 1870 to keep sand out of ladies' shoes.

adults, $2.00 for children twelve and under. Call (609) 823–6473 or check www.lucytheelephant.org for more information.

Art lovers won't want to miss **Roslyn Sailor Fine Arts,** said to be one of the largest private galleries in the world. The gallery exhibits the works of thirty-five to forty contemporary artists at a time and has an extensive art library. The gallery, at 8401 Ventnor Avenue, Margate, (609) 822–2446, is open Monday through Saturday 11:00 A.M.–5:00 P.M. and Sunday noon–5:00 P.M. in summer; call for off-season hours.

Back on the mainland in Somers Point is the oldest house in all Atlantic County, the **Somers Mansion.** The three-story brick home was built between 1720 and 1726 by Richard Somers, scion of one of the first families to settle at the mouth of the Great Egg Harbor River. The house remained in the hands of the Somers family until 1937, when it was given to the Atlantic County Historical Society.

Now the property of the State of New Jersey, the Somers Mansion has been carefully refurnished with eighteenth-century antiques to suggest its character and appearance at the time Richard Somers made it his home. Accessories, acquired over the years by the Atlantic County Historical Society, include paintings, chinaware, quilts, and samplers. The overall effect is significantly different from that encountered in most northeastern colonial restorations, which are often based upon the lives and habitations of people of very modest means; here, on the south shore of New Jersey, we begin to find the northern fringes of the plantation style. Indeed, the 3,000-acre Somers property was called Somerset Plantation . . . and Somers Point is a lot closer to Virginia than it is to Massachusetts.

The Somers Mansion, 1000 Shore Road, (609) 927–2212, is open Wednesday through Sunday 10:00 A.M.–noon and 1:00–4:00 P.M. Admission is free.

We can't pass Ocean City without visiting a reminder of what happened when lighthouse beacons weren't properly heeded. Here is the **Ocean City Historical Museum** and its roomful of exhibits concerning the wreck of the *Sindia* on December 15, 1901. The *Sindia* was a four-masted bark on the last leg of her voyage from Japan to New York. Pressing northward along the Jersey coast in the teeth of a northeasterly gale, with her officers snug in their quarters and sure that nothing was going to go wrong this close to home, the ship was at the mercy of inexperienced crewmen keeping watch above decks. Seeing a light off to port and assuming it was Sandy Hook, the helmsman rammed *Sindia* onto the bar off Ocean City. There she remains to this day, buried beneath the sand. The museum's Sindia Room tells the history of this famous wreck, with photographs, videos, charts, and articles—either retrieved from the wreck or washed up on shore—that include many beautiful pieces of Oriental pottery that never made it to the holiday tables of 1901 New York. Other rooms in the museum chronicle the landsman's life of early Ocean County. The domestic atmosphere of the era of Ocean City's 1879 founding is suggested in a series of authentically decorated Victorian rooms, complete with mannequins dressed in period costumes.

The Ocean City Historical Museum, 1735 Simpson Avenue, (609) 399–1801, is open May through October, Monday through Friday 10:00 A.M.–4:00 P.M., and Saturday 11:00 A.M.–2:00 P.M.; also in July and August, Thursday evenings 7:00–9:00 P.M., there is a lecture series open to all. In winter, hours are Monday through Friday 1:00–4:00 P.M. (winter hours subject to change). Admission is $4.00 for adults sixteen and over; Saturday admission is free for all.

Shriver's, the oldest continuously operating business on Ocean City's boardwalk, has been making saltwater taffy since 1898. The shop, on Ninth Street, (609) 399–0100, also makes great fudge.

If your beachcombing has left you empty-handed, stop at the **Discovery Seashell Museum and Shell Yard.** The museum, which exhibits and sells more than 10,000 shells and corals from around the world, is at 2721 Asbury Avenue, Ocean City, (609) 398–2316; open daily in summer. Call for hours. There is no admission fee.

Cape May

Cape May's **Stone Harbor Bird Sanctuary** is far, far smaller than the vast tracts protected by the federal government at the Brigantine and Barnegat sites, but it is no less vital to a major group of avian species. Stone Harbor is a heronry, the only one in the United States that is municipally sponsored. It's the nesting place of numerous species of the heron family, including American egret, snowy egret, Louisiana heron, green heron, black-crowned night heron, yellow-crowned night heron, and even the more recently arrived cattle egret. Another arrival, having shown up for the first time in 1958, is the glossy ibis. These dark-bronze birds, with their long, slender, downturned bills, are the only nesting species at Stone Harbor that are not members of the heron family.

The best time for birders to come to the Stone Harbor Sanctuary is between March and October. The herons, egrets, and ibis build nests and raise their young in spring; later in the season, in the final months prior to their southward migrations, the birds keep to a schedule that takes them almost en masse from their nesting areas in the sanctuary to feeding grounds in the marshes at dawn and back again to the sanctuary at dusk. Often ungainly on their stiltlike legs, herons and their kin are creatures of remarkable grace when they take wing, and to see them in such numbers at first and last light is a rare treat.

Stone Harbor Bird Sanctuary, located between Second and Third Avenues and 111th and 116th Streets, (609) 368–5102, is open all year. Visitors are restricted to the observation area adjacent to the parking lot on Third Avenue, where there are a species identification chart and coin-operated binoculars. There is no charge for parking.

Another Stone Harbor must-see is *The Wetlands Institute,* an organization dedicated to scientific research and public education concerning intertidal salt marshes and other coastal systems. Begun in 1969 by conservationist Herbert H. Mills, the institute's facilities include a main building, housing exhibits, and lecture halls; a gift shop; a library; salt-marsh and aquatic exhibits, with touch tank and touch tables with microscopes; and interactive exhibits for children. There's also a tower that offers a bird's-eye view of the surrounding salt marsh. Outdoors are a salt-marsh trail, a boardwalk, and a 100-foot pier over a tidal creek. The surrounding salt marsh is part of a 6,000-acre publicly owned tract of coastal wetlands. Guided tours and boat and kayak tours are offered in season.

The Wetlands Institute, 1075 Stone Harbor Boulevard, (609) 368–1211, is open year-round: from May 15 through October 15, Monday through Saturday 9:30 A.M.–4:30 P.M. and Sunday 10:00 A.M.–4:00 P.M.; from October 15 through May 15, closed Sunday and Monday. Admission is $7.00 for adults, $5.00 for children. The third weekend of September the institute hosts the Wings 'n Water Festival, one of the largest wildlife festivals in the United States. For information visit www.wetlandsinstitute.org.

If we were to have to pick the most tranquil and inspiring spot in Cape May County, Stone Harbor Bird Sanctuary might well be tied with *Leaming's Run Gardens and Colonial Farm* in nearby Swainton. Leaming's Run (it's named after a brook that flows through the property, which in turn is named after a whaler and early settler of Cape May) makes better horticultural use out of a scant twenty acres than any similar place we've seen. At Leaming's Run a mile-long path leads to twenty-seven individual annual gardens, each with its own theme and color scheme.

Between mid-June and early October, there is always something in bloom at Leaming's Run. August is an especially enchanting time, as the gardens attract thousands of hummingbirds—Leamings' Run has, in fact, become known as the Hummingbird Capital of the East. Given the gardens' spectacular palette of colors and the pervasive smell of honeysuckle, it isn't hard to understand the attraction they hold for the tiny, hovering birds.

A special attraction at Leaming's Run is the Colonial Farm, a small compound of log buildings that faithfully replicates a pioneer homestead of Cape May County circa 1695. Every detail of the tiny cabin, with its chimney of mud and logs, is true to the days when Cape May men like Thomas Leaming went whaling while their families waited and kept busy on farms like these.

Leaming's Run Gardens and Colonial Farm, Route 9, Swainton (Cape May Court House), (609) 465–5871, is open daily 9:30 A.M.–5:00 P.M. May 15 through October 20. Admission to the gardens and farm is $8.00 for adults, $4.00 for children ages seven through fourteen. Annual tickets, available for $20.00 per person, allow unlimited visits throughout the season.

If you don't think a stay at the **Candlelight Inn** is worth dying for, choose to stay at a time they're not hosting one of their Murder by Candlelight weekends or Chocolate Lover's weekends. The inn, a beautifully restored turn-of-the-twentieth-century Queen Anne Victorian with seven rooms, a suite, and two cottages, is decorated to a fare-thee-well with antiques, Oriental rugs, and old prints. All rooms have private baths and air-conditioning. Those in the renovated carriage house have fireplaces, Jacuzzis, and a wet bar. Guests are invited to sip sherry on the spacious wraparound veranda or soak in the hot tub on the outdoor sundeck (a truly wonderful experience on a moonlit night). A full breakfast, included in the rate, is served on antique dishes in the elegantly appointed, nineteenth-century dining room. Snacks and afternoon tea are also served. Prices range from $95 to $235. The inn is on the shore at 2310 Central Avenue, North Wildwood; (609) 522–6200 or (800) 992–2632; www.candlelight-inn.com.

Groff's in Wildwood has been serving families moderately priced meals since 1925, and the food is great. The Groff family prides itself on its desserts; among house specialties are black-bottom pie, blueberry glaze, lemon meringue, and coconut cream pie. But don't miss treats such as chicken a la Maryland. The restaurant, at Magnolia and Boardwalk, (609) 522–5474, is open Mother's Day to Memorial Day, Friday through Sunday, and Memorial Day until the third Saturday after Labor Day, daily 4:00–8:00 P.M. Take-out is available.

Wyland Whaling Wall #43, the work of international environmental muralist Wyland, is at Garfield Avenue and the Boardwalk in Wildwood.

Another Cape May Court House site worth visiting is the **Cape May County Historical and Genealogical Society Museum.** The history of Cape May County is a bit different from that of the rest of the New Jersey Shore; nearly 300 years ago this was whaling country, and many of the old Cape May families were emigrants from New England. (One of the attractions of the museum's library to genealogists, in fact, is its wealth of material that chronicles the Mayflower connections of many of the county's early inhabitants.)

The museum is quartered in the John Holmes House, which, like many very old eastern seaboard homes, is an amalgamation of structures erected at different times. The oldest section is the rear portion, believed to have been built in the mid-1700s and at one time the center of an estate that totaled nearly 400 acres. What is now the main section of the house was added just before 1800 by John Holmes, an Irish immigrant to Cape May County.

The collections of the museum generally relate to the working life of rural Cape May in the eighteenth and nineteenth centuries. In the adjacent barn are exhibits of whaling equipment, decoys, and maritime artifacts (including the lighthouse lens that formerly stood atop the tower at Cape May Point). In the museum proper are period rooms that illustrate colonial through Victorian living arrangements, a collection of early glassware, and assorted furnishings and chinaware. Most interesting, as long as you don't let your imagination wander, is the collection of surgical instruments in the medical room. These particularly relate to military medicine, and they document field surgical practices from the Revolution to the Spanish-American War. We gather that in the eighteenth century, what you did was pray for a clean hit to take you away all at once rather than leave you for the doctors to work on—a clean hit, say, from a musket such as those displayed in an adjacent room along with swords, uniforms, and other military paraphernalia, covering America's wars from the Revolution to Vietnam.

The Cape May County Historical Genealogical Society Museum, 504 Route 9, Cape May Court House, (609) 465–3535, is open Memorial Day weekend through October, Tuesday through Saturday 9:00 A.M.–4:00 P.M. (last admission 3:00 P.M.); November through May, Saturday 9:00 A.M.–4:00 P.M. (last admission 3:00 P.M.). Admission is $5.00 adults, $4.00 seniors and students ages thirteen to twenty-three, $2.00 children ages four to twelve. Guided tours by reservation only. The Genealogical Library is open Wednesday through Friday 9:00 A.M.–4:00 P.M. year-round, but be sure to call in advance.

The ***Cape May County Zoo*** is one of the Jersey Shore's biggest surprises. Perhaps it's because when we think of the shore we think of sea creatures, not landlubbers like giraffes, lions, or camels. Nor do we expect to find an African savanna where sable antelope, kudu, zebra, buffalo, ostrich, and elk roam freely.

There are more than 300 species of animals, birds, and reptiles on 128 wooded acres here, including a reptile house with four large alligators. Feeding times are Tuesday and Friday at 2:00 P.M.

The Cape May County Zoo, Route 9 and Pine Lane, Cape May Court House, (609) 465–5271, is open daily 10:00 A.M.–4:45 P.M. Admission is free, but donations are most welcome.

The town of ***Cape May,*** at the very tip of Cape May, is the sort of place that doesn't have attractions; it *is* one. Much of the "city" is a perfect period piece, a throwback to the days when a middle- or upper-middle-class vacation meant a long stay in a big hotel somewhere where the air was supposed to be good for you, and not two weeks in a car or tour bus. Cape May's career as a popular resort began very modestly just after 1800, when the only way to get here was by boat. By 1875 or so, at which time places like Atlantic City and Newport were just getting started, Cape May was a comfortable and thriving resort that could boast of having played host to presidents Pierce, Buchanan, Lincoln, and Grant. Its whaling days might have been over, but its newfound gentility and taste were sure to carry it through the next century as a place to see and be seen.

Well, not quite. Cape May City did fade as the twentieth century matured; thirty years ago, few summer vacationers or beach-weekenders ventured south of the neon-lit motels of Wildwood unless they were of a certain age. Then Cape May began to benefit from the desire of more and more travelers to get away from their kind, and also from the revival of interest in Victorian architecture. Cape May had plenty of that particular commodity, despite its notorious combustibility—private homes, hotels, cottages, and guest houses, festooned with gingerbread aplenty, had survived quite nicely into the neon-motel era, needing only paint and patrons. Cape May has gotten to be fashionable once again, even if we haven't seen any presidents rocking on the porches of late.

Today the "Nation's Oldest Seashore Resort" is a National Historic Landmark Site, with more than 600 authentically restored and preserved Victorian structures.

Perhaps the most impressive of Cape May's Victorian mansions is the **Emlen Physick Estate,** designed by the eminent Philadelphia architect Frank Furness and built in 1879. The Physick Estate belongs to that school of mid- to late-Victorian architecture called the Stick style, in which the structural features of a building were made apparent through the use of exposed exterior timbers. The result was something of a framework effect, elaborated upon by means of steep-gabled, overhanging roof planes, hooded dormers, and a broad veranda, supported by arches almost Gothic in character. A Furness signature, and a staple on finely detailed houses of the related Queen Anne and Shingle styles as well, was the use of massive, heavily ornamented chimneys—quite an ambitious approach for a beach cottage, all in all.

Tours of the Physick Estate can be arranged through the Mid-Atlantic Center for the Arts, an umbrella group that is deeply involved in local preservation and cultural affairs. The center offers a number of interesting tour packages and separate events, including forty-five-minute guided tours, historic district walking and trolley tours, and self-guided auto tours. Prices and schedules vary. The center also sponsors theater, a Victorian Week in mid-October, and a full schedule of Christmas events.

The arts center offers luncheon and afternoon tea in Twinings Tea Room, in the recently restored 1876 Carriage House on the grounds of the estate.

The Emlen Physick Estate

Lunch is served from 11:30 A.M., and an elegant afternoon tea is served from 2:00 P.M. daily (the cost for tea is $13.50 per person).

Over the past eleven years, the center has raised almost $2 million for the restoration of the **Cape May Lighthouse** in Cape May Point State Park. Built in 1859, the 157-foot 6-inch structure has 218 steps. Visitors are welcome daily April through November, and weekends the rest of the year. There is a $5.00 fee for adults, $1.00 for children.

The Mid-Atlantic Center for the Arts is headquartered at the Physick Estate, 1048 Washington Street (P.O. Box 340), Cape May 08204; (609) 884–5404 or (800) 275–4278. Contact the center for more information, or visit their Web site at www.capemaymac.org.

The innkeepers at the Victorian **Mainstay Inn by the Sea** describe their rooms and suites as ranging "from ostentatious Victorian splendor to contemporary elegance," and elegance indeed defines this magnificent Italianate villa built in 1872 as a gentlemen's gambling and entertainment club. Architectural highlights include 14-foot ceilings, elaborate chandeliers, a veranda, and a cupola. The inn has thirteen rooms and suites, all with private baths, and some with fireplaces and private porches.

The Mainstay Inn, 635 Columbia Avenue, Cape May, (609) 884–8690, www.mainstayinn.com, is open year-round. There is a three-night minimum stay in season. Rates range from $155 to $320, including breakfast and an elegant afternoon tea. The nonsmoking inn (except on the veranda) is not appropriate for small children. The inn is open from mid-March through New Year's Eve; the

Officer's Quarters suites, with living rooms, gas fireplaces, and small kitchens, are open year-round.

Each year the elegant 1840 **Washington Inn** in Cape May receives accolades as one of the region's best choices for a night out. There are five dining rooms in the 1840 plantation home, including a summer patio and one with intimate fireside seating. Contemporary American dishes include appetizers such as port-glazed pear bruschetta and Cape May crabcake, pan-seared filet mignon, and fig-and-hazelnut-crusted rack of lamb. Desserts include Chocolate Maui Tears, layered chocolate and coconut cream encased in rich dark chocolate with a rum Anglaise sauce. Entree prices range from $20 to $40. The restaurant's wine list is vast and excellent.

The restaurant is at 801 Washington Street, (609) 884–5697, and opens for dinner at 5:00 P.M. April until mid-October. Also open Friday and Saturday in March, and Thursday to Sunday in April. Be sure to make a reservation.

If you have time for only one meal at **The Mad Batter** in Cape May's circa 1882 Historic Landmark twenty-two-room Victorian Carroll Villa Hotel, opt for breakfast on the porch. If you're flexible, also stop by for lunch or dinner, which features a creative assortment of contemporary American and regional dishes. It's at 19 Jackson Street; (609) 884–9619; www.carrollvilla.com. If you're in the mood for seafood, including Cape May scallops and soft-shell crabs, scuttle down to the **Lobster House** on Fisherman's Wharf, 906 Schellenger's Landing Road, (609) 884–8296. An institution for nearly fifty years, the restaurant has a seasonal outdoor raw bar and serves cocktails aboard a docked schooner.

Akwaaba means "welcome" in a Ghanaian language, and visitors to the gracious **Akwaaba by the Sea,** an 1850s Victorian Inn, will feel most welcome indeed. Owners Glenn Pogue and Monique Greenwood have named each of the two suites and three rooms (all with private baths and air-conditioning) after prominent African Americans from Cape May, and decorated the inn with antiques and Afrocentric touches. Hearty Southern breakfasts often include crabcakes, corn bread, and cheese grits. Rates at Akwaaba by the Sea, 116 Broadway, (609) 898–1109, www.akwaaba.com, range from $150 to $165.

In 1850 a Philadelphia chemist named William Weightman built a summer home in the Second Empire style of architecture at the corner of Washington and Franklin Streets in Cape May. In 1884 his son wanted to be closer to the beach, so he bought property on Ocean Avenue, had the building cut in half, and got farmers with horses and logs to move the house. In 1962 the Reverend Carl McIntyre purchased the Weightman buildings to save them from demolition and moved them to their present site on Reading Avenue.

In January 1989 John and Barbara Girton purchased the deteriorating structures and put 103,000 hours of work and more than $3 million into restoring the property. In July 1989 they opened the first of the two buildings of the fifty-seven-room, twenty-seven-guest-room B&B *Angel of the Sea.* The restoration was fully completed in a year. In 1990 this gingerbread Victorian placed second in the National Trust for Historic Preservation's Bed and Breakfast Inns contest and has since been selected by two national bed-and-breakfast organizations as one of the top ten in the country. The inn is at 5–7 Trenton Avenue, Cape May; (609) 884–3369 or (800) 848–3369; www.angelofthesea.com. Rates range from $95 to $315 and include breakfast and afternoon tea. There is a two-night minimum on weekends, and a three- to four-night minimum on holidays and during special events.

One of Cape May's favorite stops for locals is *Tisha's,* hidden behind the Convention Hall, 714 Beach Drive, (609) 884–9119. The chef prepares American fare with Italian accents, including prime meats with unique sauces and a wonderful mussel dish. Get there early and grab an outdoor table overlooking the ocean, and be sure to bring a bottle of wine: The restaurant is BYOB. Tisha's is open for dinner; call for hours.

Each spring millions of horseshoe crabs come up the Delaware Bay to beaches near East Point Lighthouse at the mouth of the Maurice River to lay their eggs. And each year, at the same time, millions of shorebirds migrating north from South America arrive just in time to snack on the eggs, refueling for the long flight still to come. From September to November, Cape May Point becomes the Raptor Capital of North America as an estimated 50,000 migrating hawks pass over.

To learn about these—and other—avian happenings on Cape May Peninsula, visit either of the *Cape May Bird Observatory*'s two locations: Audubon North Woods Center, Cape May Point, (609) 884–2736, open daily 9:00 A.M.–5:00 P.M., or the Center for Research and Education, 600 Route 47N, Cape May Court House, (609) 861–0700, open daily 9:00 A.M.–5:00 P.M. The Birding Hotline: (609) 861–0466.

Cape May Ferry, which traverses Delaware Bay between Cape May and the picturesque town of Lewes, Delaware, is the most convenient way to travel from the Jersey Shore to Delmarva Peninsula resorts such as Rehoboth Beach, Delaware, and Ocean City, Maryland. It leaves from North Cape May and operates all year. Write Cape May Terminal, P.O. Box 827, North Cape May 08204; call (800) 64FERRY or (609) 886–1725; or visit www.capemay/lewesferry.com for a schedule and rates.

Places to Stay at the Shore

Atlantic View Inn
20 Woodland Avenue,
Avon-by-the-Sea;
(732) 774–8505;
fax (732) 869–2187
Moderate–expensive.

**Berkeley Carteret
Oceanfront Hotel**
1401 Ocean Avenue,
Asbury Park;
(888) 776–6701 or
(732) 776–6700;
fax (732) 776–9546;
www.berkeleycarteret
hotel.com.
Moderate–expensive.

Blue Bay Inn
51 First Avenue, Atlantic
Highlands;
(732) 708–9600;
www.bluebayinn.com.
Expensive.

Conover's Bay Head Inn
646 Main Avenue,
Asbury Park;
(732) 892–4664;
fax (732) 892–8747;
www.conovers.com.
Moderate–expensive.

The Flanders Hotel
11th and Boardwalk,
Ocean City;
(609) 399–1000;
www.theflandershotel.com.
Expensive.

Grand Hotel of Cape May
Ocean at Philadelphia
Avenue, P.O. Box 496,
Cape May 08204;
(609) 884–5611;

fax (609) 898–0341;
www.grandhotelcape
may.com.
Moderate–expensive.

The Hewitt Wellington
200 Monmouth Avenue,
Spring Lake;
(732) 974–1212;
www.hewittwellington.com.
Moderate–expensive.

Hotel Alcott
107–113 Grant Street,
Cape May;
(609) 884–5658 or
(800) 272–3004
Moderate–expensive.

La Maison Inn
404 Jersey Avenue,
Spring Lake;
(732) 449–0969;
fax (732) 449–4860;
www.lamaisoninn.com.
Moderate–expensive.

The Mason Cottage
625 Columbia Avenue,
Cape May;
(800) 716–2766 or
(609) 884–3358;
www.themasoncottage.com.
Moderate–expensive.

SeaScape Manor
3 Grand Tour,
Highlands;
(732) 872–7932;
www.seascapemanor
bb.com.
Moderate.

Virginia Hotel
25 Jackson Street,
Cape May;
(800) 732–4236;
fax (609) 884–1236;
www.virginiahotel.com.
Inexpensive–expensive.

Places to Eat at the Shore

Black Trumpet
Sandpiper Inn,
7 Atlantic Avenue,
Spring Lake;
(732) 449–4700
The chef/owner and the
sous-chef/co-owner serve
a small and thoughtful
American menu that
includes homemade
pastas (the black trumpet
is a house specialty); a
terrific appetizer of jumbo
lump crab, grilled shrimp,
and wild mushrooms;
and signature dishes
including fillet of fluke,
and rack of lamb. BYOB.
Lunch and dinner daily.
Expensive.

Dennis Foy's
816 Arnold Avenue,
Point Pleasant Beach;
(732) 295–0466
Mr. Foy, one of the state's
most acclaimed chefs,
presides over an open
kitchen that turns out
treats such as homemade
gnocchi, artfully prepared
scallops, and seared
sirloin. The crème brûlée
is among his masterpieces.
BYOB. Expensive.

The Ebbitt Room
Virginia Hotel,
25 Jackson Street,
Cape May;
(609) 884–5700
A romantic, sophisticated, and gracious ambience and superbly prepared and presented New American cuisine have earned the dining room high accolades. Appetizers such as rare seared beef and garlic soup and entrees including pistachio-dusted scallops and aged sirloin can be paired with a superb selection of wines. Dinner nightly. Expensive.

Europa South
521 Arnold Avenue,
Point Pleasant Beach;
(732) 295–1500
A diverse menu of Portuguese and Spanish dishes, with classics such as gazpacho, paella, and carne Alentejana (pork and clams). The dining room is cozy, and seats by the fireplace are at a premium. Early-bird specials are served Tuesday through Friday from 4:00–6:00 P.M. Lunch Tuesday through Saturday, dinner Tuesday through Sunday. Moderate.

Fromagerie
26 Ridge Road, Rumson;
(732) 842–8088
Since 1972 Hubert and Markus Peter have been serving classic French dishes with a contemporary flair in this elegant private home. True to their name, cheeses are a popular choice: The nine-cheese tasting platter is superb. Desserts are all homemade,

and the coconut cream Napolean is a stand-out. Dinner nightly. Expensive.

Golda's Anchor Inn
400 Ocean Gate Avenue,
Ocean Gate;
(732) 269–3510
The accent at this popular and casual restaurant/bar is on fresh seafood, but there are several landlubber options including a highly recommended Delmonico steak. Picky kids will love the homemade pizza. No credit cards. Lunch and dinner Tuesday through Sunday. Inexpensive.

Il Giardino Sul Mare
Wharfside Plaza, Route 9,
Forked River;
(609) 971–7699
The award-winning Italian restaurant's menu is extensive; its wine list, by the glass or carafe, moderate; and the ambience relaxed. Homemade desserts include Dark Side of the Moon, a fudge cake soaked with coffee liqueur, and cannoli and chocolate mousse cakes. Children's menu available. Lunch Monday through Friday, dinner nightly. Moderate.

Indigo Moon
171 First Avenue,
Atlantic Highlands;
(732) 291–2433
Bring along a bottle of wine to savor with your moules marinière or lobster ravioli, or spring for the five-course tasting menu ($70/person) to sample the chef's deft touch with other French dishes. But save room for the classic chocolate fon-

due. Dinner Wednesday through Sunday. Expensive.

Klein's Waterside Cafe and Grill
708 River Road, Belmar;
(732) 681–1177
Overlooking Shark River Basin, the accent at this bustling, multifaceted eatery is on a large selection of flopping fresh fish. It's served raw at the sushi and raw bar, to take home at the market, or in a large variety of preparations including chowders, crabcakes, and grilled and fried dishes. Monday is all-you-can-eat sushi night ($26.95), and early-bird specials are offered daily. The Sunday brunch ($18.95) buffet is a stand-out. Lunch and dinner daily. Moderate.

Midori
3130 Route 30, Dennisville;
(973) 537–8588
Kimono-clad waitresses at this upscale Japanese restaurant serve traditional offerings including shabu shabu, maki rolls, and seafood. There's also a sushi bar. Lunch Monday through Friday, dinner nightly. Moderate.

Schneider's Restaurant
801 Main Street,
Avon-By-The-Sea;
(732) 775–1265
"We ain't fancy, just good," state the folks at Schneider's, which has been serving good German, Austrian, and Hungarian fare for almost forty years. All the favorites, from sauerbraten to chicken Paprikash to cherry strudel, are on the menu, along with

fabulous homemade ice cream. Lunch and dinner Tuesday through Saturday. Moderate.

Tucker's Steak and Seafood House
Grand View Hotel,
800 Bay Avenue,
Somers Point;
(609) 927–3100
Ensconced in the Victorian splendor of the old Grand View Hotel, the restaurant specializes in New American cuisine, with local seafood, primed aged meat, and homemade desserts. Lunch and dinner daily in summer, closed Monday in fall. Lodging is also available. Expensive.

Other Attractions at the Shore

Allgor–Barkalow Homestead Museum
1701 New Bedford Road, Wall;
(732) 681–3806

Atlantic City Boardwalk
Atlantic City

Beach Haven Guided Walking Tours
Downtown Victorian district, Beach Haven;
(609) 492–0700

Boardwalk Hall
2314 Pacific Avenue,
Atlantic City;
(609) 449–7130

Cape May Stage
Lafayette and Bank Streets,
Cape May;
(609) 884–1341

Cape May Whale Watch and Research Center
1286 Wilson Drive,
Cape May;
(609) 898–0055

Church of the Presidents
1260 Ocean Avenue,
Long Branch;
(732) 229–0600

Glasstown Center Arts District
High Street, Millville;
(856) 327–4500

Historic Cold Spring Village
720 Route 9, Cape May;
(609) 898–2300

SELECTED REGIONAL INFORMATION CENTERS, CHAMBERS OF COMMERCE, AND VISITOR CENTERS AT THE SHORE

Atlantic City Convention and Visitors Authority
2314 Pacific Avenue, Atlantic City 08401
888–ACVISIT, www.atlanticcitynj.com

Cape May County Department of Tourism and Economic Development
4 Moore Road, Cape May Court House 08210
(609) 463–6415 or (800) 277–2297
www.thejerseycape.com

Monmouth County Department of Economic Development/Tourism
31 East Main Street, Freehold 07728
(800) 523–2587 or (732) 431–7476
www.visitmonmouth.com

Ocean County Public Affairs/Tourism
101 Hooper Avenue, P.O. Box 2191,
Toms River 08754
(732) 929–2138 for information/ questions or (800) ENJOY 33 for tourism guides
www.oceancountygov.com

Ocean Grove Chamber of Commerce
P.O. Box 415, Ocean Grove 07756
(732) 774–1391 (in New Jersey) or
(800) 388–4768 (out of state)
www.oceangrovenj.com

Ocean Grove Tourism Bureau
45 Pilgrim Pathway, Ocean Grove 07756
(732) 774–4736

Jenkinson's Aquarium
Boardwalk and Parkway,
Point Pleasant Beach;
(732) 899–1212 or
(732) 899–1659

**Millville Army Air
Field Museum**
1 Leddon Street,
Millville;
(856) 327–2347

River Belle
47 Broadway,
Point Pleasant Beach;
(732) 892–3377

Sea Girt Lighthouse
Beacon Boulevard
and Ocean Avenue,
Sea Girt;
(732) 974–0514

**St. Vladimir's Memorial
Russian Orthodox Church**
Rova Farms, 132 Perrineville
Road, Route 571, Jackson;
(732) 928–1337

Woodrow Wilson Hall
Monmouth University,
Norwood and Cedar
Avenues, West Long
Branch;
(732) 571–3400

Southern New Jersey

In a small state like New Jersey, if there is any such thing as terra incognita—a part of the state that is least understood by the people in the other parts—then surely it is southern New Jersey, called South Jersey by New Jerseyans. South Jersey properly includes the Shore, but that's not what we're talking about here. The Shore is a land unto itself, and many think they know it, whether for the right or wrong reasons. But that vast bulge of land west of the littoral, tucked between Philadelphia and Delaware Bay, is what we're after.

South Jersey contains the least densely populated part of the nation's most densely populated state, the Pine Barrens, which even most Jerseyans hadn't heard of thirty years ago. The Pine Barrens are better known and even appreciated now, thanks in part to the environmentalists' crusade that brought much of their remote, scrubby acreage under strict state development guidelines and, in some areas, outright protection. At stake in the Barrens is not only a sense of wilderness so close to civilization but also a wonderfully pure water supply in a state that desperately needs it. The Pine Barrens' great water resource is not merely on the surface, in the still rivers and ponds that bring so many canoeists down

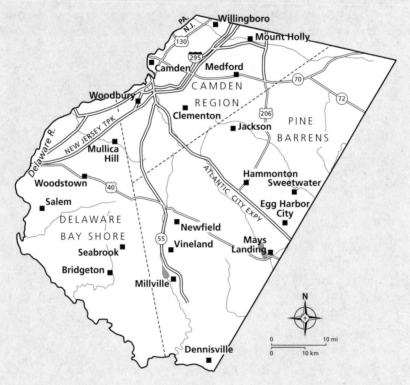

PA.
N.J.
130
295
Willingboro
Mount Holly
Camden
Medford
70
Woodbury
CAMDEN
REGION
72
Clementon
206
Jackson
PINE
BARRENS
NEW JERSEY TPK
Mullica
Hill
Hammonton
Sweetwater
Delaware R.
Woodstown
40
Egg Harbor
City
Salem
ATLANTIC CITY EXPY
DELAWARE
BAY SHORE
Newfield
55
Vineland
Mays
Landing
Seabrook
Bridgeton
Millville
Dennisville

N

0   10 mi
0   10 km

this way, but in a vast underground aquifer, which could easily
or depleted by reckless development.

In South Jersey we also find the big truck farms that produce those wu.
derful tomatoes for which New Jersey is justly famous—why else do you sup-
pose the Campbell Soup Company is in Camden? Along the "other shore" of New
Jersey, the coast of Salem and Cumberland Counties along Delaware Bay, are salt
marshes and tidal estuaries, quilted with federal and state wildlife-management
holdings. Here, at the mouths of meandering rivers like the Maurice and the
Cohansey, are towns that seem as if they belong on the eastern shore of
Maryland rather than in New Jersey, but the distance from Delaware Bay to the
Chesapeake Bay isn't very far at all.

Finally, as the bay narrows to a river and the riverbanks surrender their
marshes to wharves and factories, we approach Camden and the great bridges
to Philadelphia. Here southwestern New Jersey becomes very much like the
northeastern part of the state, a dense cluster of towns and suburbs that would
make a respectable metropolitan area anywhere else, but which are ever in the
shadow of an urban goliath across the river.

Note: The orientation in this chapter is more or less clockwise, starting in
the upper eastern corner of the region in the Pine Barrens, then heading

SOUTHERN NEW JERSEY'S TOP PICKS

Batsto	Salem Oak
Bel Haven Canoes, Kayaks and Tubes	Finn's Point National Cemetery
Renault Resort	Cowtown Rodeo
Wheaton Village	Mullica Hill
Greenwich	C. A. Nothnagle Log House
New Sweden Farmstead/Museum	Pomona Hall
Bridgeton Southern New Jersey All Sports Hall of Fame	Riverlink Ferry
	Barclay Farmstead Museum
Seabrook Educational and Cultural Center	Tandoor Palace
A. J. Meerwald	American Indian Heritage Museum
Salem Court House	

down toward the Delaware Bay Shore, and finally going up the river to the Camden Region.

Pine Barrens

Elsewhere in New Jersey, at Ringwood and at Allaire, we have come upon reminders of the days when iron mining, smelting, and forging were big industries in the state. The greatest of all New Jersey's old iron towns, however, is in the Pine Barrens, deep within the 110,000-acre Wharton State Forest. This is **Batsto,** which, in two centuries, has made the transition from busy industrial village to ghost town to major restoration.

Like the lands that surround Allaire Village, the environs of Batsto yield bog iron that can be collected on or near the surface. In 1766 Burlington attorney and provincial assemblyman Charles Read and a group of associates built a string of four ironworks in the bog-iron country of South Jersey, of which Batsto was to become the most famous. Little could he have known how famous, and how soon: Within ten years, under a later owner named John Cox, the furnace at Batsto was producing a steady stream of munitions for the Continental army. So important were the cannon and cannonballs cast at Batsto to the American war effort that the men who worked there were exempt from military service. This was a powerful inducement to owner Cox to keep the fires burning, as he was a Quaker pacifist who was initially disinclined to use his works for military production.

springtimeposies

Each April in the Pine Barrens the sand myrtle, a rare, small plant with dark, boxlike leaves and white flowers, blossoms for several weeks.

The British and their Tory allies were very much interested in what was going on at Batsto. Spies regularly reported on shipments of munitions from the works by wagon and by barge along the Mullica River, and on one occasion, in 1778, a British detachment got as close to the forges as Chestnut Neck, near the mouth of the Mullica. Nevertheless the great furnace stayed lit, and it was able to make the transition from military to peacetime production (among Batsto's domestic and commercial products of the era are two firebacks, cast to George Washington's specifications and installed at Mount Vernon).

In 1784 Batsto's great era began when the property was acquired by William Richards, who made Batsto into more than just an ironworks in the forest. It became a self-contained village, with virtually everything its workers

Sounds of Silence

We drove 5 miles east from Batsto, the restored iron-forge community in the heart of the Pine Barrens, along a dead-straight sand track that was a masterpiece of eighteenth-century surveying. Stopping at a place the map called Washington, we found nothing more than a sand-paved intersection, with a stand of pines at its center, from which other roads went nowhere through the trees. Stagecoaches once stopped here. There were taverns and schools. We got out of the car and looked into the forest, and stood still long enough to surprise a white-tailed deer. The wind gusted; there was a dry whisper of pine needles. We had found the eye of the Jersey storm, here in abandoned Washington, and save for that whisper it was a place of unearthly and un-Jerseylike quiet.

needed—store, residences, stables, sawmill, icehouse, and farm. Richards also built the structure that still dominates Batsto today, the stuccoed mansion. Richards retired in 1809, but his son and grandson carried on. The furnace itself was rebuilt in 1829, and in 1846 the first Batsto glass factory was erected.

Although glassmaking at Batsto was profitable enough for a second glass factory to be built in 1848, the great iron furnace was shut down for good that year. The reason was the same as at Allaire: Pennsylvania coal was too cheap for New Jersey charcoal to compete. The furnace was dismantled in 1855. Twelve years later the glassworks went out of business, and in 1874 fire leveled half of Batsto village.

Batsto was purchased by Philadelphia industrialist Joseph Wharton in 1876. When his initial plan to dam the local streams and rivers and sell the water to Camden and Philadelphia failed, he built a sawmill and underground silo, enlarged the mansion and transformed its appearance to reflect the Italianate

The Hat That Wasn't

Look on a detailed map of the Pine Barrens, and you'll find a place called Ong's Hat. Like many communities in that part of the state today, Ong's Hat is just a lonely crossroads that wouldn't even qualify as a ghost town. But what about that name?

According to the late South Jersey historian Henry Charlton Beck, the Ong in question was one Jacob Ong, who traveled frequently in the Mullica River valley in the early 1700s. He built a little cabin at one of his stopping places and called it a "hoet," as any Dutch speaker would. The word is related to the English "hut," but it's similar enough to "hat" for the corruption to have crept onto New Jersey maps and stayed there.

Green-Tomato Pie

Here's an unusual recipe, using unripe Jersey tomatoes, that was popular long ago down in the Pine Barrens.

Prepare crust for a two-crust pie, using your favorite recipe. Line a pie pan with the bottom crust, and roll out the top crust and have it ready.

Dice six or eight green tomatoes, depending on size (there should be enough to fill the pie shell amply). Cut a half lemon into $\frac{1}{8}$-inch pieces, rind and all. Put half of the diced tomatoes into the pie shell, dust with flour, add half of the lemon, and sprinkle with five heaping tablespoons of sugar. Repeat the procedure, finishing with six heaping tablespoons of sugar. Put the top crust on the pie, sealing well. Bake at 400°F for 30 to 40 minutes, or until the crust is golden. If a toothpick inserted into the pie shows the tomatoes are still firm, cover the rim of the pie with foil to prevent burning as baking completes.

style of architecture, and cleared vast areas of land to cultivate crops, including cranberries. By the end of the nineteenth century, Batsto had been transformed into a "gentleman's farm."

After Wharton died in 1909, the State of New Jersey had a chance to buy his property for $1 million. State officials said yes, but the voters, feeling frugal, said no. Now the stage was set for the complete dereliction of the Batsto buildings. What nature was accomplishing slowly, the U.S. Air Force proposed to finish quickly in 1954, when plans were announced for a jet-support depot that would have done for the Pine Barrens what the Port Authority's jetport scheme almost did for the Great Swamp. The state opposed the Air Force proposal, as did environmentalists and those who wished to save what was left of Batsto village. This time New Jersey opened its purse: For $3 million, the entire tract was purchased. Thus was Wharton State Forest created. Restoration of the village

AUTHORS' FAVORITE ATTRACTIONS IN SOUTHERN NEW JERSEY

A. J. Meerwald	Renault Resort
American Indian Heritage Museum	Seabrook Educational and Cultural Center
Batsto	
Finn's Point National Cemetery	Wheaton Village

began in 1958 and has continued ever since.

Batsto today offers visitors a look at what life in a nineteenth-century Pine Barrens village was like. All summer long interpreters can be found in the workers' houses and such key buildings as the mansion and the sawmill. The crafts of weaving and pottery making are also demonstrated. Across the Batsto River milldam from the village are the general store and 1852 post office (open in summer), the gristmill and barns, a visitor center with interpretive exhibits and museum shop, and the Batsto Mansion itself.

muddywaters

The next time you're paddling along the rivers of the Pine Barrens, note the dark, brownish color of the water. The soil in the Barrens is highly acidic, and iron and organic contents leach out from it into the rivers and streams.

Historic Batsto Village, off Route 542 at 4110 Nesco Road in Hammonton, (609) 561–0024, is open daily throughout the year. The visitor center is open from 9:00 A.M. to 4:30 P.M.; the village grounds are open dawn to dusk. Interpretive programs are offered daily Memorial Day to Labor Day and Wednesday through Sunday from September through May. Call ahead for schedule information. The village is closed Thanksgiving and Christmas. Donations for the mansion tour are welcome. A parking fee is in effect weekends and holidays from Memorial Day through Labor Day.

Beyond the village spreads *Wharton State Forest,* with its splendid facilities for hiking, camping, canoeing, horseback riding, hunting, and fishing.

The Jersey Devil

They didn't just pull the name of New Jersey's hockey team out of thin air.

There is a "Jersey Devil," at least in persistent folklore. Described as having the head of a horse, the wings of a bat, and a dragonlike body, the creature has been the terror of the Pine Barrens for more than 250 years. According to legend, a Mrs. Leeds, of Estellville (though there are variations in the woman's name and town), learned she was pregnant for the thirteenth time and swore that if she had to have another child, "Let it be the devil." She got her wish, giving birth to a monstrosity that let out a screech, then flew up the chimney and into legend.

Accused over the years of every crime from raiding chicken coops to souring milk to killing whole ponds full of fish with its poisonous breath, the monster at one time carried a reward on his head of $100,000, dead or alive. But no one has ever been able to catch him: The Jersey Devil is still out there, raising hell.

The Great Paisley Boom

Look on a map of South Jersey's Pine Barrens and you won't see a city named Paisley. But in the late 1880s, real-estate promoters touted the "magic city" of Paisley as a place where colleges would soon jostle against conservatories, where artists and authors would count doctors and composers among their neighbors, and where agriculture and manufacturing alike would boom. There were offices selling Paisley properties in several major cities—in all, 13,000 lots on 1,400 acres were on the market.

Some 3,000 eager buyers took the bait, at prices of around $375 per acre (the promoters had paid roughly a hundredth of that amount), and waited for construction to take off. Trouble was, just about all of them waited. By 1890 there were twelve modest buildings in Paisley—and that was the high point of its development. It's all still Pine Barrens.

Camping is permitted year-round—both at developed areas and at seven primitive sites. Nine cabins, with indoor toilets, showers, hot and cold water, and bunks, are available for public use. For information on camping and other facilities in Wharton State Forest, call (609) 561–0024 or write 4110 Nesco Road, Hammonton 08037.

What better way to appreciate the wilderness of the Pine Barrens than by taking a backcountry canoe trip along Upper Toms River as it winds and twists through typical Pine Barrens foliage? There are numerous places to rent canoes and kayaks throughout the area; most will help you arrange your trip—whether for two hours or two weeks—and provide transportation. Just to mention a couple: *Mick's Canoe Rental, Inc.,* in Chatsworth (mailing address: Box 45, Route

TOP ANNUAL EVENTS IN SOUTHERN NEW JERSEY

Note: Schedules may vary; call ahead.

Apple Farm Arts and Music Festival, Elmer; May; (609) 358–2472

Red Bank Jazz & Blues Festival on the Navesink, Red Bank; June; (732) 741–0055

Delaware Bay Day, East Point Light, Matt's Landing, Port Norris, Bivalve and Shellpile; June; (609) 785–2060

New Jersey State Fair, Cherry Hill; July; (800) 749–3247

Chatsworth Cranberry Festival, Chatsworth; October; (609) 726–9237

Grand Christmas Exhibition, Wheaton Village, Millville; late November/early January; (609) 825–6800

563, Jenkins 08019); (609) 726–1380 or (800) 281–1380. *Pine Barrens Canoes and Kayak Rental,* 3260 Route 563, Chatsworth, (609) 726–1515 or (800) 732–0793, has half- and full-day rentals from April to the end of October.

Just past Mick's Canoe Rental, keep a sharp eye out for *Jenkins Chapel.* It's easy to miss—it's the Garden State's smallest church. The nondenominational chapel, established by Episcopalians and run by Methodists, seats just twenty-eight. Services are held Sundays at 10:45 A.M.

There are few things on earth—or water—more relaxing than floating down a river in a tube. The river sets the pace and does the work; you just lie back and relax. *Bel Haven Canoes, Kayaks and Tubes,* in addition to renting canoes and kayaks, also rents tubes and will launch you on a two- or four-hour float down one of the nearby rivers. Cost varies on the number of people in your group: There needs to be at least three persons, and the price is $15 per person. Life jackets, tubes, and transportation to and from the river are provided; bring along your own rope for tubing. Refreshments must be in soft packaging or thermoses; no cans or bottles are allowed. The operation is open from May through August, Tuesday through Sunday 9:00 A.M.–5:00 P.M. Call for off-season hours. Bel Haven is on Route 542, Green Bank; (609) 965–2205 or (800) 445–0953.

takeahike

The well-marked 50-mile Batona Trail wanders through the heart of the Pine Barrens, passing near Batsto Village and connecting Wharton State Forest, Lebanon State Forest, and Bass River State Forest. For a camping permit (issued only for designated sites), contact one of the State Forest offices.

Estell Manor County Park, 3 miles south of Mays Landing on Route 50, is the site of the ruins of Estellville Glassworks, an early-nineteenth-century glass factory. The ruins have interpretive signs, and visitors can get an idea of how glass was made from 1825 to 1877. The center has educational displays and a live animal exhibit. The 1,672-acre park is open daily dawn to dusk. The nature center is open weekdays 8:00 A.M.–4:00 P.M., and weekends and holidays 10:00 A.M.–4:00 P.M. Closed major holidays. Admission is free. Call (609) 645–5960 for information. The park is part of the Atlantic County Division of Parks and Recreation, 109 State Highway 50, Mays Landing.

With the addition of the luxury, forty-five-room Tuscany House Hotel and an eighteen-hole Vineyard Golf Course, Renault Winery has morphed into *Renault Resort.* The winery itself has a fascinating history. Louis Renault came to southern New Jersey from Reims, France, in 1864, and the winery—surrounded by acres of vineyards—has been in business ever since. It even operated round-the-clock during Prohibition, when the proprietors made a 44-proof "medicinal tonic" under special government license (Jersey folk always believed in the salubrious effects of a good tonic). Today Renault produces Chablis, Cabernet Sauvignon, Colombard, Riesling, May wine, and even champagne—the winery was, in fact, the largest American maker of champagne before California and New York took over the lead.

Renault offers an excellent guided tour, which covers wine making and storage, as well as a visit to the firm's museum of glassware and antique wine presses and other equipment, and finishes with a participatory visit to the tasting room.

Guests can choose from two restaurants. Joseph's serves Mediterranean fare, with dishes such as veal Napoleon, seafood paella, and homemade pasta dishes; lunch and dinner served daily. Saturday and Sunday the Gourmet Restaurant in the winery serves entrees such as herb-crusted veal medallions and chicken and lobster paillard; dishes are accompanied by wine samplings. Sunday brunch is served at both restaurants.

Renault Winery, 72 North Bremen Avenue, Egg Harbor City, (609) 965–2111, is open Monday through Saturday (except Thanksgiving, Christmas, New Year's Day, and Easter) 10:00 A.M.–5:00 P.M., Sundays and holidays noon–5:00 P.M. Guided tours are offered weekdays 11:00 A.M.–4:00 P.M., Saturday 11:00 A.M.–8:00 P.M., and Sunday noon–4:00 P.M. Admission is $3.00 for adults, free for those under eighteen.

Legend has it that **Sweetwater Casino** was once *the* place to go to play high-stakes poker. Now it's the place to go to sit, have a drink and/or meal, watch the Mullica River roll by—or maybe ride the pontoon boat *Sweetwater*

Carranza Monument

Deep in the Pine Barrens, on an unnamed road in desolate Tabernacle Township, a monument adorned with an Aztec eagle and a Spanish inscription marks the spot where a twenty-three-year-old Mexican aviator named Emilio Carranza died on July 13, 1928. Carranza, a Mexican military hero who had made a goodwill flight from Mexico City to Washington and New York, had just left Long Island's Roosevelt Field on what he hoped would be a nonstop return flight when his Ryan Monoplane went down in a thunderstorm. His body was returned to Mexico—and his final, fatal flight was commemorated with what surely must be New Jersey's least-visited monument.

Each year, on the anniversary of his crash, a ceremony is held at the site in his honor. It's organized by the members of American Legion Post 11, which recovered the aviator's body. A word to the wise: There are rumors that the monument is haunted, so it may be best to visit during daylight hours.

Lady, which sails every half hour on weekends. This is a popular meeting spot, and reservations aren't accepted for parties of fewer than nine, so relax and soak up the wonderful Pine Barrens atmosphere. The menu includes fried lobster, shrimp scampi, and beef Wellington, and a children's menu is available. Friday, from 5:00 to 9:30 P.M., a $16.95 Pasta and Seafood Frenzy includes a pasta buffet, peel-and-eat shrimp, snow crab legs, and salad bar. Lunch is served Monday through Saturday; dinner is served nightly. Live entertainment is provided on weekends. An $11.50 early bird special is served between 11:30 A.M. and 6:00 P.M.

Be sure to bring home some of the restaurant's Casino Cheese—an interesting blending of cheddar and spices—first made here in 1971. You'll find the restaurant at 2780 Seventh Avenue; (609) 965–3285.

Southern New Jersey seems to be a place that attracts people of vision determined to launch new enterprises. Batsto had Read and his ironworks; Egg Harbor City had Renault and his winery; and just outside Vineland there were whole communities founded by industrious Russian-Jewish immigrants who developed farms and a clothing factory. In Millville a pharmacist named R. T. C. Wheaton set up a glassmaking business that thrives to this day, but Wheaton, Incorporated, now the world's largest family-owned producer of glassware, is not Wheaton's only legacy. His contributions are remembered as well at **Wheaton Village,** a museum and crafts complex that is one of this area's most popular attractions.

The heart of Wheaton Village is the Museum of American Glass, a modern exhibit building that houses a collection of more than 6,500 examples of artistic and utilitarian glassware, ranging from goblets to paperweights, from Mason jars to the world's largest bottle. The museum traces the development of trends in American household glassware, from the roughly crafted glass of colonial times, through the gorgeous stained-glass creations of Louis Comfort Tiffany, to today's handcrafted and mass-produced articles.

In the re-created 1888 Wheaton Glass Studio, artisans employ traditional skills to fashion vases, pitchers, bottles, and other useful and ornamental articles, all of which are for sale in the Wheaton Village stores. Glassblowing demonstrations are given at 11:00 A.M., 1:30 P.M., and 3:30 P.M. For an extra charge, one of Wheaton's craftspersons will even guide you as you shape molten glass into your own paperweight.

Other Wheaton Village attractions include the Down Jersey Folklife Center, focusing on the rich and diverse traditions of New Jersey's eight southern counties; an old-time general store, stocked with museum-quality wares that aren't for sale and penny candy that is; a nineteenth-century Tin Shop, with a working resident tinsmith; the Stained Glass Studio, with artists-in-residence using traditional techniques; an 1876 schoolhouse; demonstrations of pottery making,

Craftsmen demonstrate the art of glassblowing
at the Wheaton Glass Studio.

glass lampworking, and wood carving; and The Gallery of Fine Craft, which features one-of-a-kind American crafts, with a series of special exhibitions that change regularly throughout the year. The 1880 Palermo Railroad Station, typical of rural depots of its era, is more than just a static exhibit—it's a station where you can board a train pulled by the *C. P. Huntington,* a half-scale replica of an 1863 Southern Pacific wood burner. The ¾-mile trip circles the museum grounds every half hour from 11:00 A.M. to 4:00 P.M. April through December.

Wheaton Village, 1501 Glasstown Road, Millville, (856) 825–6800 or (800) 998–4552, is open April through December (open some holidays),

Tuesday through Sunday 10:00 A.M.–5:00 P.M. Admission is $10.00 for adults, $9.00 for senior citizens, $7.00 for children ages six to eighteen. The Web site is www.wheatonvillage.org.

If you're a Matchbox car collector, you know how rare a #41 Ford GT Superfast is. And #22 Pontiac Superfast red. They're on exhibit—along with more than 29,000 other Matchbox vehicles and products—at the *Matchbox Road Museum & Collector Shoppe* on Pearl Street in Newfield; (856) 697–2800 or (800) 976–7623. The museum and shop are usually open Monday through Friday 9:00 A.M.–4:00 P.M., weekends and evenings by appointment. Admission is free.

Delaware Bay Shore

One of the state's finest salt marshes is nestled amid 5,000 acres of forest and reed thickets at *Dennis Creek Wildlife Management Area* in Dennisville. The mile-long Jake's Landing Road, which leads to the area, passes through a densely pined portion of Belleplain State Forest. The tidal creek, which flows into nearby Delaware Bay, is a popular gathering spot for waterfowl such as Canada geese, goldeneyes, and hooded mergansers and is also an excellent spot for crabbing and fishing.

Cape May National Wildlife Refuge is a welcome resting place for migratory birds about to cross the 12-mile-wide mouth of Delaware Bay. The refuge, now comprising more than 8,000 acres, will ultimately protect 16,700 acres of wildlife habitat on Cape May Peninsula. It's strategically located on the Atlantic Flyway, and its 5-mile stretch along the bay is recognized as one of the major shorebird staging areas in North America, providing a critical habitat for hundreds of thousands of migratory birds each year, as well as for other wildlife, including forty-two mammal species, fifty-five reptile and amphibian species, and numerous fish and shellfish.

In addition to May and early June, when the shorebirds arrive (see the sidebar "Red Knots"), one of the most exciting times to visit the refuge is during the annual raptor migration in fall, when great numbers of fifteen raptor species, including peregrine falcons, ospreys, and sharp-shinned hawks, land to rest and refuel.

The refuge has two separate divisions: the Delaware Bay Division in Middle Township, which extends along the Delaware Bay, and the Great Cedar Swamp Division, which straddles Dennis and Upper Townships. Stop at Refuge Headquarters to pick up a map and find out the best places for wildlife viewing.

Cape May National Wildlife Refuge Headquarters, 24 Kimbles Beach Road, Cape May Court House 08210, (609) 463–0994, is open weekdays 8:00 A.M.–4:00

P.M. If the headquarters is closed when you arrive, pick up a brochure at the information kiosk. The refuge is open daily from sunrise to sunset. Admission is free.

Heading northwest toward the narrow upper part of Delaware Bay, it's easy to follow the main roads through Bridgeton and miss one of southern New Jersey's best-kept secrets. This is the village of **Greenwich,** nestled a few miles from the mouth of the Cohansey River and looking for all the world as if it has just been transported from coastal New England. Appearances aside, it does differ in one important respect: It was laid out in the 1680s by John Fenwick, a Quaker. The fine, straight street Fenwick had surveyed was called Ye Greate Street, and so it is called today. This is where the best of Greenwich's early buildings are. These include the 1730 brick **Nicholas Gibbon House,** with an interior hardly altered over 250 years; the 1771 **Friends Meeting House;** and the **Sheppard House,** facing the Cohansey River at the foot of Ye Greate Street. The oldest part of this last structure dates from 1683. From this point a ferry was operated across the Cohansey River from 1767 to 1838. On nearby Market Lane there's a monument to a 1774 event that is as suggestive of New England as the local architecture; here a gang of firebrands, disguised to look like Indians (just as their Boston Tea Party counterparts were), burned a consignment of English tea.

Tours of the colonial homes and other historic buildings of Greenwich are given at various times throughout the year; the Gibbon House is open on a somewhat more regular basis. For information contact the Cumberland County Historical Society (headquartered in the Gibbon House), P.O. Box 16, Ye Greate Street, Greenwich 08323, (856) 455–4055.

Red Knots

There aren't too many places to put up for the night along New Jersey's Delaware Bay shore, and aside from a few steamed crab stands, there aren't many places to pull off the road for lunch either. But each May, hungry travelers by the tens of thousands descend upon the Delaware beaches for a much-needed rest and a big, nourishing meal. These are the migratory shorebirds called red knots, and they are heading north from their South American wintering grounds to Canada's subarctic tundra, where they nest and breed. The birds' New Jersey banquet consists of a superabundance of horseshoe crab eggs, freshly laid in the wet sand. It's been estimated that if it weren't for the migrating shorebirds and their need for a midflight protein binge, New Jersey would be paved with horseshoe crabs. And if anything happened to the bay's ecological balance to decimate the population of those primitive creatures, the red knots and other shorebird species would be seriously imperiled.

In 1638 a company of Swedes and Finns landed in the New World and set up a structure called Fort Elfsborg, near present-day Salem. The fort didn't last long, but the Scandinavian influence has survived in southern New Jersey to this day. In 1988, to commemorate the 350th anniversary of the first Swedish settlement in America, the New Sweden Company, Inc., erected *New Sweden Farmstead/Museum* in nearby Bridgeton. The farmstead is an exact reproduction of a seventeenth-century farmstead built by the early Swedish and Finnish colonists. It consists of seven log structures: a blacksmith shop, a storehouse, a threshing barn, a stable, a residence, a barn, and a sauna/smokehouse. Construction was supervised by a technical assistance team from Sweden, and most of the furnishings are authentic.

New Sweden Farmstead/Museum is at City Park on Mayor Aiken Drive off Commerce Street. For more information contact The New Sweden Farmstead/Museum, Inc., 50 East Broad Street, Bridgeton 08302, (800) 319–3379 (recorded information). The farmstead is open from mid-May through Labor Day, Saturday 11:00 A.M.–5:00 P.M. and Sunday noon–5:00 P.M. Admission is $3.00 for adults, $1.50 for children ages six through twelve, and free for children under six. There is a $5.00 admission fee for a family of four.

Also at City Park is the *Cohanzick Zoo,* New Jersey's first public zoo and one of the few in the United States that operates without an admission charge. Free admission, however, hasn't affected the quality or quantity of the exhibits; all the animals you'd expect to see are here—more than one hundred in modern, naturalistic exhibits. For information call (856) 455–3230, ext. 242 or 262. The zoo is open daily 9:00 A.M.–4:00 P.M.

The Bridgeton Southern New Jersey All Sports Hall of Fame Museum, dedicated to individuals and teams of all sports from southern New Jersey, exhibits a huge collection of photos, equipment, scrapbooks, and trophies. A Golden Glove belonging to baseball Hall of Famer Willie Mays is on display here, as are trophies of Olympic athlete John Borican. Baseball stars "Goose" Goslin and Sparky Lyle and boxing legend Rocky Graziano are remembered. It's on Burt Avenue and Babe Ruth Drive, Bridgeton; (856) 451–7300. Call for hours. Admission is free.

In the spring of 1944 Charles Franklin Seabrook, founder of the largest processor of frozen food in the world, invited a Japanese Relocation Committee to visit South Jersey. He needed workers, and the more than 110,000 Japanese Americans interned in camps because they were deemed "enemy aliens" were eligible for farm work as a result of the War Relocation Authority's seasonal leave policy. Seabrook offered the Japanese Americans jobs, and during the next two years more than 2,500 came from ten relocation centers nationwide.

The Ultimate Honor

There are twelve rest stops on the New Jersey Turnpike, each named for a famous native or resident of the Garden State. In alphabetical order:

- Clara Barton (American Red Cross founder)

- Grover Cleveland

- James Fenimore Cooper

- Woodrow Wilson (who was also governor, and president of Princeton University)

- Thomas Edison

- John Fenwick (Quaker founder of first permanent English settlement in New Jersey, at Salem, 1675)

- Alexander Hamilton (founded Paterson)

- Joyce Kilmer

- Vince Lombardi

- Molly Pitcher (Revolutionary war heroine)

- Richard Stockton (signer of Declaration of Independence)

- Walt Whitman

The farm, which operated around the clock and packed one hundred million pounds of frozen, canned, and dehydrated vegetables a year, also supplemented its workforce with workers from other countries, including Estonia, Romania, Germany, Scotland, Puerto Rico, and the Caribbean. In the 1940s and 1950s it was the most culturally diverse rural area in the country. In 1994, on the fiftieth anniversary of the arrival of the Japanese Americans, the *Seabrook Educational and Cultural Center* was opened to preserve Seabrook's rich history.

Exhibits at the center focus on three major areas: the historical role that the Seabrook Farms Company played in the area's settlement and employment, the various ethnic groups who settled and/or worked there, and community activity. Among the displays at the center are a large-scale model of what the village looked like in the 1950s, photographs, and oral histories.

The Seabrook Educational and Cultural Center, Upper Deerfield Township Municipal Building, 1325 Route 77, Seabrook, (856) 451–8393, is open Monday through Thursday (except on holidays) 9:00 A.M.–2:00 P.M. There is no admission fee.

The **A. J. Meerwald,** an authentically restored Delaware Bay oyster schooner built in Dorchester, New Jersey, in 1928, sets sail from various ports along the Delaware River from mid-April through mid-October. The public sailings are a part of the Bayshore Discovery Project, whose mission is to help educate the public about the culture, history, and natural resources of the Delaware Estuary. Both daytime and sunset sails are offered aboard the tall ship, and fares for the two-and-one-half-hour morning and afternoon sail are $30 for adults, $25 for seniors, and $15 for ages three to twelve. Evening sails are $35 for each passenger. The project is headquartered in Bivalve, which is also home to its *Delaware Bay Museum.* For a schedule and/or information, contact the Bayshore Discovery Project, 2800 High Street, Port Norris (Bivalve) 08349; (856) 785–2060. For reservations and/or a schedule, call (800) 485–3072, or visit www.bayshorediscoveryproject.org.

Following what is now no longer the bay but the Delaware River proper, we come to *Salem,* at one time the site of Fort Elfsborg and later, like Greenwich, settled by Quakers (1675) associated with the colonial enterprise of John Fenwick and William Penn. Feisty little Peter Stuyvesant, the Dutch master of New Amsterdam (later New York) and the New Netherland colony, rousted the Swedes from their New Jersey holdings in 1655; little did he know that he was merely the middle fish in a gulp-gulp-gulp scenario. The big fish, of course, was dear Britannia.

Many years later Salem City was the site of an event important to the future development of New Jersey. One day in 1820 a man named Robert Gibbon Johnson—a descendant of the Gibbons who built the fine brick house on Ye Greate Street in Greenwich—walked up the steps of *Salem Court House,* turned to face a gathered crowd, and ate a tomato. He *ate a tomato,* fresh from his own garden, right before a horror-stricken multitude that fully expected him to crumple dead on the spot. Johnson proved his point: Tomatoes weren't poisonous. The way was clear for New Jersey—with a little help from as-yet-unarrived Neapolitans, who already knew how good *pomodori* were—to take its rightful place as tomato grower of the world, pizza maker, stacker of cans . . . *pace,* Carl Sandburg.

You can still see the courthouse where this landmark event took place. Much altered and added to over the years, it still stands at the corner of Broadway and Market Street, downtown. If you care to go inside, it's open 9:00 A.M.–noon and 1:00–4:00 P.M. on weekdays. There is no tomato monument, but since the building represents an amalgam of styles from 1817 to 1908, it does offer more than passing interest in its own right. There is, however, a tomato festival in Salem. Held in late September, it's appropriately named after Robert Gibbon Johnson. For information call the Salem Chamber of Commerce at (856) 299–0299.

The Salem Oak

If there is a spiritual center to Salem, and a spot best suited for beginning a walking tour to take in some of its more than sixty colonial and Victorian-era homes, the **Friends Burying Ground,** on West Broadway opposite Oak Street (with its many fine Victorian homes), is surely the place. Here, where many of the earliest settlers of Salem and the lower Delaware Valley lie buried, stands the majestic **Salem Oak.** Estimated to be at least 600 years old, this white oak is the last of the vast forest of trees that covered the site of Salem town when John Fenwick arrived. According to legend this is the tree beneath which Fenwick sat when he signed his initial treaty with the leaders of the local Delaware Indian tribe. When last measured, the Salem Oak stood 88 feet tall, a dimension easily matched by the spread of its branches. The trunk is 21 feet 6 inches in circumference.

The best source of information on the historic houses of Salem, including maps and pamphlets for a self-guided walking tour, is the Salem County Historical Society. Every other spring the society sponsors an open house, taking in most of the town's important sites. For information contact the society at 79–83 Market Street, Salem 08079, (856) 935–5004. The society's museum, in the 1721 Alexander Grant House, is open Tuesday through Saturday noon–4:00 P.M. Admission is $3.00.

At **Finn's Point National Cemetery** there are markers in memory of 2,704 men who died during the Civil War; 2,436 of them were Confederate soldiers who had been interred at a prison camp on nearby Pea Patch Island. Many of them had been captured at the Battle of Gettysburg. There are two monuments here: In 1879 the U.S. government erected a marble memorial to the memory of Union soldiers interred here who died while serving as guards at the camp, and in 1936 a Grecian-type columned cupola was placed over it. In 1910 the government inscribed the names of the Confederate dead on bronze plates and affixed them to the base of an 85-foot obelisk-type structure of reinforced concrete with Pennsylvania white granite facing.

In the northwest corner of the cemetery, thirteen white marble headstones mark the burial places of World War II German prisoners of war who died while in custody at Fort Dix. And in another section are markers for fifty veterans who served in World War II, Korea, or Vietnam.

The cemetery was at one point a small part of the Finn's Point Military Reservation, erected by the government in 1896 in anticipation of the Spanish-American War. The name was changed to Fort Mott in 1897 in honor of Maj. Gen. Gershom Mott, commander of the New Jersey Volunteers during the Civil War. Today, visitors can tour the fortification at Fort Mott State Park, as well as the cemetery. For information contact Fort Mott State Park, 454 Fort Mott Road, Pennsville 08070, (856) 935–3218.

If you don't mind leaving the state for a bit, after visiting Fort Mott State Park, hop aboard the **Three Forts Ferry** for a short ride to two Delaware forts: Fort Delaware on Pea Patch Island, which was used to house those Confederate prisoners during the Civil War (and now home to the largest heron rookery on the East Coast); and Fort DuPont, at the 322-acre Fort DuPont State Park. This fort, which also dates back to the Civil War, housed several hundred prisoners from Rommel's Afrika Korps during World War II.

Lyme Disease

As New Jersey's deer population increases, so does the number of deer ticks, which can cause Lyme disease. To reduce your chances of being bitten, follow these precautions:

- Wear loose-fitting, light-colored clothing that will help you to see the ticks more easily. A long-sleeved shirt and hat also are recommended.

- Stay on trails and keep out of densely foliated areas.

- Leave as little skin exposed as possible.

If you do find a tick on you, don't panic. Pull it off slowly, making sure to remove it entirely. If you suspect you've been bitten, check with your physician.

The *Three Forts Ferry,* (302) 834–7941 (Fort Delaware) or (856) 935–3218 (Fort Mott), operates from mid-April until mid-September, 10:00 A.M.–4:00 P.M. No pets other than service animals are allowed on the ferry. No bikes or pets are allowed on Pea Patch Island. Tickets are $6.00 for adults and $4.00 for children ages two through twelve. Call or check the Web site (www.destate parks.com) for the schedule.

Southern New Jersey might seem an incongruous place to find a professional rodeo, but every Saturday night from Memorial Day through September, ***Cowtown Rodeo*** in Woodstown, the longest-running Saturday night rodeo in the country, hosts some of the finest riding east of the Mississippi by both cowboys and cowgirls. The rodeo is on Route 40 (mailing address: Route 2, Box 23A), Woodstown 08098, (856) 769–3200. Gates open at 6:00 P.M., and the show starts at 7:30 P.M.; tickets are $12.00 for adults and $6.00 for children twelve and under.

Cowtown Bawl, Inc., one of the state's largest flea markets, is held every Tuesday and Saturday—rain or shine—throughout the year on the rodeo grounds from 8:00 A.M.–4:00 P.M. Opened in 1926, the market moved to its present location in 1940, and today it attracts almost 700 dealers and up to 40,000 people a day. Among the wares: antiques, collectibles, crafts, and fresh produce. For information call (856) 769–3000 or 769–3202.

It will come as no surprise to learn that Swedesboro was settled by Swedes in the middle of the seventeenth century. They came to the area to farm, and soon after their arrival they began constructing the state's first Lutheran house of worship. In 1784, after the original log cabin building burned down during the American Revolution, they built what is now ***Trinity Episcopal Old Swedes Church*** (it became Episcopal in 1786).

Today the brick Georgian building is open for tours by appointment. Also on the grounds are the early 1700s Schorn log cabin, moved here from nearby Racoon Creek, and a wonderful old cemetery.

The grounds of Trinity Episcopal Old Swedes Church, 209 Kings Highway and Church Street, (856) 467–1227, are always open. The church is open for tours Monday through Friday 10:00 A.M.–4:00 P.M. and Sunday afternoon after services. Call for an appointment to tour the church at other times.

The continental menu changes with the seasons at ***Swedes Cafe Bar and Restaurant*** in Swedesboro, but almost everything else in the inn has been restored and historically preserved to resemble, as closely as possible, the original seventeenth-century tavern. Some of the appointments are a bit more modern: The hammered tin ceiling in the dining room and the mahogany mirror in the porch room are only one hundred years old. Entrees include rack of lamb, roast duck, and sesame-crusted seared tuna. A bar menu is also available, which includes great barbecued spare ribs. The restaurant, at 301 Kings Highway, (856) 467–2052, serves lunch Friday and dinner nightly 5:30–10:00 P.M.

The tiny village of **Mullica Hill** is a mecca for lovers of antiques and crafts. Residents have turned their homes, or at least part of them, into shops, and now more than seventy line Main Street (Route 45), selling everything from samplers to homemade quilts to Depression glass. **King's Row Antique Center,** at 46 Main Street, is a good place to begin. It's open daily. At **Murphy's Loft,** 53 North Main Street, you can browse through 50,000 used, out-of-print, and collectible books. The bookshop is open daily 10:00 A.M.–6:00 P.M. Stop in for a homemade brownie at **Mirenda's Bakery,** at 195 Main Street, open Tuesday through Friday 8:00 A.M.–5:00 P.M. and Saturday 8:00 A.M.–4:00 P.M. The **Harrison House** serves breakfast, lunch, dinner, late-night snacks, and home-baked goods daily 6:00 A.M.–11:00 P.M. For a map or more information, contact Mullica Hill Merchants Association, P.O. Box 235, Mullica Hill 08062; (856) 881–6800; www.mullicahill.com.

Clementon Amusement and Splash World Water Parks combines high-tech thrills with old-fashioned charm to offer a fun day for the whole family. In business since 1907, they have wisely kept enough of their original attractions to bring a smile to grandma's lips and incorporated enough new rides and activities to keep the kids happy. The Classic Carousel, with antique-style horses, hearkens back to a gentler age, as does the *Clementon Belle* showboat, which circles the lake. But they've also got one of the largest and best log flumes in the country, a ten-story Ferris wheel, and thrill rides including Thunderbolt and Falling Star to keep the scream level up.

Attractions at Splash World include Caribbean Cove, a pirate ship, and a float down Endless River, past waterfalls and rock formations.

Clementon Amusement and Splash World Water Parks, 144 Berlin Road, (856) 783–0263, is open seasonally. Call for hours. A combined day-long admission fee costs $27.76 (including tax); $20.55 after 4:00 P.M. Children under 36 inches (with shoes) are admitted free, and there's a 20 percent discount for seniors. Separate admissions are available

snakesnackin'

Rattlesnakes were a major threat to early settlers. To protect themselves when they knew they'd be passing through snake country, they'd sometimes drive several hogs in front of them. The hungry swine, protected by coats of bristles and a lining of fat, would scarf up the snakes like popcorn. In the absence of a hog, it is recommended that those who confront an angry rattler back away.

for each park. Admission includes parking and all shows (including a lion and tiger show).

In the mood to do some picking? Gloucester County is loaded with U-Pick-It farms. To mention just a few: ***Mood's Farm Market,*** Route 77, Mullica Hill, (856) 478–2500, for apples, blackberries, blueberries, cherries, grapes, nectarines, pears, plums, raspberries, and snap beans; closed Sundays. ***U-Pick,*** at the junction of Route 45 and Route 538, Mullica Hill, (856) 478–2864, for peaches, apples, snap beans, okra, black-eyed peas, and eggplants; open daily in season. ***Patane's Farm,*** 100 Democrat Road, Gibbstown, (856) 423–2726, for cantaloupes, cucumbers, eggplants, squash, tomatoes, turnip greens, peppers, and watermelons. Call ahead to see what's in season.

What's alleged to be the oldest log cabin in the United States, believed to have been built shortly after the first Swedish settlers arrived in this country, is the ***C. A. Nothnagle Log House*** in Gibbstown. Although the actual year of construction is unknown, it is estimated to have been built between 1638 and 1643. The cabin, attached to the home of Doris and Harry Rink, is at 406 Swedesboro Road. The Rinks are generally available to show folks around, but do call ahead, (856) 423–0916, to make sure they're home.

Camden Region

Like it or not, many of South Jersey's Quakers were dragged into the upheaval of the American Revolution. James Whitall and his wife, Ann, kept a comfortable farm along the Jersey side of the Delaware, just 5 miles south of Philadelphia. Their house, built on land along the river bluffs, may have seemed ideally situated in peacetime, but for many of the same reasons, it became a strategic site once hostilities began. The Continentals, wishing to defend the heights of Red Bank (not to be confused with the city of Red Bank, near the Atlantic coast), appropriated James Whitall's apple orchard for the construction of ***Fort Mercer*** and commandeered part of the house itself for the officers' quarters. The immediate British threat was not only from the occupied city of Philadelphia, but from the warships that patrolled the Delaware. The rebels were especially concerned that the naval and land forces not be allowed to unite.

On October 22, 1777, as Rhode Island volunteers were still finishing the earthwork defenses of Fort Mercer, 1,200 British and Hessian troops attacked the rear of the fort. Inside were only 400 Americans, but they had been warned of the attack by Jones Cattell, who ran from Haddonfield to alert the Continental commander, Col. Christopher Greene. Colonel Greene ordered his troops—many of them free blacks—to wait until the last possible minute to fire. Just as the Hessians reached the base of the earthen ramparts, Greene's men let fly a ferocious volley of grapeshot and musket balls. Four hundred Hessians fell dead or wounded. Again they tried; again they were repulsed. As he lay dying, the Hessian commander, Count Donop, supposedly told his American captors, "I die a victim of my ambition and the avarice of my sovereign."

The pair of unsuccessful Hessian charges upon Fort Mercer lasted barely a half hour, but the engagement between barge-mounted American guns and the British warships in the river carried on into the next day. Ann Whitall had tried to ignore the violence flaring all around her, and she continued her spinning in a room on the second floor of her home. When a British cannonball pierced the upper north area of the attic wall and rolled downstairs to where she was sitting, it is said Ann scolded the British, saying, "If thee would not fight, thee would not hurt." Later when her house was requisitioned to serve as a field hospital, she worked hard to nurse all of the wounded.

Despite the success of Fort Mercer's defenders, General Washington eventually decided that he could not afford to commit enough men to the task of maintaining it. After the position was abandoned, the British overran and looted Whitall's property. The Quaker billed the Continental Congress for compensation, which was never received.

From the return of James and Ann in 1778 until 1897, three generations of Whitalls lived in the stout stone-and-brick house on the heights above the Delaware. The surrounding property was acquired by the United States government in 1872 (hence the name of the municipality—National Park, New Jersey), but it was turned over to Gloucester County authorities in 1905. Since then it has been managed as a park in commemoration of the Battle of Red Bank.

Aside from the preserved and partially reconstructed earthworks of Fort Mercer, the principal attraction of **Red Bank Battlefield** is the restored **Whitall House.** Today the house looks much as it did in the peaceful days before the Revolution, when James Whitall ran his farm from the little first-floor office that faced the river; elsewhere within the 1748 structure (the stone portion is said to have been built by Swedish settlers even earlier) are a formal parlor, a great room with a large hearth, a huge kitchen located in the stone wing, and bedrooms. The furnishings are all in keeping with the period, as are the kitchen gardens and small orchard outside. On a late October day, the windfallen apples give off their winy smell, which must have been a welcome change from the stench of black powder and blood.

The Red Bank Battlefield, 100 Hessian Avenue, National Park, (856) 853–5120, is open all year during daylight hours. The Whitall House is open in summer, Wednesday through Sunday 1:00–4:00 P.M. Donations are accepted.

In Camden stands the **Walt Whitman House,** where the Good Grey Poet lived from 1884 until his death in 1892. This two-story frame building is the only home Walt Whitman ever owned, and he was able to pay the $1,750 that it cost only because of the unexpectedly large amount of money he earned from sales of the seventh edition of *Leaves of Grass.* Whitman had been boarding with his brother in Camden; when he moved into his own house, he had no furnishings other than a bed, a chair, and his books. Partially paralyzed from a series of strokes, he needed a housekeeper as well as a household. He found both when he engaged a widow, Mrs. Mary Davis, to move in with her own furniture and see to the cooking and cleaning in return for free rent. Whitman himself was by then a poor man, living largely on the generosity of his friends for the last eight years of his life.

Visitors to the Whitman House can see the poet's sparse furnishings, many of his books, and an interesting array of memorabilia, including photographs, letters, and documents.

The Walt Whitman House, 330 Mickle Boulevard, (856) 964–5383, is open Wednesday through Saturday 10:00 A.M.–noon and 1:00–4:00 P.M., and Sunday 1:00–4:00 P.M. Admission is free.

If you want to make a pilgrimage to Whitman's grave, head over to **Harleigh Cemetery,** which donated a plot to the poet. He paid for the mausoleum, which he shares with his mother and brother. There's a black granite monument with his likeness on it, and his own elegy:

> I BEQUEATH MYSELF TO THE DIRT
> TO GROW FROM THE GRASS I LOVE,
> IF YOU WANT ME AGAIN LOOK FOR ME
> UNDER YOUR BOOT SOLES.

Haiku poet Nick Virgilio is also buried here in a grave overlooking the lake. A lectern is etched with his poem "Lily/out of the water/out of itself."

The Harleigh Cemetery, 1640 Haddon Avenue, (856) 963–0122, is open daily 7:30 A.M.–4:30 P.M.

Another Camden site worth a visit is **Pomona Hall,** headquarters and museum of the Camden County Historical Society, located at the Southeastern edge of town near the Collingswood border. Pomona Hall is a handsome Georgian brick structure, built in 1726 by prominent Quaker Joseph Cooper Jr., and expanded in 1788 by his descendant Marmaduke Cooper. Inside are fine examples of eighteenth- and nineteenth-century furnishings and colonial kitchen equipment. The holdings of the society's adjoining museum include Indian artifacts, Civil War memorabilia, representative tools associated with preindustrial crafts, fire-fighting equipment, and antique toys. A special exhibit chronicles the days, just after the turn of the twentieth century, when Camden was the home of the Victor Talking Machine Company. If you've ever heard the voice of

Enrico Caruso transcend the decades through the medium of a brittle black disk, you can bet that it was recorded at the Victor studios in Camden.

The Camden County Historical Society's Museum and Pomona Hall and Library, Park Boulevard and Euclid Avenue, (856) 964–3333, is

passthepopcorn

In 1933 the world's first drive-in movie theater opened its "doors" in Camden, featuring *Wife Beware* with Adolphe Menjou.

open Wednesday through Friday 9:30 A.M.–4:30 P.M., and Sunday 1:00–5:00 P.M. Admission is $2.00 for the tour and $1.00 for the library.

The New Jersey State Aquarium in Camden (One Riverside Drive; 609–365–3300 or 800–616–JAWS), is hardly off the beaten path. With parking for 2,200 cars, it's one of the state's major tourist attractions. Nevertheless, it's easy to miss an extremely pleasurable side trip that departs from the aquarium—the **Riverlink Ferry.** This ferry crosses the Delaware River in twenty minutes and deposits passengers at Penn's Landing in downtown Philadelphia. The riverfront park has a tree-lined promenade, an amphitheater with live entertainment, and a sculpture garden. Several attractions are within walking distance. For a schedule and/or information: Riverbus, Inc., P.O. Box 327, Camden 08101; (215) 925–LINK or (800) 634–4027.

"Big J," the country's largest and most decorated battleship, now has a permanent home on the Delaware River just south of the aquarium.

The 887-foot 7-inch *Battleship* **New Jersey,** built in 1940 at the Philadelphia Navy Yard, served in World War II, Korea, Vietnam, and the Persian Gulf. The Iowa Class ship's motto was "Firepower for Freedom," and firepower it had in spades—its nine 16-inch guns could hit targets 23 miles away. When at war, its crew numbered from 2,500 to 2,900.

Self-guided tours of the floating museum are offered daily April through September 9:00 A.M.–5:00 P.M., and daily October through December 9:00 A.M.–3:00 P.M. The museum is also open daily in March 9:00 A.M.–3:00 P.M. and in January and February, Friday through Monday 9:00 A.M.–3:00 P.M. Tickets are $13.50 for adults and $9.00 for children ages three to eleven, seniors, and service veterans. Guided tours are also offered. An expanded, two-hour Firepower Tour includes information on the ship's weapon system and a visit to the Combat Engagement Center. Tickets for this tour are $17 for adults and $11 for seniors, veterans, and children ages six to eleven. The tours are given at 10:00 A.M., noon, and 1:00 and 3:00 P.M.

If you can round up thirty-nine friends, consider signing up for Sea by Day, Lights by Night, an overnight encampment aboard Big J, which includes a sail to Philadelphia. Groups get a tour and sleep aboard the ship.

For general information and directions to Battleship *New Jersey,* 62 Battleship Place, Camden, call (866) 877-6262 or visit the Web site www.battleship newjersey.org.

Amid the urban bustle of Cherry Hill sits ***Barclay Farmstead Museum***—a living-history museum dedicated to preserving a way of life that is quickly disappearing in New Jersey. The centerpiece of the thirty-two-acre farm on the north branch of the Cooper River is a three-story brick Federal farmhouse, built in 1816 by a Quaker farmer and completely furnished with period antiques. There are also an operating forge, barn, and blacksmith shop; a corn crib; a Victorian springhouse; and a museum shop. The farmstead, at 209 Barclay Lane, Cherry Hill, (856) 795–6225, is open Tuesday through Friday noon–4:00 P.M. and the first Sunday of each month 1:00–4:00 P.M.; closed Mondays and national holidays. Admission is $2.00 for adults and $1.00 for children and seniors.

Near Barclay Farmstead on Covered Bridge Road is ***Scarborough Covered Bridge,*** one of two remaining covered bridges in the state, and the first to be built in New Jersey in ninety-three years. It was dedicated on February 14, 1959.

The shrimp vindaloo at the ***Tandoor Palace*** is spicy and hot, just the way a good vindaloo should be. Less intrepid diners can choose from other Indian and Pakistani dishes, such as chicken tikka or lamb *rogan josh.* Everything is delicious and inexpensive. The restaurant, in Plaza 30 Shopping Center, 328 White Horse Pike, Clementon, (609) 435–1234, is open for lunch and dinner daily. There is a luncheon buffet, and dinner buffet Monday through Wednesday (regular menu also available).

The Cirelli family has been making ice cream since 1913, and much of their success is attributed to the fact that they use only the freshest organic ingredients. Judge for yourself at ***Leo's Ice Cream Company,*** 7 Tomlinson Mill Road, Medford; (856) 797–8771. Open noon–10:00 P.M. in summer; call for off-season hours.

It's rumored that the Jersey Devil—a phantom beast that has plagued South Jersey since colonial times—has been spotted in the area of the ***Jackson Museum,*** housed in a more than 150-year-old schoolhouse. The schoolhouse was formerly on the property of Six Flags Great Adventure. In 1984 Six Flags donated the building to the Jackson Heritage Preservation Society, which paid to have it moved to a site behind the town's municipal building. Today the museum exhibits artifacts from the inland, forested section of Ocean County. The museum, open by appointment, is on Don Connor Boulevard, Jackson, (732) 928–1539.

Perhaps the most cheerful thing that can be said about Burlington County Prison is that it's now a museum. But from 1811 until 1965 it incarcerated men and women guilty of every crime from debt to murder. Today the ***Burlington County Prison Museum*** is a National Historic Landmark, and visitors can see the prison yard where those convicted of capital crimes were hung, the workshop where trades such as broom and basket making were taught, the exercise yard with its 20-foot wall, and the cells where prisoners were locked up after being deloused. Graffiti throughout the building depict efforts to keep up hope as well as spirals into despair.

The Burlington County Prison Museum, on Route 541 in Mount Holly, is operated under the auspices of the Burlington County Parks Department (609–265–5858). It's open Thursday through Saturday 10:00 A.M. to 4:00 P.M. and Sunday noon to 4:00 P.M. Admission is $4.00 for adults and $2.00 for children.

For thousands of years people of the Powhatan nation have inhabited the coastal areas of the mid-Atlantic. The oldest written treaty in North America (1646) was between the Powhatan Confederacy and England. The ***American Indian Heritage Museum,*** the only Indian-owned-and-operated museum in New Jersey, tells the history of these people and the part they played in shaping the United States. The museum tour includes a visit to the outdoor re-creation of a traditional ancestral woodland village and an opportunity to see live buffalo. The art gallery exhibits contemporary paintings, sculpture, pottery, drawings, photographs, and wood carvings. The museum, on the Rankokus Reservation, Rancocas Road, Rancocas (mailing address: P.O. Box 225, Rancocas 08073), (609) 261–4747, is open the first and third Saturday of the month (closed December to February) 10:00 A.M.–3:00 P.M. and by appointment on Tuesday and Thursday. Festivals are held in May and October. Admission is $5.00 for adults, $4.00 for senior citizens, and $3.00 for children.

Places to Stay in Southern New Jersey

Haddonfield Inn
44 West End Avenue,
Haddonfield;
(856) 428–2195 or
(800) 269–0014;
fax (856) 354–1013;
haddonfieldinn.com.
Moderate–expensive.

Hilton Cherry Hill
2349 West Marlton Pike,
Route 70, Cherry Hill;
(856) 665–6666;
fax (856) 662–1414;
www.hilton.com.
Moderate–expensive.

Iris Inn at Medford
45 South Main Street,
Medford;
(609) 654–7528;
fax (609) 714–0277
Inexpensive–moderate.

Isaac Hilliard House B&B
31 Hanover Street,
Pemberton;

(800) 371–0756 or
(609) 894–0756;
www.isaachilliardhouse.com.
Inexpensive–moderate.

Penny Royal Manor
68 North Main Street,
Mullica Hill;
(856) 478–0236
Inexpensive–moderate.

Ramada Inn and Conference Center
399 Monmouth Street,
Hightstown;
(609) 448–7000;
www.ramada.com.
Moderate–expensive.

The Victorian Lady
301 West Main Street,
Moorestown;
(856) 235–4988
Moderate.

Places to Eat in Southern New Jersey

Crystal Diner
2009 Brunswick Avenue,
Lawrence;
(609) 392–3500
Everything one looks for in diner fare is on the menu, but the Turkish owners have raised the bar with an outstanding selection of entrees including mammoth portions of lamb chops, large steaks, and well-prepared fish. Open 24/7. Inexpensive–moderate.

Elements Cafe
517 Station Avenue,
Haddon Heights;
(856) 546–8840
The upscale bistro serves an eclectic menu of New American dishes with French, Asian, and Latin influences. There are small- and large-plate offerings, and an extensive selection of hearty, homemade soups. Lunch Monday through Saturday, dinner Tuesday through Saturday. Moderate–expensive.

Food for Thought
129 Marlton Crossing,
Marlton;
(856) 797–1126
An eclectic menu ranging from an appetizer of roasted duck pierogies and carmelized onions in a fig demi-glaze to entrees such as tilapia fillet crusted with crab and horseradish. High tea is served Saturday noon–3:00 P.M. Lunch Tuesday through Saturday, dinner nightly. Expensive.

Harrison House Diner and Restaurant
North Main Street,
Mullica Hill;
(856) 478–6077
The original 1963 Swingle diner has been contemporized, but the extensive menu, with everything from chipped beef on toast to build-your-own burgers and homemade meat loaf, remains classic diner fare. Don't forget the cappuccino and smoothies. Open 24/7. Inexpensive–moderate.

Hennessey Tavern
191 Paris Avenue,
Northvale;
(201) 768–7707
The owner named the restaurant for his wife, actress Jill Hennessey. It's a kid-friendly pub with a cozy, fireplaced dining room, a menu of comfort foods, a TV broadcasting sports programs, and a good selection of microbrews. Open daily for lunch and dinner. Inexpensive.

SELECTED REGIONAL INFORMATION CENTERS, CHAMBERS OF COMMERCE, AND VISITOR CENTERS IN SOUTHERN NEW JERSEY

Camden County Office of Public Affairs Court House
520 Market Street, Camden 08102
(856) 225–5431
www.camdencounty.com

Cherry Hill Regional Chamber of Commerce
1060 Kings Highway North,
Cherry Hill 08034
(856) 667–1600
www.cherryhillregional.com

Delaware River Region Tourism Council
(856) 757–9400
www.visitsouthjersey.com

Pinelands Commission
P.O. Box 7, New Lisbon 08064
(609) 894–7300
www.state.nj.us/pinelands

Salem County Visitor Center
New Market Street, Salem 08079
(856) 935–9242

Italian Bistro
Route 38 and Chapel
Avenue, Cherry Hill;
(856) 665–6900
Brick-oven pizza, home-
made pasta and calzones,
and an excellent selection
of well-prepared entrees.
Lunch and dinner daily.
Moderate.

La Familia Sonsini
202 Old Marlton Pike,
Medford;
(609) 654–5217
Italian and authentic New
Orleans dishes. BYOB.
Dinner Tuesday through
Sunday; Sunday brunch.
Moderate.

Miel Patisserie
Village Walk Shopping
Center, 1990 Route 70E,
Cherry Hill;
(856) 424–6435
Fabulous French pastries
and desserts, and home-
made sorbets and ice
cream. Take-out. Open daily.
Inexpensive.

Molly Pitcher Inn
88 Riverside Avenue,
Red Bank;
(732) 741–6333
The view from the dining
room of this small luxury
hotel overlooking the
Navesink River is lovely, as is
the sophisticated menu that
changes with the seasons.
An excellent Sunday brunch
is served at 11:00 A.M. and

1:30 P.M., and jackets are
required after 5:00 P.M.
Lunch and dinner Tuesday
through Sunday. Expensive.

Restaurant Nicholas
160 Route 35 South,
Middletown;
(732) 345–0077
The menu changes with the
seasons at this award-winning New American dining
destination that offers two-
and three-course selections,
as well as a more elaborate
six-course tasting menu. The
restaurant's wine list is as
sophisticated as its cuisine,
and a vegetarian menu is
also offered. There's a fine
cheeseboard and dessert
menu. Dinner Tuesday
through Sunday. Expensive.

Other Attractions in Southern New Jersey

Amalthea Cellars
209 Vineyard Road,
Atco;
(856) 768–8585

Bridgeton Historic District
50 East Broad Street,
Bridgeton;
(856) 451–4802

Camden Children's Garden
Delaware River Waterfront,
3 Riverside Drive, Camden;
(856) 365–8733

Finn's Point Lighthouse
Supawana Meadows
National Wildlife Refuge,
Fort Mott and
Lighthouse Roads,
Pennsville;
(856) 935–1487

Garden State Discovery Museum
2040 North Springdale
Road, Cherry Hill;
(856) 424–1233

Glasstown Center Arts District
High Street,
Millville;
(856) 327–4500

Holocaust Education Center
1301 Springdale Road,
Cherry Hill;
(856) 751–9500

Indian King Tavern Museum
233 Kings Highway East,
Haddonfield;
(856) 429–6792

Nail House Museum
1 Mayor Aitken Drive,
Bridgeton City Park,
Bridgeton;
(856) 455–4100

Potter's Tavern
West Broad Street,
Bridgeton;
(856) 451–4802

General Index

Special Indexes

Art Galleries

Lodgings

Parks/Natural Areas

Restaurants

Zoos

About the Authors

William G. Scheller was born in Paterson, New Jersey, where several generations of his family worked in the local locomotive, silk, and aircraft industries. He attended Paterson schools and both St. Peter's Preparatory School and St. Peter's College in Jersey City.

Mr. Scheller is the author of more than twenty books, including *New York Off the Beaten Path, Country Walks Near New York,* and *The Hudson River Valley.* His articles have appeared in the *Washington Post Magazine,* the *Christian Science Monitor, Islands,* and *National Geographic Traveler.* Along with his friend and occasional collaborator, New York photographer Chris Maynard, Mr. Scheller was profiled in a *New Yorker* "Talk of the Town" piece for having canoed the length of New Jersey's Passaic River and for circumnavigating (also by canoe) Manhattan Island. The two also collaborated on *Manifold Destiny,* a guide to cooking on car engines.

Kay Scheller is a co-author of *New York Off the Beaten Path,* and a contributor to National Geographic's *Crossing America* and the *Insight Guides* to Boston, New England, and New York State. Ms. Scheller was a co-author of the *New England* volume in National Geographic Society's *Driving Guides to America* series.

The Schellers are the authors of *Best Vermont Drives: 14 Tours in the Green Mountain State* and *Best New Hampshire Drives: 14 Tours in the Granite State,* published under their own Jasper Heights Press imprint.

The Schellers live in northern Vermont.